## Cleveland On Foot . . .

"A superb introduction to our neighborhoods and natural areas"—*Northern Ohio Live*

"Useful for beginners and people who are new to this area. For experienced hikers . . . the book is a fun way to add variety when planning outings."
—*Explorer*, Cleveland Museum of Natural History

"A straightforward, no-nonsense guide that should be in every hiker's glove compartment."
—*Ohioana Quarterly*

"User-friendly . . . Informative"—*Currents*

"It's tough to get lost with a book like this."
—WEWS TV-5 News

# Cleveland On Foot

## 3RD EDITION

**50 Walks & Hikes
in Greater Cleveland**

Patience Wilson Cameron

GRAY & COMPANY, PUBLISHERS
CLEVELAND

Gray & Company, Publishers
1588 E. 40th St., Cleveland, OH 44103
(216) 431-2665

www.grayco.com


Library of Congress Cataloging-in-Publication Data
Cameron, Patience Wilson
Cleveland on foot: a guide to walking and hiking in Cleveland and vicinity / Patience Wilson Cameron. —3rd ed.
Includes bibliographical references
1. Hiking—Ohio—Cleveland Metropolitan Area—Guidebooks.
2. Walking—Ohio—Cleveland Metropolitan Area—Guidebooks.
3. Cleveland Metropolitan Area (Ohio)—Guidebooks. I. II. Title.
GV199.42.032C543  1998       97-53763


ISBN 1-886228-15-9

Printed in the United States of America

# Contents

Preface to the Third Edition . . . . . . . . . . . . . . . . . . . . . . . . . . . . . . . . . . . . 7
Acknowledgments . . . . . . . . . . . . . . . . . . . . . . . . . . . . . . . . . . . . . . . . . . . 8
Introduction . . . . . . . . . . . . . . . . . . . . . . . . . . . . . . . . . . . . . . . . . . . . . . . 11

**I.   Hiking Preparation** . . . . . . . . . . . . . . . . . . . . . . . . . . . . . . . . . . 13

**II.  Hiking Resources** . . . . . . . . . . . . . . . . . . . . . . . . . . . . . . . . . . . . . . 21

**III. Easy Urban and Suburban Walks**
  1. Downtown Cleveland: Art and Architecture . . . . . . . . . . . . . . . 31
  2. Downtown Geology: Every Stone a Story . . . . . . . . . . . . . . . . . 41
  3. Downtown Cleveland: More Public Art . . . . . . . . . . . . . . . . . . 49
  4. Ohio City . . . . . . . . . . . . . . . . . . . . . . . . . . . . . . . . . . . . . . . . . 55
  5. Lakewood and Lake Erie Shore . . . . . . . . . . . . . . . . . . . . . . . . 60
  6. Tremont . . . . . . . . . . . . . . . . . . . . . . . . . . . . . . . . . . . . . . . . . . 65
  7. Brooklyn Centre: Community in Renaissance . . . . . . . . . . . . . . 76
  8. Riverside Cemetery . . . . . . . . . . . . . . . . . . . . . . . . . . . . . . . . . 82
  9. University Circle . . . . . . . . . . . . . . . . . . . . . . . . . . . . . . . . . . . 91
  10. Lake View Cemetery . . . . . . . . . . . . . . . . . . . . . . . . . . . . . . . . 96
  11. Cleveland Heights: History Walk . . . . . . . . . . . . . . . . . . . . . . 104
  12. Cleveland Heights: Architecture Walk . . . . . . . . . . . . . . . . . . 109
  13. Shaker Heights and Shaker Lakes . . . . . . . . . . . . . . . . . . . . . 116
  14. Chagrin Falls: Victorian Village . . . . . . . . . . . . . . . . . . . . . . . 120
  15. Berea and Baldwin-Wallace College . . . . . . . . . . . . . . . . . . . 130
  16. Bratenahl: A Lakeshore History Walk . . . . . . . . . . . . . . . . . . 138
  17. Rocky River: Lakefront and Residential Walk . . . . . . . . . . . . 148

**IV. Easy Trail Hikes**
  18. Hach-Otis Sanctuary State Nature Preserve . . . . . . . . . . . . . . 155
  19. Ohio & Erie Canal Towpath Trail, CVNRA . . . . . . . . . . . . . . 158
  20. Ohio & Erie Canal Reservation . . . . . . . . . . . . . . . . . . . . . . . 162
  21. Big Creek Reservation, Lake Isaac . . . . . . . . . . . . . . . . . . . . . 165
  22. Bradley Woods Reservation . . . . . . . . . . . . . . . . . . . . . . . . . . 168
  23. Garfield Park Reservation . . . . . . . . . . . . . . . . . . . . . . . . . . . . 172
  24. Huntington Reservation . . . . . . . . . . . . . . . . . . . . . . . . . . . . . 177
  25. Euclid Creek Reservation . . . . . . . . . . . . . . . . . . . . . . . . . . . . 180
  26. Rocky River Reservation (North) . . . . . . . . . . . . . . . . . . . . . . 183
  27. Oak Hill . . . . . . . . . . . . . . . . . . . . . . . . . . . . . . . . . . . . . . . . . 186
  28. Hinckley Reservation: Worden's Ledges . . . . . . . . . . . . . . . . 189
  29. South Chagrin Reservation: River Walk . . . . . . . . . . . . . . . . . 193

**V.  Moderate Trail Hikes**
  30. Mentor Marsh State Nature Preserve:
      Kerven and Wake Robin Trails . . . . . . . . . . . . . . . . . . . . . . . . 197
  31. Mentor Marsh State Nature Preserve:
      Zimmerman / Buckeye Trail . . . . . . . . . . . . . . . . . . . . . . . . . . 202
  32. Bedford Reservation: Tinker's Creek . . . . . . . . . . . . . . . . . . . 205
  33. Rocky River Reservation (South) . . . . . . . . . . . . . . . . . . . . . . 208
  34. North Chagrin Reservation: Hemlock Trail . . . . . . . . . . . . . . 213
  35. Mill Stream Run Reservation . . . . . . . . . . . . . . . . . . . . . . . . . 218

## VI. Moderately Strenuous Trail Hikes

36. North Chagrin Reservation: Buckeye Trail Loop .............. 221
37. North Chagrin Reservation: Squire's Castle .................. 224
38. South Chagrin Reservation: Buckeye Trail Loop .............. 228
39. Bedford Reservation: Buckeye Trail from Egbert ............. 232
40. Bedford Reservation: Buckeye Trail from Sagamore Grove ..... 235
41. Hinckley Reservation: Whipp's Ledges ...................... 235
42. Virginia Kendall Park: Ritchie Ledges / Pine Grove Loop ...... 242
43. Virginia Kendall Park: Ice Box Cave / Boston Run Trail ....... 246
44. Punderson State Park: Stump Lake ......................... 249
45. Punderson State Park: Pine Lake .......................... 252

## VII. Strenuous Trail Hikes

46. Three Waterfalls, CVNRA ................................ 255
47. Jaite to Boston Mills, CVNRA ............................ 259
48. Brecksville Reservation: Buckeye Trail to Pinery Narrows ..... 263
49. Brecksville Reservation: Buckeye Trail to Jaite ............... 267
50. Brecksville Reservation: Deer Lick Cave Loop .............. 271

Appendix ...................................................... 276
Bibliography .................................................. 277
Index ........................................................ 279

# Preface to the Third Edition

The third edition of *Cleveland On Foot* is dedicated to Harry M. Cameron, my dear husband, good friend and confidante, and collaborator on previous editions, who died at home of heart failure on Christmas Eve, 1996. He was a generous, wise, and clear-thinking man who loved to hike in the great outdoors. Together we produced the first edition of *Cleveland On Foot* in 1992 as a joint retirement project after two years of planning. We knew the trails of Northeast Ohio well. And, after of hiking in other cities that had guidebooks for local trails, we realized that Cleveland lacked a hiking guide. So we decided we would fill this need.

Never in our wildest dreams did we expect *Cleveland On Foot*—our modest, self-published endeavor—to enjoy the popularity that it has over the last six years. Harry would be happy to know that all copies of both the first and second editions have sold out. With the help of many loyal hiking friends, I have revised, updated, and rewalked all 45 chapters, and added 5 new chapters to the book. I could not have completed this project without the generous support of the local hiking community, my friends and neighbors, and my family. Contributors' names are listed in the acknowledgments.

The original goal of this guide remains the same—to share Northeast Ohio's beautiful trails and parks, and interesting urban and suburban areas, with as many people as possible. Harry's favorite quotation from Henry Adams was the following: "Chaos is the law of nature, order the dream of man." It was our dream to share the natural world with others by organizing our favorite walks and hikes in a book that would guide people to the splendor of the great outdoors.

My hope is that you will have many happy hours of walking and hiking in Greater Cleveland while enjoying the area's sheer abundance of natural beauty in all the seasons. I also hope you will discover, as we did, the immense pleasure that can be derived from the healthy exercise and refreshing peace of mind that walking and hiking bring.

Patience Wilson Cameron
February 1998

# Acknowledgments

There are quite a few people I wish to thank for helping me complete this book during a most difficult year. Many hiking friends in the Cleveland Hiking Club and Buckeye Trail Association (and other hiking groups) participated in this revised and updated edition of *Cleveland On Foot* by reviewing and rewalking the text's hikes as needed, and by helping to correct and update hike maps. The contributors include:

Sylvia Banks; Jerry Berner, president of the Cleveland Hiking Club; Georgie and David Gray; Emily Gregor, past president of the Buckeye Trail Association; Jean Znamenek; LaFronza Hardy; Art Harvey; Judy Biscan; Elizabeth McQuaid; Michael and Lidia Murphy; Shirley Pashall; Saul Isler; Richard Kana; Lynn Schreiber; Warren Davis; Louis Shainker; Jim Sprague, statewide trail coordinator for the Buckeye Trail Association; and Patricia Spoth.

The contributors listed below deserve grateful, extra-special thanks for their research and compilation of new hikes for this third edition of *Cleveland On Foot:*

Bill Manthey, Berea; Earl Waltz, Jean Weil, Tom Barensfeld, and George Lupone, Bratenahl; Michael Morgenstern, Rocky River.

Grateful thanks as well to Jane Christyson at the Cleveland Metroparks' marketing office, who made available some great images, which are included in the Cleveland Metroparks hikes featured in this edition of *Cleveland On Foot*; and to many the talented photographers who contributed images, which are identified throughout the book.

I wish also to thank my grandson Jonathan Cameron, who provided companionship on the walk through Chagrin Falls, and my friend (and hardy hiker) Elinor Polster, who accompanied me on the new downtown chapter and on several walks and hikes in Cleveland Metroparks and the Cuyahoga Valley National Recreation Area.

Others who aided me in one way or another were Walter Lennartz, longtime member of the Cleveland Hiking Club, and Sarah Clague, artist in residence at the Jewish Community Center.

Lastly, lest I leave someone out, I wish to thank all the members of my family, my neighbors, my friends, my hiking and birding companions, and the clergy and members of my church—St. Paul's Episcopal in Cleveland Heights—for their support, encouragement, and understanding.

# Cleveland On Foot

## 3RD EDITION

# Disclaimer

This guide was prepared on the basis of the best knowledge available to the author at the time of publication. However, because of constantly changing trail conditions due to natural or other causes, the author disclaims any liability whatsoever for the condition of the trails described herein, for occurrences happening on them, or for the accuracy of the descriptions. Users of this guide are cautioned not to place undue reliance upon the continuing validity of the information contained herein, and to use this guide at their own risk.

Please note that the walks and hikes from earlier editions that have been included in this edition were reviewed and rewalked by the author and contributors. New chapters were reviewed and rewalked in their entirety by the author. Contributors are noted at the end of each chapter and in the acknowledgments.

# Introduction

This book has been developed primarily for newcomers to Cleveland who have both the time and interest to explore it on foot. There are undoubtedly many in the Cleveland area for whom these excursions will provide a new and enjoyable experience. As the title implies, all the activities described here are walking tours or hikes.

This book is also for people who have lived in Cleveland for many years, possibly all their lives, but who perhaps have never learned about the wonderful hiking opportunities that abound in our area. The activities described can be enjoyed in as little as an hour or two, or as long as a full day.

Please check the descriptions carefully. I hope there are no errors or omissions, but if some have crept in please send a note and let me know how I can improve this guide next time. If the descriptions are satisfactory, I'd like to know that, too.

Hopefully, this book will encourage you to partake of the special joy that comes from walking and hiking, the sharpening of the senses that makes one feel more alive. I hope you have as much pleasure taking these walks and hikes as my husband and I have had in describing them to you, and that this guide will be only the start on a lifelong adventure in hiking.

## What Is in this Guide?

The walks and hikes described here are categorized by degree of difficulty for the average walker and hiker.

**Easy Urban and Suburban Walks** are located in and around the city of Cleveland and its suburbs. They are short walks of one to five miles, often with features of historic, scenic, architectural, or other unusual interest to enjoy. They usually follow sidewalks and involve no exertion beyond the pace and distance you set for yourself. They are also generally suitable for children.

**Easy and Moderate Trail Hikes** are located in the parks surrounding Cleveland, some in Cleveland Metroparks, and many including stretches of the blue-blazed Buckeye Trail (BT). They are usually three to five miles or more and may ascend or descend some hills. They may have uneven footing or obstacles such as stream crossings, but they are suitable for average and more experienced hikers in good health.

**Moderately Strenuous and Strenuous Trail Hikes** are also located in the Cleveland Metroparks, Cuyahoga Valley National Recreation Area (CVNRA), or state parks. They usually cover about 10 miles or more over hilly or rough terrain, on the BT or other marked trails. Some of these hikes are in remote areas and require sturdy boots and a day pack with food and liquid. On these hikes there may be steep ascents and descents, and stream crossings without the aid of bridges.

## Why Walk?

Years ago everyone walked out of necessity—to work, to school, to the store. Taking a stroll was a common pastime. Nowadays, having grown up with all sorts of transportation available, we seem to have far less need to walk. But there is value in taking to the woodland trails or even to the neighborhood sidewalks to get away from a frenetic modern lifestyle. Hikers have learned to love the peacefulness and rhythm of walking and hiking. We appreciate the benefits of physical exercise and the mental relaxation that ensues from participating in this sport. This guide will introduce you to some of the treasures and pleasures of Northeast Ohio that you can easily observe on foot.

When out walking, slow down and observe. Look for wild animals and their footprints, many kinds of birds in all their splendor, trees, wildflowers, mushrooms, and a wide variety of ferns, cloud formations, and stunning views.

How do you get started? Mental attitude is most important. The hardest part is making a determined effort to get out, perhaps alone, or with a friend or an organized group. Once you get past all the excuses you can invent for not walking, you will soon find yourself anxious to go outdoors and begin exploring. We have beautiful days for outdoor exploring in Northeast Ohio in every season.

> . . . . my mind, set free by space and solitude and oiled by the body's easy rhythm, swings open and releases thoughts it has already formulated. Sometimes, when I have been straining too hard to impose order on an urgent press of ideas, it seems only as if my mind has slowly relaxed; and then, all at once, there is room for the ideas to fall into place in a meaningful pattern.
>
> —Colin Fletcher, *The Complete Walker*

# Hiking Preparation

The most basic item to take with you on a hike or walk is a map of the area. This guide contains a map for each hike it describes. Cleveland Metroparks provides free trail maps and information about hiking at all four of its nature centers—in the Rocky River, Brecksville, Garfield Park, and North Chagrin reservations—and at ranger headquarters in Mill Stream Run Reservation and Look About Lodge in South Chagrin Reservation. More information about Cleveland Metroparks can be found in Section II, "Hiking Resources."

Maps of trails in the Cuyahoga Valley National Recreation Area (CVNRA) are available at park headquarters in Jaite and at the three visitor centers: Canal Road, Hunt Farm, and Happy Days. More information about the CVNRA is also found in Section II.

For city walks, we suggest the maps published by the American Automobile Association (216-361-6000) and the street atlases published by Commercial Survey Company (216-771-3995). Other Cleveland maps and atlases are also available—look for them at most area bookstores.

Mentioned throughout this introduction and listed in Section II are organizations from whom more hiking maps can be obtained. These sources will enable you to expand your hiking information beyond that contained in this guide.

The key to successful and enjoyable hiking is advance planning. Before starting out, read through the hike descriptions and familiarize yourself with the features, landscape, and terrain you will encounter on the walk or hike.

It is a good practice to take a compass with you as a guide should you become lost. Even if you are unsure how to read maps, a compass is invaluable in the woods. It always points close to north in this part of the country and thus helps you travel in a chosen direction.

If, despite your best efforts, you become lost while hiking, try to retrace your footsteps. This often gets you back to a missed turn in the trail. When following blazes, glance up frequently to be sure you are still on the route. (A blaze is a mark, usually on a tree, to indicate a trail.) Look down, also, to see the trodden footpath and footprints of others who have gone this way before you. Or just stop completely, look around, and go back to the last blaze. Position yourself alongside the tree or post with the last mark painted on it and look in all directions. Often you'll spot the trail going in an entirely different direction. If you are with others, shout or blow on your whistle to attract attention to your location. If all else fails, follow a stream downhill to its entry into a larger body of water. This is a useful method to get you out of the woods and often back to an identifiable landmark. Distances on our listed hikes are generally so short that you will not find it difficult to reach one of the access roads shown on the maps.

## Group Hiking

Hiking alone poses dangers such as getting lost or becoming injured without assistance available. To lessen these hazards, hike with a partner or in a group. Group hiking, for most people, is also simply more fun and companionable.

When in a group, stay together. A rule of thumb is that the last person in line always keeps the person ahead in sight. If you find yourself last and unable to keep up, the group is going too fast and you need to notify the person ahead to get word of your predicament to the designated leader. The leader is responsible for all the hikers in the group and should adjust the pace or wait at intersections for everyone to regroup, or decide how a slower hiker may return to the starting point.

Trail courtesy on a group hike includes the following: 1) allowing faster hikers to proceed ahead of you; 2) holding back branches for the closely following hiker; 3) warning the person behind you of danger ahead, such as a tree root or deep hole; 4) assisting other hikers, if they wish, in crossing streams or making their way over rough terrain; and 5) warning of an approaching car, bicycle, or horse when on a roadway, All-Purpose Trail, or Bridle Trail.

## Clothing and Footwear

When hiking and walking, comfort is of utmost importance. Most people have found the greatest ease in wearing layers of clothing that can be removed or added as temperatures change. You will need to experiment with kinds and combinations of clothing to find those that are most comfortable for you in different weather conditions. On a cool day while waiting for a group hike to start, resist the temptation to don heavy clothing that will soon need to come off after the hike starts and you start perspiring.

In hot weather, cotton keeps the body cooler than synthetic fabrics. Wool in cool weather has proven again and again to provide the greatest warmth, even when it gets wet. Veteran hikers wear cotton next to the skin, with the next layer a cotton or wool shirt that can be buttoned up or down, and sleeves that can be rolled up or down as needed.

Long pants help you avoid leg scratches, insect bites, and poison ivy. An umbrella or waterproof jacket will protect you against the inevitable rain that falls when walking or hiking. Wear a hat to protect your head from sun, low branches, and rain. The head is the best regulator of body temperature, so applying or removing a hat will often provide instant relief from cold or heat.

Proper socks provide insulation, padding, and skin comfort. Most hikers prefer to wear two pairs—a thick outer wool sock and a thin cotton or propylene inner sock. The exact combination of weight and thickness depends upon what kind of hiking or walking you are doing and upon the boot or shoe being worn. Some people wear one pair of socks with cushioned insoles that fill out the shoe space and provide extra comfort.

Sometimes you will find you need to carry an extra pair of socks to change into after getting your feet wet, a precursor of the dreaded foot blister. Some dedicated hikers apply rubbing alcohol to their feet before a difficult hike, followed by talcum powder or a medicated foot powder to help keep the feet dry. Applying moleskin or similar protection to a reddened pressure area often prevents a blister from forming. If an area of the foot starts to get painful, apply moleskin right away. And remember that nothing is more pleasurable on a hot day than bathing tired feet in a cool stream for a few moments. Try it sometime.

Boots are the single most important piece of equipment you will acquire and the most difficult to choose. Waterproofed hiking boots that are sturdy and comfortable and have non-slip soles will serve you well on most woodland trails. Sturdy running or walking shoes are most comfortable on sidewalks and paved paths.

Talk to experienced hikers about the advantages and disadvantages of different types of boots. Stick with a tried and true brand. Try on new boots using both pairs of socks you expect to wear while hiking. Be sure the boots fit your feet comfortably, provide adequate support for your ankles, and allow a little space beyond the toes for downhill hiking. As with boots, when selecting a walking shoe, search until you find the best-fitting shoes for your feet. If you expect to do winter hiking, apply a snow sealer to footwear when new and periodically thereafter to protect them from water and keep the leather supple.

## Food and Liquid

No stream, pond, lake, river, or other body of water in our area of Northeast Ohio is safe to drink from without water treatment. Always carry a canteen of water or fruit juice with you when you hike or walk, especially on a warm day. Apples or oranges to quench thirst and replace lost body liquids are handy also. You will lose body fluids quickly when hiking, not only through perspiration but through expiration. This is true even on winter hikes; you can become dehydrated quickly and not even suspect it until unusual fatigue sets in. When perspiring heavily, take small sips of liquid often for optimal body metabolism rather than gulping a large amount at once.

During a walk or hike that lasts several hours, you will wish to carry food—a sandwich, fruit, raw vegetable snacks, a trail mix of raisins, nuts, and dried fruit, hard candy, or a high-energy bar to provide the nourishment needed for this energetic sport. Eating small amounts frequently rather than a large amount at once provides a steady flow of fuel to your body without overloading your digestive system.

## First Aid

Anyone entering the woods needs to be prepared for emergencies. A turned ankle, an eyeball scratch, a bruised elbow, a heel blister, or a deep briar scratch—all of these can occur when walking or hiking in the woods. On a group hike the leader is usually responsible for carrying first aid equipment.

The amount of first aid you take depends upon the type and length of the hike and the number of people on the outing. Adhesive bandages will take care of small scratches, blisters, and cuts. As mentioned, moleskin is best applied to foot blisters or hot spots. A roll of two- or three-inch elastic bandage will handle a sprained wrist, ankle, or knee. Small sterile gauze squares and tape can stem a bleeding cut or patch an eye. Aspirin, alcohol pads, insect and tick repellent, sun lotion, and other items can also be included as needed.

## What to Carry

The length, difficulty, and location of the hike will help you determine what to carry and how. Pockets will hold a map, compass, and some food; a belt will carry a canteen and a pedometer to measure your hike; a belt pack will carry first aid, snack food, a small flashlight, a knife, and tissues; and a day pack will hold all of these items plus clothing, a hat or bandanna, rain gear, and a camera. Eventually, each hiker will determine how much is necessary and comfortable to carry.

It is a good idea to carry a flashlight with you on short winter days to aid you in finding the trail if darkness descends. A whistle is useful for calling attention to yourself in case of emergency. Always carry personal identification, and before you leave notify someone as to where you are hiking and when you expect to return.

Bird-watching is a fast-growing hobby. You may wish to carry binoculars and a bird identification book such as the National Geographic Society's *Field Guide to the Birds of North America* (see bibliography).

Identifying wildflowers is also a pastime of many hikers, but please leave the flowers where you find them. It may be tempting to carry out wildflowers, but they will wilt before you get them home. It is more fun to take along a wildflower book and study the flower right where it grows, and more enriching to look at its leaves, petals, and the other intricate and fascinating parts, as well as the environment in which it lives. A very helpful flower identification book is Lawrence Newcomb's *Wildflower Guide* (see bibliography).

## Safety

Safety is one of the prime considerations in hiking. Consider it whenever you are out alone or with a group. If a situation seems unsafe to you, avoid it. Note any caution reminders on the trail and in the trail descriptions in this guide. They are suggestions for your protection.

When on a paved trail, keep to the right to allow bicyclists, joggers, runners, and faster hikers to pass on the left. On road hikes, make a habit of facing traffic as you walk, and walk in single file if traffic is heavy. On bridle trails, when a horse and rider approach, trail safety requires that you stop immediately, step off to the side of the bridle path, and remain quiet and still until they are well beyond you. This behavior prevents a fearful horse from rearing up and injuring you or the rider. And, for obvious reasons, always watch your step on bridle trails.

When going out in wet, icy, or snowy weather you might find that normally benign trails, sidewalks, and black-topped paths have become treacherous. Many hikers find it helps to have a walking stick and they never go out without their "third leg." This support helps maintain an easy rhythm and provides substantial help in going up and down slopes. It can also be useful in beating a path through overgrown terrain and in crossing streams. A disadvantage of a walking stick is the extra weight. Often you can pick up a suitable stick on the trail when you need one and leave it at the trailhead for the next hiker to use.

## How Long to Walk

Try to take one of the easy, shorter hikes in this guide if you are a novice, to see how your body reacts. Are you sore and aching the next day? You will find you may need to work gradually into the longer and more strenuous hikes. You are the judge of the type and length of your outing. Most persons find they can gradually increase their distance by mentally challenging themselves: "I did three and a half miles today . . . I'm going to do four miles next time." Listen to your body.

## Pace

Most walkers and hikers who start out slowly soon build up their endurance and speed to about 2 to 2.5 miles per hour. The approximate times listed in this guide are calculated for the "average" hiker. But there may be times when you would like to go slower to enjoy the birds, flowers, trees, waterfalls, colorful foliage, or magnificent views. Your legs, lungs, and heart will tell you the proper pace for you to walk. It is usually better to go at a slow, steady pace for several hours than to speedhike for one or two. You'll see more, of course, by slowing your pace. If the group you are hiking with consistently goes faster than you, then consider hiking with another group or select slower hikes. An important aspect of pacing is maintaining an easy rhythm, one that can take you along for hours without your awareness of the passage of time.

## Resting

There is no formula for frequency of rests while on a walk or hike. As with taking in food, it is usually much more effective to take short, frequent rest stops, especially when ascending a steep hill, rather than an occasional long rest. Lunch and snack stops provide a natural opportunity to rest, as does contemplating a view. When public facilities are not available, a call of nature away from the trail is a chance to stop. Remember always to bury excrement and tissues.

## Walking Uphill and Downhill

Hiking uphill requires a slower pace. It takes some practice to take small, steady steps upward with very brief rests until the top is reached. If you find your heart is pounding rapidly or you are gasping for breath, you need to stop right then until it resumes a slower beat, then slowly continue your ascent and stop for a longer rest at the top. Try placing your boot flat on the slope when going up, avoiding rocks as much as possible. This maneuver stretches and strengthens the calf muscles so they will help you more the next time you ascend a slope or hill.

Downhill walking is easier on your heart but harder on your knees because you are using different muscles in descending. Go downhill slowly, making sure your footing is secure. Again, as you descend, avoid coming down on rocks, slippery mud, leaves, or tree roots. Take advantage of firmly rooted trees to assist you, checking their reliability before trusting them to help you descend. Some hikers find their walking stick very useful in walking downhill.

## Carrying In and Carrying Out

Why do some people discard trash on the trail? Are they immune to the unsightly view of cans, bottles, paper, foil, and plastic that spoils our pleasure in nature's beauties? The volume of trash left behind by increasing numbers of trail users is of genuine concern. Part of your responsibility in hiking and walking and enjoying our great outdoors is to carry *out* whatever you carry *in*. Many dedicated hikers take along a small trash bag and routinely pick up litter and recyclable cans as they walk. Some hiking clubs and other outdoor organizations regularly schedule trail clean-up hikes. These days the carry in/carry out philosophy means carrying out *more* than you carry in. If everyone did this, consider how much we would enhance the walking experience for all.

## Staying on the Trail

It is important to stay on the trail no matter how easy it may be to take a shortcut. If one leaves the designated trail, pathways are started that others will follow, creating new areas for unwanted soil erosion.

The need to respect private property is also essential. Stay on designated trails, paved paths, and sidewalks. As mentioned above, when walking on a paved All-Purpose Trail, it is best to walk to the right. All of the walks and hikes in this guide are in areas specified for public use and do require one to remain on the pathway or trail described.

## Trail Sense

Part of trail sense is plain common sense, but some of it has to be developed. It means the sense not to get lost, and, if temporarily disoriented, to find one's way back. Even a well-marked trail will occasionally have a lapse. As discussed earlier, the only thing to do is walk a short distance in the most likely direction, then return to the last marker until the continuation is found.

When disoriented, the worst thing to do is yield to panic. Sit down until you have calmed down, and decide on a course to follow. Observation is the key. Observe the terrain and the features through which you are walking. Much of the woodland has similar features, so it is often difficult to remember where you have walked. After a while one fallen tree may look like another you have passed previously. Is it? Is the ground well trodden? This seems to be the trail . . . but is it the one you came on? Trails along streams and ravines are easy to retrace. Brook crossings help orient you, and certain features observed can be unique and memorable.

Even if you are not particularly friendly with a compass, it helps to keep you walking in the proper direction. It is all too easy to walk in circles without being aware of it. Use the sun for direction and your watch to tell you how long you have walked.

You will find that your trail sense will develop naturally as you enjoy discovering the beautiful parks and woodlands in Northeast Ohio.

## Buckeye Trail Tree Blazes

Typical Buckeye Trail blazes: a single blaze indicates the hiking trail is straight ahead. The tree on the right shows two blazes, the upper blaze indicating the direction of turn.

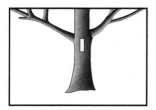 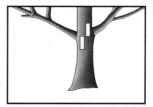

Casey Batule/Cleveland Metroparks

# Hiking Resources

A variety of the walks and hikes included in this guide were selected from the many resources below. There are, however, many more walks available in the facilities described than could possibly be included here. I hope you will take advantage of these hiking opportunities on your own and obtain information from the organizations listed here.

## City of Cleveland

Located on the shores of Lake Erie and divided by the Cuyahoga River, Cleveland—a city of half a million people—has much to offer visitors and residents alike. It is a thriving metropolitan area with many older and restored ethnic neighborhoods and lovely tree-shaded suburbs. The University Circle area contains an unusual concentration of cultural facilities. And the vast Cleveland Metroparks system, often called the "Emerald Necklace," circles the city with green spaces.

The walks and hikes listed in this guide will lead you to these and other outstanding areas of scenic natural beauty or historical distinction.

Information about the city of Cleveland can be obtained from the Convention & Visitors Bureau of Greater Cleveland, Terminal Tower, Cleveland, OH 44114 (216-621-4110), or from the Greater Cleveland Growth Association, Tower City Center, Cleveland, OH 44114 (216-621-3300).

## Cleveland Metroparks

Cleveland Metroparks, established in 1917, celebrated its 75th anniversary in 1992. The park district currently consists of 19,636 acres of land in five counties and is governed by a three-person board of park commissioners that oversees the 14 reservations and connecting parkways, as well as Cleveland Metroparks Zoo and RainForest. The tax district for Cleveland Metroparks includes all of Cuyahoga County and Hinckley Township in Medina County.

Hiking trails are an integral part of Cleveland Metroparks. Many trails were built or improved during the Depression era by Works Progress Administration (WPA) and Civilian Conservation Corps (CCC) crews. The fine craftsmanship is still evident in many of the parks' shelters, stone walls, bridges, steps, and benches.

Cleveland Metroparks includes the following 14 reservations: Bradley Woods, Huntington, Rocky River, Big Creek, Mill Stream Run, Brecksville, Bedford, Garfield Park, South Chagrin, North Chagrin, Euclid Creek, Hinckley, Brookside, and Ohio & Erie Canal. This guide describes a selection of hikes in several of them. Naturalists in the five nature and outdoor education centers (Brecksville, Garfield Park, North Chagrin, Rocky River, and Look About Lodge in South Chagrin) can provide information and maps of the parks. The reservations are generally open from 6 a.m. to 11 p.m. every day of the year. A few buildings and special facilities, such as the Cleveland Metroparks Zoo and RainForest, may have varying hours and charge admission fees. An overview map of Cleveland Metroparks is shown below:

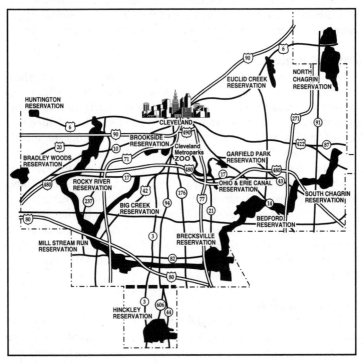

Map courtesy of Cleveland Metroparks

*The Emerald Necklace*, a monthly listing of Cleveland Metroparks activities, including hikes, is a free publication for residents of Cuyahoga County and Hinckley Township. For this publication, and for information about the parks, write or call: Cleveland Metroparks, 4101 Fulton Pkwy., Cleveland, OH 44144-1923 (216-351-6300; phone line available 24 hours). In the event of accidents or emergencies, call the ranger headquarters at 440-243-0442.

## Lake Metroparks

Lake Metroparks consists of 25 parks including about 4,000 acres throughout Lake County. The following parks have hiking trails: Chagrin River Park, Chapin Forest Reservation, Children's Schoolhouse Nature Park, Concord Woods Nature Park, Girdled Road Reservation, Hell Hollow Wilderness Area, Hidden Valley Park, Hogback Ridge, Indian Point Park, Lake Farmpark, Lakeshore Reservation, Paine Falls Park, Penitentiary Glen Reservation, Riverview Park, and Veterans Park.

Information about Lake Metroparks can be obtained from Lake Metroparks, Concord Woods, 11211 Spear Rd., Concord Township, OH 44077 (440-256-7275 or 800-227-7275).

## Headlands Beach State Park

Headlands Beach State Park and Headlands Dunes State Nature Preserve are located in Painesville Township in Lake County, just west of Fairport Harbor. These parks are directly on Lake Erie and offer pleasant beach walking. Walking on the dunes is permitted, but visitors are asked not to walk on any growing plants.

Ohio's statewide Buckeye Trail begins (or ends) in Headlands Beach State Park and is marked with two-by-six-inch blue rectangles (called "blazes") painted on trees or posts. Information about the park can be obtained from Headlands Beach State Park, 9601 Headlands Rd., Mentor, OH 44060 (440-352-8082).

## Mentor Marsh State Nature Preserve

Mentor Marsh State Nature Preserve consists of 644 acres of land and is jointly owned by the Ohio Department of Natural Resources (ODNR) and the Cleveland Museum of Natural History. It is located 3.5 miles west of Painesville on SR 283 and 0.5 mile north on Corduroy Rd. The blue-blazed Buckeye Trail is identified here as the Zimmerman Trail. There are other short hiking trails in the preserve accessible from local roads; these are described in chapters 30 and 31. Information can be obtained from Mentor Marsh State Nature Preserve, 5185 Corduroy Rd., Mentor, OH 44060 (440-257-0777).

## Hach-Otis State Nature Preserve

Hach-Otis State Nature Preserve is in Willoughby Township, 1 mile east of Willoughby Hills. Managed by the Ohio Department of Natural Resources (ODNR) and the Audubon Society of Greater Cleveland, Hach-Otis can be reached by going east on US 6, then 200 yards north on SR 174, and east on Skyline Dr. to a dead end where parking is available. Short boardwalks and trails provide spectacular views of the Chagrin River 150 feet below (see ch. 18). More information can be obtained from one of the following: Ohio Department of Natural Resources (ODNR), Division of Natural Areas and Preserves, Bldg. F, Fountain Square, Columbus, OH 43224 (614-265-6453; local 440-563-9344), or the Audubon Society of Greater Cleveland, 216-861-5093.

## Punderson State Park

Punderson State Park is located about 30 miles east of Cleveland in Geauga County, near the junctions of SR 87 and SR 44. The main entrance to the park is on SR 87, 1 mile west of this junction. A stately Tudor manor house provides guest rooms, dining rooms, and meeting rooms (440-564-9144). The 996-acre park also has housekeeping cabins, a camping area, an outdoor swimming pool, and Punderson Lake for boating, swimming, and fishing. Hiking trails surround the golf course and the glacially formed lakes and traverse the wooded hills and open fields. Two such hikes are presented in chapters 44 and 45. Information can be obtained from Punderson State Park, Box 338, 11755 Kinsman Rd., Newbury, OH 44065-9684 (440-564-2279 or 440-564-2201).

## Nelson-Kennedy Ledges State Park

Nelson-Kennedy Ledges State Park is located north of the town of Nelson on SR 282 in the northeast corner of Portage County. This small 167-acre park has interesting hiking trails that wind through caves and ancient ledges formed 350 million years ago. Information is available from Punderson State Park at the above address and phone number.

## West Branch State Park

West Branch State Park is near the town of Campbellsport on SR 14, east of Ravenna. It offers 5,352 land acres and 2,650 water acres for recreational enjoyment. The Buckeye Trail follows the perimeter of Kirwan Lake over rolling terrain with ever-changing views for a challenging hike of over 8 miles. Information about facilities in the park can be obtained from West Branch State Park, 5708 Esworthy Rd., SR 5, Ravenna, OH 44266-9659 (330-296-3239).

## Cuyahoga Valley National Recreation Area

The Cuyahoga Valley National Recreation Area (CVNRA), created in 1974, is a 33,000-acre natural valley administered by the National Park Service of the U.S. Department of the Interior. It preserves a beautiful 22-mile corridor of pastoral green space between Cleveland and Akron. It is easily accessible to residents of both cities for active recreation, for education, for study of nature and history, and for that refreshment of body and spirit so needed by those of us who are city dwellers. The Cuyahoga River, remnants of the Ohio and Erie Canal and its towpath, and the historic Cuyahoga Valley Scenic Railroad extend down the center of the CVNRA. Miles of trails are found throughout the CVNRA, including those in Cleveland's Bedford and Brecksville reservations, and Akron's Furnace Run, Deep Lock Quarry, O'Neil Woods, and Hampton Hills MetroParks. The 19.5-mile Ohio & Erie Canal Towpath Trail is open to hikers, bicyclists, and joggers between Rockside and

Bath roads. (In the fall of 1998 the Towpath Trail will extend another six miles north of Rockside Rd.) Hikes in the CVNRA vary in difficulty; some are described in this guide. An overview map of Cuyahoga Valley National Recreation Area is shown below.

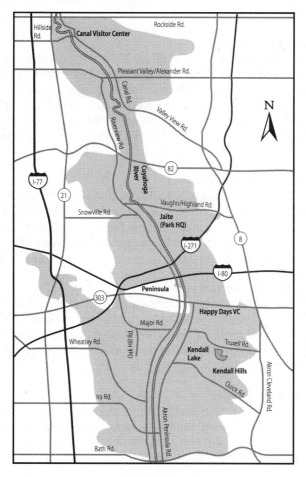

Cuyahoga Valley National Recreation Area

The National Park Service (NPS) maintains headquarters in the small historic town of Jaite on Vaughn Rd. at Riverview. The NPS buildings, painted yellow, are the restored former homes of Jaite paper mill workers. Information can be obtained from the National Park Service, 15610 Vaughn Rd., Brecksville, OH 44141-3018 (440-526-5256).

Park rangers at three visitor centers provide scheduled programs, visitor assistance, trail maps, and information about the CVNRA. Canal

Visitor Center is located in an old restored house near Hillside Rd., at 7104 Canal Rd., Valley View, OH 44147 (216-524-1497). Happy Days Visitor Center is in Virginia Kendall Park on SR 303, east of the town of Peninsula and west of SR 8 (330-650-4636 or 800-257-9477). Hunt Farm Visitor Center is at Bolantz and Riverview Rds. These centers are open from 9 a.m. to 5 p.m. daily.

## Holden Arboretum
The Holden Arboretum is a unique 2,800-acre private preserve of natural woodlands, horticultural collections, display gardens, ponds, fields, and ravines. A daily admission fee is charged to non-members who wish to use the many resources and trails available at Holden. Membership information is available from Holden Arboretum, 9500 Sperry Rd., Kirtland, OH 44094-5172 (440-946-4400 or 440-256-1110).

## Geauga Park District
The Geauga Park District publishes trail maps of Whitlam Woods, Eldon Russell Park, Big Creek Park, Metzenbaum Park, Swine Creek Reservation, and Best Wildlife Preserve. Information can be obtained from Geauga Park District, 9160 Robinson Rd., Chardon, OH 44024 (440-286-9504 or 440-285-2222).

## Lorain County Metro Parks
Lorain County Metro Parks offers hiking trails in the Black River, French Creek, Vermilion River, Wellington Creek, and Carlisle reservations. Information and maps are available from Lorain County Metro Parks, 12882 Diagonal Rd., LaGrange, OH 44050 (440-458-5121 or 800-LCM-PARK).

## Findley State Park
Findley State Park is in Lorain County near Wellington on SR 58. It offers hiking trails and recreational swimming and boating on Findley Lake. Information is available from Findley State Park, 25381 SR 58, Wellington, OH 44090 (440-647-4490).

## Metro Parks Serving Summit County
Created in 1921, Metro Parks consists of over 6,600 acres of land in a series of parks with hiking trails of varying lengths and degrees of difficulty. The parks in Summit County are Cascade Valley, Deep Lock Quarry, Firestone, Furnace Run, Goodyear Heights, Gorge, Hampton Hills, Munroe Falls, O'Neil Woods, Sand Run, Seiberling Naturealm, Silver Creek, and the 23-mile Bike and Hike Trail. For more information contact Metro Parks Serving Summit County, 975 Treaty Line Rd., Akron, OH 44313 (330-867-5511).

## Portage Lakes State Park

Portage Lakes State Park is near SR 93 and SR 619, close to Akron. It consists of 1,000 land acres with hiking trails and 2,520 water acres. Information is available from Portage Lakes State Park, 5031 Manchester Rd., Akron, OH 44319-3999 (330-644-2220).

## Tinker's Creek State Nature Preserve

Tinker's Creek State Nature Preserve is located in both Portage and Summit counties and has several short hiking trails surrounding seven ponds. From Twinsburg the preserve is 2 miles south on SR 91, then east on Old Mill/Davis Rd. Adjacent to it is Tinker's Creek State Park containing a 10-acre manmade lake for water recreation and one short hiking trail. Information about both parks is available from: Tinker's Creek State Park, 5708 Esworthy Rd., SR 5, Ravenna, OH 44266-9659 (330-562-5515).

## Eagle Creek State Nature Preserve

Eagle Creek State Nature Preserve in Nelson Township is a 441-acre park in Portage County with a bird observation blind, boardwalk, and a system of trails. It can be reached from Garrettsville by going 2 miles northeast on Center Rd., then 1 mile south on Hopkins Rd. Information is available from the Ohio Department of Natural Resources (see address under Hach-Otis State Nature Preserve).

## Sierra Club

The Sierra Club's Northeast Ohio Chapter can be reached by calling 440-843-7272. This group holds regular meetings and offers hiking, canoeing, and other outings for its members. Environmental education and conservation are major interests of the Sierra Club.

## Buckeye Trail Association

The Buckeye Trail (BT) is a blue-blazed 1,200-mile-long trail extending around the perimeter of the state of Ohio, from Lake Erie in the north, to Cincinnati in the south, to Toledo in the west. Much of the BT is on country roads, but a large portion of it goes through city and state parks, canal towpaths, forests, woods, and other public and private lands.

Along the BT the light blue two-by-six-inch blaze is painted at frequent intervals on trees, fence posts, telephone poles, and other permanent objects. If the trail makes a turn, either a blue arrow is used or a special double blaze is designated, with the upper blaze offset in the direction toward which the trail turns (see p. 19).

This Ohio footpath was put together by volunteers of the Buckeye Trail Association (BTA) who conceived the idea, planned, laid out, and blazed the routes, and today take care of maintaining the trail. The BTA sells maps and guides for many portions of the trail, holds annual and chapter meetings, and publishes a bimonthly newsletter called *The Trailblazer*. A recently formed Northeast Ohio Buckeye Trail group schedules monthly hikes. To obtain information or to join, write to Buckeye Trail Association, Inc., Box 254, Worthington, OH 43085.

## Cleveland Hiking Club

The Cleveland Hiking Club (CHC), founded in 1919, celebrated its 75th anniversary in 1994. It is one of the largest and oldest continually operating hiking clubs in the country. The CHC offers many opportunities for large group hiking. The club publishes its own schedule and requires that six club hikes be completed before membership is obtained. For information send a self-addressed stamped envelope to Cleveland Hiking Club, P.O. Box 347097, Cleveland, OH 44134-7097.

## Other local and national resources

After getting started with walking and hiking in Northeast Ohio by means of this guide or others, you may wish to consider joining a hiking organization as you get more involved in the sport. The foregoing sections have listed many local organizations to write to for information and maps. In addition, the organizations listed below may offer you an opportunity to do more walking, expand your knowledge and enjoyment of nature, participate in volunteer trail maintenance work, and, of course, enjoy the friendship and fellowship of others who love walking and hiking and the out-of-doors.

*American Hiking Society*, 1015 31st St. N.W., Washington, DC 20007

*Appalachian Mountain Club*, 5 Joy St., Boston, MA 02108

*Appalachian Trail Conference*, Box 807, Harpers Ferry, WV 25425

*Cleveland Museum of Natural History*, Wade Oval, Cleveland, OH 44106 (216-231-4600)

*Cuyahoga Valley Trails Council, Inc.*, 1607 Delia Ave., Akron, OH 44320

*Keystone Trails Association*, Box 251, Cogan Station, PA 17728

*Nature Conservancy Ohio Chapter*, 1504 West First Ave., Columbus, OH 43212 (614-486-4194)

*North Country Trail Association*, Box 311, White Cloud, MI 49349

*Ottawa National Wildlife Refuge*, 14000 West SR 2, Oak Harbor, OH 43449 (419-898-0014)

*Rails-to-Trails Conservancy Ohio Chapter*, Suite 307, 36 West Gay St., Columbus, OH 43215 (614-224-8707)

*Wilderness Center*, 9877 Alabama Ave. S.W., Box 202, Wilmot, OH 44689-0202 (330-359-5235)

# Descriptions and Map Symbols

In this guide paragraph numbers in the trail descriptions correspond to numbers on the maps. Mileage in the trail descriptions is approximate. Measurements were made with a pedometer set to an average gait; as gait changes with terrain, slight variations are inevitable. Please note that the maps are not drawn precisely to scale. Each map features a legend explaining the symbols used on that map.

Stokes Wing of the Cleveland Public Library

# Easy Urban and Suburban Walks

# 1 Downtown Cleveland
## Art and Architecture

**Distance:** 4 miles

**Walking time:** 3 hours

**Description:** This walk is on sidewalks and requires crossing many busy streets. It is best taken on weekdays when public buildings are open.

**Directions:** I-90 eastbound to Exit 171B (Ontario Ave.); north on Ontario to Public Square. OR, I-90 westbound to Exit 173C (Superior Ave.); west on Superior to Public Square. Tower City Parking located adjacent to and beneath Tower City Center. Access to parking area is off Huron Rd. near Ontario Ave. RTA trains stop terminate at Tower City Center's lower level.

**Parking & restrooms:** At Tower City Center.

In the last 10 years, the city of Cleveland has made a remarkable recovery from urban decline and decay with major building projects. Encompassing both new construction and renovations, these projects include the Key Center skyscraper, the Rock and Roll Hall of Fame and Museum, the Great Lakes Science Center, Jacobs Field, Gund Arena, the new Cleveland Browns stadium, the Warehouse District, and Playhouse Square. All of these stunning updates and additions to downtown Cleveland represent major attractions that bring people into the city. Many of the older buildings, however, still remain as important architectural landmarks.

This walk will introduce many of Cleveland's distinctive historical buildings and some of the major public art on display both outside and inside public buildings. Chapter 2, Downtown Geology, describes a walk focusing on some of the building stones and fossils to be found in the heart of the city. Chapter 3, Downtown: More Public Art, takes the walker to some of the outdoor (and indoor) works of art placed in strategic locations around Cleveland.

Often building tours are available by individual or group arrangement and are so noted in the descriptions.

**1.** Start the tour by viewing the two levels of shops in Tower City

Center. This building complex was created from a former railroad station, completed in 1930 when Terminal Tower was built. Terminal Tower was then the second-tallest building in the world and has been Cleveland's landmark ever since. (On weekends its enclosed 42nd-floor observation deck is open to the public for a unique view of the city. For information call 216-621-7981.) A 1990 renovation and expansion added new concourse space, many shops and offices, and the Ritz-Carlton Hotel. The fountains in the Skylight Concourse and between the escalators in Tower Court are of especial interest.

Note the elaborate portico at the building's exit to Public Square, with rosettes on the vaulted ceiling, vast windows, and allegorical murals—all recently refurbished. The 1930 murals by Jules Guerin surround the top of the portico. They depict transportation, industry, commerce, and the four elements: earth, air, fire, and water. Note the sloping roofs that remain over the ramps that formerly led down to the trains.

Leave Tower City Center at the Public Square exit.

**2.** Public Square was laid out in 1796 when Moses Cleaveland arrived to survey the Western Reserve of Connecticut. Standing in the southwest quadrant of the square is an 1888 James G. C. Hamilton statue of Cleaveland showing him with a compass and surveyor's staff. (It has been said that the "a" was left out of Cleaveland's name when it would not fit into a newspaper masthead!)

In the northwest quadrant is a statue of Tom L. Johnson, a beloved and influential mayor of Cleveland (1901–09), who is remembered as an opponent of vested interests. Sculptor Herman Matzen, a longtime instructor at the Cleveland Institute of Art who carved many of Lake View Cemetery's beautiful monuments (see ch. 10), shows Johnson seated with a copy of Henry George's *Progress and Poverty,* a tract that inspired the mayor to work for social change. (Johnson dedicated this quadrant to freedom of speech, encouraging Clevelanders to speak their minds from this location anytime.) Plaques on either side of the stature contain a poem written in Johnson's memory.

Most prominent in the southeast quadrant is the 1894 Soldiers and Sailors Monument by artist and architect Levi Tucker Scofield. This lofty memorial, surrounded by four massive bronze statues representing different branches of the armed forces (infantry, artillery, cavalry, and navy), is dedicated to the 10,000 Cleveland-area servicemen who served in the Civil War. The interior of this 125-foot-high structure is open to the public from 9 a.m. to 4 p.m. daily except Sundays.

**3.** From Public Square walk north to Old Stone Church, an 1834 Presbyterian Church rebuilt in 1855 and again in 1884 after being severely damaged by fires. Recent chemical cleaning of the church's exterior has brought out details in the original, locally quarried Berea Sandstone (see ch. 15). The entrance to the church is at Old Stone Center, around the corner at 1380 Ontario (216-241-6145). Tours are

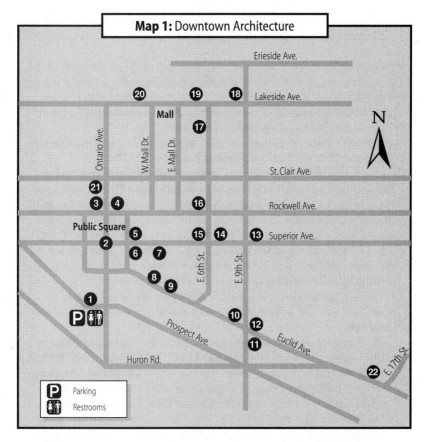

**Map 1:** Downtown Architecture

offered to see the large Tiffany and LaFarge stained-glass windows and the beautiful oak interior designed by architect Charles Schweinfurth. A small booklet available at the entrance to the nave describes these gorgeous windows in detail. The building is open Mon–Fri, from 9 a.m. to 4:30 p.m. Please stop by the reception desk for permission to enter the nave.

**4.** Opposite Old Stone Church is the old (1890), reddish sandstone Society for Savings building (now KeyBank), which has been incorporated into the new (1992) Key Tower. This complex combines the old bank, the Marriott Hotel, and a 57-story office tower—Cleveland's (and Ohio's) tallest building at 888 feet.

The old building, Cleveland's first skyscraper, was designed by John Wellborn Root. The bank is a heavy, fortress-like structure with granite pillars and arched windows. An ornate lamp fixture at one corner was designed by the Winslow Brothers Co. of Chicago; its wrought-iron post with curving iron vines supports an acorn-like glass basket containing an incandescent light. In 1879 Cleveland became the first U. S.

city to light its streets electrically using local inventor Charles Brush's flicker-free arc lamps. (Brush Electric Co. later became part of General Electric.)

Inside the old building are a beautiful stained-glass ceiling, marble columns, and murals depicting the goose that laid the golden egg by English painter Walter Crane. Here also are murals by Louis P. Szanto and Andrew B. Karoly. This artwork is described in detail in small, glass-enclosed cases at the center of the room.

At the Rockwell St. entrance of the new lobby is a large abstract painting called *Promenade du Sceptique* by Frank Stella (1974).

**5.** Turn south to Superior Ave. The red, polished-granite BP America building, built in 1985, faces west at 200 Public Square. Its eight-story atrium with indoor waterfall, plantings, and granite stairway was planned to conform to the sloping grade of the site and offers fine views of Public Square through its high glass windows. *Primal Energy*, a 1985 abstract wire and metal work by artist Richard Lippold, is suspended in the Superior Ave. lobby. In the Euclid Ave. lobby is *Étoile VIII* (1983), a brushed stainless-steel suspension by artist George Rickey.

Across Public Square is the eye-catching facade of the former May Company building with its prominent terra-cotta clock and ornamental detail.

**6.** Also on Public Square at Superior Ave. is the Old Federal Building (1910), identified across the top facade as "United States Post Office, Custom House, and Court House." This was Cleveland's first post office, and from here home delivery of mail originated in 1863—the first ever in America. No longer a post office, it now houses most of Cleveland's federal courts. The exterior figures, *Jurisprudence* on the left and *Commerce* on the right, were created in 1910 by sculptor Daniel Chester French, the designer of the Lincoln Memorial in Washington, D.C. One side of the *Jurisprudence* figure portrays a mother holding her baby (symbolizing protection); the other side a felon in chains (symbolizing justice). *Commerce* shows a figure with one arm on a globe and an ore ship in the other. To her right is Electricity and to her left, Steam. Each corner eagle high up on the roof is carved from a single block of granite and has a 20-foot wingspan.

In 1903, Chicago architect Daniel Burnham planned an elaborate mall and civic center for Cleveland. Massive stone buildings, similar in design with impressive interiors and ornate details, were to surround a central mall. Of all the buildings in the so-called "Group Plan," the Old Federal Building was the first to be completed. Only six more were finished: the Cuyahoga County Courthouse (1912), Cleveland City Hall (1916), Public Auditorium (1922) and Music Hall and North Lobby (1927), the Cleveland Public Library (1925), and the Cleveland Board of Education (1930). (Public Auditorium and the Music Hall are now part of the Cleveland Convention Center.) The ornate lamps and statues on the exterior of the Old Federal Building are characteristic of the Group Plan buildings. The Mall consists of Mall A, with Marshall Frederick's *Fountain of Eternal Life* (often referred to as "War Memorial Fountain"), and Malls B and C extending from Rockwell north to Lakeside, between East and West Mall drives.

**7.** Continue east on Superior to the Arcade, the only enclosed structure of its kind in the United States when it opened in 1890. Designed by architects John Eisenmann and George H. Smith, it joins Euclid Ave. on the south with Superior Ave. on the north, one level below. Its 400-foot-long, 100-foot-high glass-roofed, five-story atrium was built by Detroit bridge builders. This forerunner of the suburban shopping mall is sandwiched between two solid nine-story office buildings. The grand marble stairways and elegant interior details are immediately impressive. The central bridge was added in 1900 and the staircase at the Superior end in 1930. Note the mosaic floor and, overhead, the gargoyles.

Walk through the Arcade to the Euclid Ave. exit and walk east on the south side of Euclid.

**8.** Two smaller arcades were built in Cleveland to protect shoppers from the city's cold, windy winter weather. The Euclid Arcade, at 510 Euclid Ave., was built in 1911. It is a 440-foot-long, one-story terra-cotta passageway to Prospect Ave., formerly connected to the demolished Colonial Hotel.

**9.** At 530 Euclid Ave. is the slightly smaller Colonial Arcade (1898), also 440 feet long but with a second-story balcony and a Classical-style glass roof. This arcade also led to the old Colonial Hotel. It has been refurbished.

**10.** Continue east on Euclid Ave. to E. 9th St., where there are several prominent banking institutions. At the northwest corner is National City Center, constructed in 1980 with an open pedestrian plaza and a fascinating kinetic sculpture called *Triple L Excentric Gyratory (Gyratory III)*, designed by George Rickey. The blades of its three arms move slowly and randomly without regard to the velocity of the high winds that whip across this intersection.

**11.** The ornate white-granite building on the southeast corner of E. 9th and Euclid (presently closed) is identified on its upper facade as Cleveland Trust Co. This 1908 building's exterior is highly decorative, with a beautiful portico of columns. Pediment sculptures by Karl Bitter represent Banking flanked by Land and Water, the "mainsprings of wealth." When and if this structure reopens, it is worth viewing the interior, with its magnificent 85-foot-high rotunda with Tiffany-style dome of blue, green, and yellow stained glass. There are 13 columned bays with murals by Francis D. Millet depicting life in the Midwest, as well as bronze railings, marble floors and walls, and original banking desks, grilles, and doorways.

**12.** On the northeast corner of E. 9th and Euclid is Huntington

Bank, with one of the largest and most impressive bank lobbies in the United States. Built in 1924 to resemble a Roman basilica, this 30-acre room is L-shaped with entrances on Euclid, E. 9th, and Chester. The three-story-high ceiling with skylights, marble columns, standing brass light fixtures, and allegorical murals by Jules Guerin are all exceptional. The murals depict patriotism, justice, industry, and architecture, with background scenes of Cleveland and the Great Lakes.

**13.** Walk north on E. 9th St. to Superior Ave. On the northeast corner is the Cathedral of St. John the Evangelist, headquarters of the Catholic Diocese of Cleveland. Originally built in 1852, this French Gothic–style center was substantially rebuilt and refurbished, with a new tower added in 1948. The beautiful 1,500-seat cathedral contains decorative columns, stained-glass windows, stucco walls, a handcut wooden altar, statues from France, and a Lady Chapel with an impressive marble altar and small stained-glass windows.

**14.** Go west one block on Superior. Bank One Center, completed in 1991, is on the left. The massive Federal Reserve Bank of Cleveland is on the right. The Henry Hering sculpture at its Superior Ave. entrance is *Energy in Repose,* a bronze statue of a muscular laborer (modeled after Charles Atlas) who symbolizes the vast resources of the federal banking system resting in vaults until needed by the country's financial network.

Flanking the entrance on E. 6th St. are the figures of *Security* on the right and *Integrity* on the left. The sculpture on the right is armored and crowned with oak leaves, and clasps a sword and lockbox. The figure on the left is crowned with olive leaves and holds sealed documents and a rod symbolizing the oath of responsibility.

This grand building of pink granite and marble was designed in 1923 to resemble an Italian palace, with marble curbstones to mark its boundary. The interior has beautiful marble floors, walls, and pillars, and decorative iron screens representing each Federal Reserve district. This bank has one of the world's largest vault doors, which can be seen only on a Friday afternoon tour. For information call 216-579-2125.

**15.** Cross E. 6th St. to the block-long Cleveland Public Library. Third largest in the country, after the Library of Congress and the New York Public Library, the Cleveland Public Library was the first to create the system of placing books on open shelves for public browsing.

The main library building is closed for renovations at present. Adjacent to it is the Louis Stokes Wing, opened in 1997. These two buildings are separated by the Eastman Reading Garden designed by Maya Lin, the well-known architect of the Vietnam Veterans Memorial in Washington, D.C.

When the main library building reopens in late 1998 or early 1999, take a look inside to view the marvelous marble staircases, painted lobby ceiling, light fixtures, and clock globe at the entrance. Three-story Brett Hall, a huge reading room, has four unusual murals within its portals: straight ahead (north) is *The City in 1833*; to the right is *Sommer's Sun*; on the rear (south) wall is *Public Square;* and to the west is *Night Sky:Cleveland 1978*. A free pamphlet at the reference desk describes these murals in more detail. A tour of the library can be scheduled by calling 216-623-2800.

**16.** From the library walk north on E. 6th St. to the Board of Education Building, the last Group Plan building to be built (1930). Walk west on Rockwell to Memorial Plaza and the main facade of the Board of Education Building. A 1932 statue of Abraham Lincoln by Cleveland's Max Kalish stands on the west side of the plaza (Mall A). This naturalistic figure shows President Lincoln delivering his memorable Gettysburg Address, which is engraved on a plaque below. Enter the Board of Education Building at the Mall A entrance to view the beautiful marble lobby.

The striking *Fountain of Eternal Life* (also known as "War Memorial Fountain") was designed in Art Deco style in 1964 by a former Clevelander, Marshall M. Fredericks. Restored in the 1980s, this image memorializes area service personnel who died in World War II and the Korean War. The 35-foot bronze statue of a young man emerging from flames and reaching toward the heavens rises from a hollow, filigreed sphere depicting the ancient superstitions and fears that often underlie war. Four massive granite carvings surround the statue and represent the world's great civilizations.

**17.** The long Cleveland Convention Center complex that lies along E. 6th St. between St. Clair and Lakeside Aves. consists of Public Auditorium (1922) and the Music Hall and North Lobby (1927). An addition with much-enlarged display space and a new mall entrance was added in 1964. The complex was completely renovated in 1988, and the Convention Center is now used frequently for gatherings of all kinds. The huge Public Auditorium has 11,500 seats, all with an unobstructed view of the stage; the smaller Music Hall seats 2,800.

**18.** Walk east on Lakeside Ave. At the green just past E. 6th St. is a bronze statue of a young George Washington looking toward the west, created by William McVey in 1973.

Across the street in tiny Willard Park is the massive freestanding artwork called *Free Stamp*. Designed in 1985 by Claes Oldenburg and Coosje van Bruggen for the SOHIO (now BP America) Building on Public Square, it was to have been a "contemporary paraphrase" of the nearby Soldiers and Sailors Monument on Public Square. *Free Stamp* was to have been placed face down in front of the BP America building, but because of disagreements, BP gave it to the city, which had it redesigned and turned on its side for this location. It was finally installed in 1991 after much controversy.

Beyond *Free Stamp* (across E. 9th St.) is North Point, an office building at 1001 Lakeside. At the entrance stands *Symphonic Suite,* an interesting 1990 bronze grouping by Mike Cunningham consisting of six stylized musicians with painted and patined surfaces.

**19.** Directly west of *Free Stamp*, on Lakeside Ave. and E. 6th St., is the grand Cleveland City Hall, designed by J. Milton Dyer. This majestic building was recognized in 1983 by the American Institute of Architects as one of the outstanding city halls in the nation. From its stately portico to its magnificent rotunda, City Hall is an impressive treasure to view. The stunning interior features a two-story-high barrel-vaulted ceiling, skylights, marble floors, walls, and columns, murals, and bronze lamps and gates. Displayed here is Archibald Willard's masterpiece painting *The Spirit of '76*, restored in 1987. Much of the interior of City Hall was renovated in the 1970s. The beautiful mayoral suite contains fine-grained oak walls and five painted tapestries showing scenes of early Cleveland. The handsome city council chambers, among the largest and most elegant in the country, boast a gold-leaf ceiling, chandeliers, hand-carved English oak paneling, and a large Ivor Johns mural—*Where Men and Minerals Meet* (1928)—symbolizing Cleveland's importance as a shipping, mining, and industrial center. Tours of City Hall may be arranged by calling 216-664-2000.

North of City Hall on Erieside Ave. is the new I. M. Pei–designed Rock and Roll Hall of Fame and Museum, and, adjacent to it, another new institution, the Great Lakes Science Center (GLSC). Across Erieside Ave. from the GLSC is the new Cleveland Browns Stadium (under construction as of this writing, and scheduled to open in 1999). Further up E. 9th St. (at its northern terminus, past the Rock Hall) is the *Steamship William G. Mather*—a floating maritime museum—and Voinovich Park. All of these sites are worth visiting because of their close proximity.

**20.** Proceed west on Lakeside Ave. to the Cuyahoga County Courthouse, another one of the Group Plan buildings. This one has a gorgeous columned portico with statues of important legal figures along the cornice, and statues of Alexander Hamilton and Thomas Jefferson in front. The 10 marble cornice statues were made by Karl Bitter and other sculptors in 1911 to represent important episodes in the evolution of the British and American legal systems.

The six figures above the main entrance on Lakeside Ave. from left (west) to right (east) depict men who influenced the development of law in England: Archbishop of Canterbury Stephen Langton (1150–1228), who won the signing of the Magna Carta; Simon de Montfort (1200–1265), who established the House of Commons; King Edward I (1239–1307), who implemented judicial reform; John Hampden (1594–1643), who authored the Petition of Rights; Lord Chancellor John Somers (1651–1716), the force behind the passage of the Declaration of Rights; and William Murray, Earl of Mansfield (1705–1793), who contributed to the development of commercial law.

The four statues above the north entrance represent historical figures who played a significant role in our legal heritage: Moses (moral law); Roman emperor Justinian (civil law); Alfred the Great (common law); and Pope Gregory IX (canon law). The bronze figures on each side of the north entrance are of U.S. Chief Justice John Marshall (1755–1835) and Ohio Chief Justice Rufus P. Ranney (1813–1891).

The grand 1911 sculptures of Thomas Jefferson and Alexander Hamilton that flank the main entrance steps are also by Karl Bitter. Although in life these two men had a rancorous relationship, here they are seated side by side. However, there is a great contrast in their portrayal. Jefferson, author of the Declaration of Independence and our first secretary of state, embraced individual rights; Hamilton, our first secretary of the treasury and prime mover in the ratification of the U. S. Constitution, personified power and prestige. Bitter shows Hamilton sitting up straight and looking imperious; he is holding a hat, gloves, and a walking stick and wearing elegant slippers fastened with ribbons. Jefferson, in contrast, seems deep in thought and wears heavy buckled shoes and rumpled clothes; some crumpled papers hang loosely from his right hand while his left arm rests casually on the back of the chair.

The elegant marble hall inside the courthouse has a beautiful vaulted ceiling and large murals on the second floor at either end—*The Constitutional Convention, September 17, 1787* by Violet Oakley (1915) at the north end, and *King John Signing the Magna Carta at Runnymede, 1215* by Frank Brangwyn (1913) at the south end.

On the east side of the hall is a marvelous curving marble stairway with a Tiffany stained-glass window in the center entitled "Justice." Designed by Frederick Wilson and Charles Schweinfurth in 1913, this beautiful window memorializes famous legal figures.

**21.** From the courthouse walk south on Ontario, returning to Public Square and Tower City Center. Along the way note the ornate Standard Building at 1370 Ontario with its distinctive terra-cotta starburst design on the exterior panels.

**22.** An optional extension of this walk will take you to a historically and culturally interesting section of Cleveland a few blocks east of downtown. Playhouse Square on Euclid Ave., between E. 14th St. and E. 17th St., is Cleveland's magnificently restored theater district. The Allen, Ohio, State, and Palace theaters were once homes to vaudeville, movies, and legitimate theater; today they house the Cleveland Ballet, Cleveland Opera, Great Lakes Theater Festival, and many other performing arts groups. Resplendent with marble staircases, ornate ceilings, and crystal chandeliers, the State's 320-foot lobby is one of the world's longest. Here are four 50-foot murals painted by James Daugherty in 1921–22.

Free guided tours of the complex are offered once a month, from 10 a.m. to noon on Saturday and Sunday, except in January and August. Call 216-771-4444 for more information.

# 2 Downtown Cleveland
## Geology: Every Stone a Story

**Distance:** Less than a mile

**Walking time:** Varies, but allow 2 hours

**Description:** This walk does not cover a very large area but requires adequate time to fully examine the buildings, stones, and fossils. It can be shortened, of course, to accommodate whatever time is available to you. There are some busy street crossings. Because entrance to a few public buildings is necessary, it is best to take this walk on a weekday. Bring a small magnifying glass, if possible, to allow for closer scrutiny of fossil details.

**Directions:** I-90 eastbound to Exit 171B (Ontario Ave.); north on Ontario to Public Square. Or, I-90 westbound to Exit 173C (Superior Ave.); west on Superior to Public Square. Tower City Parking located adjacent to and beneath Tower City Center. Access to parking area is off Huron Rd. near Ontario Ave. RTA trains stop at Tower City Center's lower level.

**Parking & restrooms:** Available at Tower City Center.

Most of the information for the following walk was adapted from *Guide to the Building Stones of Downtown Cleveland: A Walking Tour* (Ohio Division of Geological Survey Guidebook No. 5, 1992) by Joseph T. Hannibal and Mark T. Schmidt. Hannibal, a geologist and Curator of Invertebrate Paleontology at the Cleveland Museum of Natural History, also provided additional information and carefully reviewed this chapter for accuracy.

Much of the city of Cleveland is spread over a giant prehistoric valley carved over 2 million years ago, and later widened and deepened by erosion from several different advancing glaciers that covered this area during the Ice Age, which lasted from about 2 million years ago to about 12,000 years ago. These glaciers and several ancient lakes predating Lake Erie left layers of material that now fill this valley with silt, clay, and sand. The bedrock supporting Cleveland's tall buildings is more than 200 feet below the surface at Public Square. The area on either side of the Cuyahoga River known as the Flats was formed by the cutting action of the present Cuyahoga River.

In erecting Cleveland's larger structures, builders have used both local rocks and stones imported from various parts of the world. Architects selected specific stone types for the exteriors and interiors of

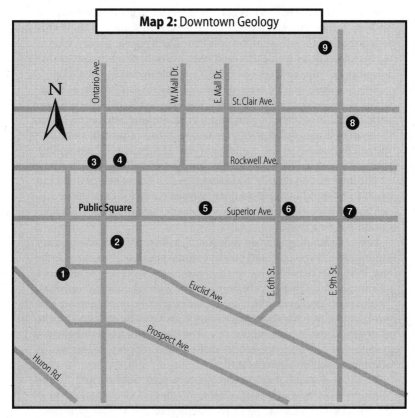

Map 2: Downtown Geology

buildings based on the stone's ornamentation (color, texture, and pattern), durability, workability, and, of course, cost and availability.

Many of Cleveland's familiar downtown buildings are made of a wide variety of geologically interesting building stones. These rocks, many with fossils embedded in them, provide a fine opportunity for allowing your mind to wander back to prehistoric times and trying to imagine how the earth was when it was in a far different stage of development from its present one.

**1.** Begin the walk at Tower City's exit to Public Square (see ch.1, note #1 for a description of Tower City).

The beautiful Tennessee marble flooring in the portico is from the Holston Formation in the Knoxville, Tennessee, area. This rock was formed in the Ordovician Period (505 to 438 million years ago), when that area was inundated by an inland sea. The small white blobs in the stone are organisms that once lived in the warm sea. In geologic terms, marble is a limestone or dolomite that has been recrystallized below the earth's surface due to heat and pressure. This limestone, however, has not been recrystallized, so it is not a true marble in geological terms. In builders' terms, though, marble can be described simply as somewhat soft carbonate rock that can be polished. The irregular black seams in the marble, called stylolites, formed when portions of the limestone dissolved away, with dark, concentrated, insoluble materials remaining.

The Botticino marble walls in the lobby were also formed as limestone, at the bottom of a warm sea that covered Italy in the Jurassic period (208 to 144 million years ago). What appear to be round circles in the marble are coated grains, formed by grains of sand or small fossils rolling around in the shallow sea and accumulating surrounding layers of calcium. These spheres now are cut through and appear flat.

The information desk in the inner lobby has side panels of Botticino marble and a top of Verde Antique, a trade name for dark-green serpentine-rich rock containing iron and magnesium, often used as a decorative building stone.

Leave the building and take a close look at its exterior, made of Salem Limestone, a frequently used building stone quarried in southern Indiana. It consists mostly of the calcium carbonate skeletons of billions of marine animals. These can be seen with or without a magnifying lens. The fossil organisms in the limestone lived in the warm, shallow sea that once covered Indiana about 325 million years ago. The dark gray blocks of stone underfoot (surrounded by red blocks) are of flame-roughened granite that has been treated to make it less slippery. When wet, it becomes darker and quite beautiful.

**2.** Cross Public Square to the 125-foot-high Soldiers and Sailors Monument on the southeast quadrant, with its 15-foot statue, *Liberty*, at the top. Dedicated in 1894 to commemorate the 10,000 men from Cuyahoga County who served in the Civil War, the monument was designed by the architect Levi T. Scofield. In front of each of the building's four outer walls are bronze sculptures representing the four branches of the service—the infantry, artillery, cavalry, and navy.

Take a look up at the blackish gray stone in the column and exterior of the monument. It is polished Quincy (Massachusetts) Granite that is probably of Mississippian age (formed 360 to 320 million years ago). Each of the 10 blocks that compose the column weighs about 14 tons. The reddish stone used for the outer steps and for the platform at the top of the stairs is Grimsby Sandstone from Medina, New York, estimated to be 438 to 408 million years old. The curved markings you see on the platform at the top of the steps represent wave ripples in the sand, frozen by the action of geologic forces.

Much of the light beige stone of the monument is Berea Sandstone quarried locally in Amherst, Ohio, and is around 360 million years old. This sandstone formed as deposits of beach sand, shallow marine sand, or sand dunes. It is a very hard rock useful in building. What looks like long horizontal grooves along the inner side of the small west pedestal is inclined layering of the sand created during its formation. Geologically, the sand grains in this sandstone are much like those found in beach sand at Edgewater Park.

A United States Geological Survey bench mark is embedded in the stone rail on the northwest side of the monument, marking its location 668 feet above sea level.

**3.** Cross Public Square to Old Stone Church (First Presbyterian Church) at the corner of Ontario St. and Rockwell Ave. Built in 1853 of Berea Sandstone, it is the oldest building in downtown Cleveland; its light gray color (formerly dark black due to air pollution) is the result of a recent chemical cleaning. Note the small marks on the facing stones made by stoneworkers' brushhammers. The exterior sandstone was mined in Carlisle Township, Lorain County. The massive bell mounted on the sidewalk dates from 1865.

It is well worth the time to visit the interior of this church, elaborately redesigned by the architect Charles Schweinfurth in 1884 after a disastrous fire. The entry is through the office of Old Stone Center, 1380 Ontario St. (216-241-6145). Note the gorgeous mahogany paneling, graceful carvings, barrel-vaulted ceiling with structural tresses, Holtkamp organ, and magnificent stained-glass windows. Artist John LaFarge designed the Amasa Stone window on the south wall and Louis Comfort Tiffany designed two of the windows on the west wall—*Beside the Still Waters* and *I Am the Resurrection and the Life*. Tiffany also created two of the windows on the east wall—*The Sower* and *The Recording Angel*. A pamphlet describing Old Stone Church and its art and architecture is available in the office area.

**4.** Walk across Ontario St. to the reddish Society for Savings building (now KeyBank), Cleveland's first skyscraper, which opened in 1890 with five-foot-thick ground-floor walls that help support the 10-story structure. Attached to the southwest corner of the building is an elaborate wrought-iron post supporting an ornate, acorn-shaped street lamp. It is one of Cleveland's original street lights in a city that was among the first to electrify its roads.

The base and low columns of the building are Graniteville granite from Iron County, Missouri; dating back about 1.3 billion years it is one of the oldest stones used in Cleveland's buildings. The deep reddish stone used in the upper portion is Jacobsville Sandstone from Houghton County, Michigan. This rock is composed of tiny grains of quartz and feldspars, and its reddish color is derived from hematite. More stoneworkers' brushhammer marks are easily visible.

As you walk east toward the entrance to the new 57-story Key Tower, note the clever glass connector between the old and new structures. At 888 feet, Key Tower (originally known as Society Tower) is now Cleveland's (and Ohio's) tallest building, and the tallest structure between New York City and Chicago. The facing on the tower's lower floors is

Napoleon Red granite from Sweden; on the upper floors it is pre-Triassic Stony Creek granite from Branford, Connecticut, more than 245 million years old. The sidewalk in front is flame-roughened Stony Creek granite that, on a rainy day, turns a handsome dark color.

Purplish Rosso Levanto marble from Turkey adorns the interior lobby floor. This stone was formed in the early Tertiary period (66.4 to 1.6 million years ago). The gorgeous Breccia Pernice marble walls in the lobby are from the Mt. Pastello region of Italy and are Jurassic (208 to 144 million years old). These limestone walls contain large and small fragments with small fossils within, to create unusual rock embedded in rock.

Walk toward the bank of elevators serving floors 24–39 and note the light and dark orange marble walls. The marble is Rosso Verona from the Venice area of Italy and is Jurassic in age. Some of the circular nodules are ammonite fossils. An ammonite is an extinct type of cephalopod with a multichambered shell through which a siphuncle (tube) passes. The chambers of ammonites were separated by complex partitions (see photo 1). A 4-inch ammonite can be found on the north side of the bank of elevators serving floors 24–39, between the two elevators to the west and about seven feet from the floor. Another ammonite, about the same size, lies in the marble on the south bank of elevators (serving floors 13–23), toward the east side, in the third marble panel from the east opening, about two feet above the floor.

Photo 1: Ammonite

To see the splendid interior of the original building's grandly restored banking hall, turn west to the entrance to the old Society for Savings. Fourteen stone columns support a 26-foot-high ceiling enclosing a spectacular stained-glass skylight. Two beautiful Walter Crane murals depict the story of the goose that laid the golden eggs, and two other murals by Szanto and Karoly illustrate the fable of the sons' buried inheritance. In small glass-enclosed cases are descriptions of the artwork.

**5.** The next stop is at what is generally considered to be Cleveland's most beautiful building—Cleveland Public Library—built in 1923–25. Walk south on Public Square one block to Superior, and east on Superior to the block-long library on the left. (See ch. 1, note #15 for more information about the library.)

The exterior stone is white Murphy marble (also called Cherokee marble) from Tate, Georgia, which has suffered considerably from general weathering, acid rain deterioration, and rough cleaning methods. Because of this erosion, concrete balusters supporting the upper railing in the building's front have replaced the original marble columns. Murphy marble is Cambrian in age, formed 570 to 505 million years ago. The main entrance steps are made of North Jay (Maine) Gray granite. The main library building is closed for renovations until late 1998. Many of the library's materials and services have been moved to the adjacent Louis Stokes Wing, newly opened in 1997. When the main library reopens, it is anticipated there will be a major reorganization of departments between the two buildings.

Just inside the entrance of the main building are Tennessee marble floors with top, side, and bottom views of stylolites, formed where the rock was sutured back together after portions of the limestone dissolved away. Note the beautiful Botticino marble walls and staircases, painted ceiling, light fixtures, and clock globe at the entrance. Straight ahead is the entrance to three-story Brett Hall, originally the general reading room and now the general reference room. The travertine flooring has now been covered with carpeting. When the library opened in 1925, travertine, a porous freshwater limestone, was ideal for absorbing the noise created by the many footsteps echoing in this majestic room. The hall is lighted by splendid windows.

Take the impressive marble stairway up to the third floor. On the second floor note the striking architecture of the surrounding buildings, visible through the windows. These openings were strategically designed to enable librarians and visitors to enjoy pleasant outside views while working inside.

The John Griswold White collection of valuable rare books is located in room 323. When visiting this room it is necessary to leave identification with the librarian in charge in order to look at the interesting fossils here. Just inside the entry door, take a close look at the round corals in the limestone door trim. This beautiful marble was found in Ozora, Missouri, and is a 380-million-year-old Devonian rock that was created from remnants of a shallow-water coral reef.

Go to the far east end of the room to the left door frame of the door marked "Staff Only," and look about four and a half feet up from the floor. Here you will see a fossil of rugose coral, about two inches in diameter, appearing in cross section as a small round formation with spokes (see photo 2). It is also called horn coral because it is cone shaped and sometimes superficially resembles a horn. In the marble windowsills are many more smaller horn corals. Before leaving this room, be sure to see the exhibit of many rare and unusual chess sets in the glass cases.

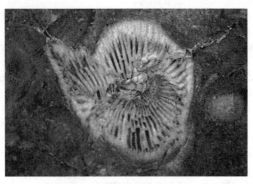

Photo 2: Rugose coral (horn coral)

Leave the White Room to go downstairs to the second floor hallway near the History Room. Here, in the Botticino marble wainscoting, are good examples of coated grains. These five-millimeter-wide formations appear as flat, round fossils with concentric layers of calcium carbonate that enclose tiny grains. In some cases there is even a tiny, comma-shaped snail inside. As mentioned earlier, coated grains were formed by the tumbling action of waves in shallow water that caused accretions to gradually build up around the tiny fossils.

Next, step inside the History Room (room 210) to see another fossil, foraminiferans. These small half-inch-diameter fossils are embedded in the cream-colored limestone marble windowsills. Foraminiferans are types of one-celled organisms with hard supporting structures consisting of many chambers. Fossilized, they appear as tightly wound spirals. A good example is found in the third windowsill from the reference desk, at the east end of the sill.

Between the main library building and the Louis Stokes Wing is the Eastman Reading Garden, named for Miss Linda Eastman. (See ch. 8, note #4.) An L-shaped pool and water sculpture in the garden were designed by Maya Lin, the architect of the Vietnam Veterans Memorial in Washington, D.C.

New York architect Malcolm Holzman designed the Louis Stokes Wing in Beaux Arts style to fit into the boxy Group Plan buildings in an interesting way. (For a description of Cleveland's Group Plan see ch. 1, note #6.) The glass exterior of the Stokes Wing represents the lamp of knowledge. U. S. congressman Louis Stokes remains a strong supporter of library needs and member of the board of directors. Many artists produced distinguished art for the new wing. Information about the art is available at the main desk. The building is open from 9 a.m. to 6 p.m. Monday through Saturday, and 1–5 p.m. Sundays. It is closed Sundays in the summer (216-623-2800).

**6.** Leave the Louis Stokes Wing and continue east on Superior Ave.to E. 6th St. to reach the Federal Reserve Bank on the corner. This imposing, fortress-like building was designed in 1923 by architects Frank Walker and Harry Weeks to resemble a grand Italian palace. It is clad on its lower portion with a reddish gray Moose-a-Bec granite from Maine, a 408- to 360-million-year-old Devonian rock. The upper portion is a beautiful pink Murphy marble with dark streaks (called Etowah marble by builders) from the Tate area of Georgia and is Cambrian in age (570 to 505 million years old). The handsome statues, *Security* on the right and *Integrity* on the left, are also of Murphy marble, as are the curbstones that mark the bank's territory.

It is worthwhile going inside the Federal Reserve Bank to admire the gorgeous marble floors, the gold Sienna walls and columns with prominent veins of calcite, and the hand-painted cathedral ceiling. (See ch. 1, note #14 for more information on the Federal Reserve Bank.) Other features of the building can be seen on a Friday afternoon guided tour by calling 216-579-2125.

**7.** Continue walking east on Superior Ave., past the new annex to the Federal Reserve Bank, to E. 9th St. On the northeast corner is the Cathedral of St. John the Evangelist, the headquarters of the Catholic Diocese of Cleveland. Originally built in 1848–1852, this French Gothic–style church features an exterior of multicolored Tennessee Crab Orchard stone (Crossville Sandstone) from Cumberland County, Tennessee, from the Pennsylvanian period (320 to 286 million years old). Its unusual red, brown, and orange patterns have been created by iron oxides. Its sheen, which is visible on a sunny day, is due to small fragments of mica within the rock. The church's exterior trim and statues are of Salem Limestone, containing tiny calcified organisms. On the small north wall next to the square tree planter, and visible at about eye level, are straight and curved tubular burrows, or channels, up to two centimeters wide and 24 centimeters long. These interesting tubes were made by organisms churning through shoal sediments in the sea, leaving behind trace fossils.

Take a look inside this gorgeous cathedral, seating over 1,500 people. The interior features decorative columns, beautiful stained-glass windows, stucco walls, a handcut wood altar, and statues imported from France. The Lady Chapel in the south transept contains an impressive marble altar lit by small stained glass windows.

**8.** Continue walking north on E. 9th St. to One Cleveland Center at 1375 E. 9th, near St. Clair Ave. This handsome, "silver chisel" building, completed in 1983, contains many easily visible fossils that stand out in the polished Champlain Black marble (Crown Point Limestone) in the lobby. The honed grayish base and low walls of the building's exterior are made of the same stone, but it has deteriorated markedly due to acid rain and has split off along stylolites, where jagged cracks have developed in the limestone along its seams. This limestone comes from Isle La Motte, Vermont, and is Ordovician in age (505 to 438 million years old).

Step inside the lobby and look on the wall opposite the down escalator near the elevators for a large snail fossil called maclurites. It is about 10 centimeters in diameter (see photo 3). Also embedded in this beautiful black stone are smaller nautiloid cephalopods containing many chambers separated by thin partitions (see photo 4).

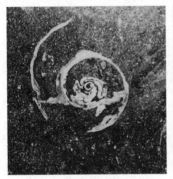

Photo 3: Maclurites          Photo 4: Nautiloid Cephaloid

**9.** From here you may return to Tower City Center by retracing your steps, going south on E. 9th St. and west on Superior Ave., or you may wish to stop in at the Galleria at Erieview, the spectacular glass-enclosed shopping arcade at St. Clair and E. 9th St.

From the Galleria it is an easy walk north past Lakeside Ave. to the I. M. Pei-designed Rock and Roll Hall of Fame and Museum, and the Great Lakes Science Center just west of the Rock Hall. The new Cleveland Browns stadium is expected to open in 1999. The Rapid Transit Authority's waterfront line includes a stop at E. 9th St. that will return you by train to Tower City Center, if desired.

There are many other interesting building stones in downtown Cleveland that invite exploration. If you wish to continue your investigation, please refer to the Hannibal and Schmidt publication mentioned at the beginning of this chapter; it is available at the Cleveland Museum of Natural History's gift shop, The Ark in the Park (216-231-4600).

This chapter was prepared with the generous assistance of Dr. Joseph T. Hannibal, Curator of Invertebrate Paleontology, Cleveland Museum of Natural History. It was reviewed and rewalked by the author.

# 3 Downtown Cleveland
## More Public Art

**Distance:** 3.8 miles

**Walking time:** 2 ½ hours

**Description:** This walk is on sidewalks and requires crossing many busy streets. Use CAUTION at wide intersections and cross only at signals. Since most of the buildings are closed on weekends, it is best to take this walk on a weekday, if possible.

**Directions:** I-90 eastbound to Exit 171B (Ontario Ave.); north on Ontario to Public Square. OR, I-90 westbound to Exit 173C (Superior Ave.); west on Superior to Public Square. Tower City Parking located adjacent to and beneath Tower City Center. Access to the parking area is off Huron Rd. near Ontario Ave. RTA trains stop at Tower City Center's lower level.

**Parking & restrooms:** At Tower City Center.

Cleveland's public art in the downtown area is well worth seeing. Chapter 1 describes much of the city's unusual art collection both inside and outside public buildings, and generally north and east of Public Square. This chapter continues the exploration of art on foot, generally south and west of Public Square. These impressive artistic pieces are often located in unexpected places. Some of the art is old, some very new. All is interesting. Much of the information in this chapter is adapted from the Committee for Public Art's booklet, *A Walking Tour and Guide to Public Art in Downtown Cleveland* (1995).

**1.** Start the walk at Tower City Center. (For a description of the art in the center, see ch. 1, note #1.) Exit at Public Square and turn right (southeast) on Ontario St. Pass Prospect Ave. and at North Garage, cross Ontario St. to the Garden at Gateway. Cross Huron Rd.

**2.** On the corner of Huron Rd. and Ontario St. near the entrance to Gund Arena is Nancy Dwyer's *Meet Me Here* (1994). These large block letters carved from red granite are 18 inches high and serve as convenient seats to rest on. They also function as a humorous landmark for spectators who might become separated from their companions.

Continue along Ontario past Gund Arena. This site is where the NBA's Cleveland Cavaliers play basketball and many other sporting and entertainment events occur. Turn left at Gateway Plaza. Gateway is a 28-acre sports and entertainment complex built in 1994. Gund Arena and

Jacobs Field, the home of the Cleveland Indians baseball team, are located here. Gateway was the original name of the development project that gave rise to Jacobs Field and Gund Arena.

**3.** *Sport Stacks: Gateway Plaza Columns* were designed by R. M. Fisher in 1994 to provide a futuristic look and yet relate to the nearby industrial area of Cleveland. At 80 and 92 feet tall, these steel columns incorporate doorways in their design and provide ventilation and emergency exits for the large service area underneath the plaza. At night, concentric rings of blue light radiate from the towers with amber lights beneath them that make the structures appear to float.

Pass Gate A and take a peek inside beautiful Jacobs Field behind the fencing, then continue east on Gateway Plaza to Gate C.

**4.** At this corner is another of Nancy Dwyer's artworks, *Who's On First?* (1994). These carved, red granite block letters also serve as seating and pay tribute to Abbott and Costello's classic comedy routine, the first recording ever to be enshrined in the Baseball Hall of Fame.

Here also is a bronze statue of Bob Feller, the Cleveland Indians' winningest pitcher, who played with the team throughout his career (1936–1956, except for 4 years in the military during World War II). Signed when he was only 16, Feller pitched three no-hitters and 12 one-hit games in his career with the Indians.

Return along Gateway Plaza to E. 6th opposite Gate A. Along the east side of Gund Arena is another sidewalk sculpture, *Market Place/Meeting Place: An Urban Memorial* by Angelica Pozo and Penny Rakoff (1994). This piece commemorates the history of this strategic site alongside the river, and of Central Market, which opened here in 1856. The mosaic frieze around the base of the work depicts the colorful fruits, vegetables, meats, fish, and dairy and bakery products once sold here. The top of the piece (which also serves as seating) contains captioned tiles fired with sepia-toned photographic images that recall the area's rich history as a neighborhood with homes and churches and a market center. The four keystones contain bits of glass, crockery, and dishes dug from the site by archaeologists before Gateway was constructed.

**5.** Continue on Gateway Plaza to Ontario St. and turn right (northwest) to Huron. Carefully cross at Huron Rd. and Ontario St. to the sidewalk alongside Tower City Center's west side.

**6.** Turn right at W. 3rd St. and left at W. Prospect to the MK-Ferguson Building, the former Main Post Office. The murals at the entrance off Prospect were painted in 1936 by J. J. Greitzer, with sponsorship from one of President Franklin D. Roosevelt's New Deal programs. The Art Deco interior lobby has been beautifully restored. Still remaining are the bas relief sculptures on the walls, echoed in the panels at the counters. Also remaining are the former post office windows for stamps, money orders, parcel post, general delivery, and so forth. The

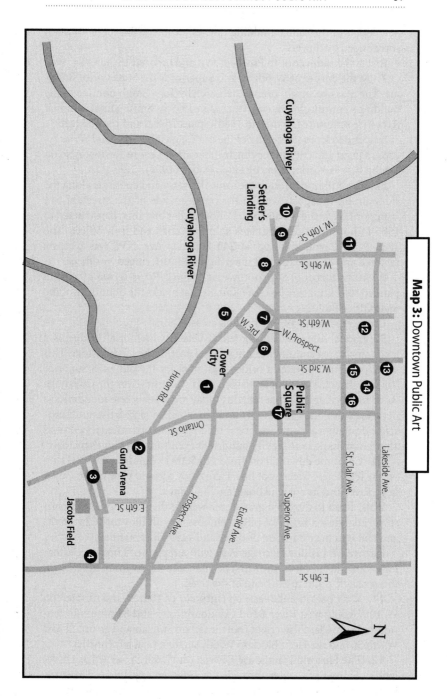

**Map 3:** Downtown Public Art

new lobby in this office building houses an interesting pole fountain surrounded by flowers.

Exit at the same door to Prospect Ave. and turn left to Superior Ave.

**7.** At the corner of W. 6th St. and Superior is the State Office Building. The massive, bright orange steel arch by Tony Smith dominates the building's entrance. *Last,* constructed in 1979 as Smith's final Minimal Art–style sculpture (he died in 1980), spans 75 feet and rises 35 feet.

Suspended from the ceiling of the building's lobby is *Cloud Series IV, 1981,* a linen and cotton weaving by fiber artist Lenore Tawney. Also on exhibit here is *Passing Years* by Hugo Robus (1952).

Exit the building through the same doorway and continue along the sidewalk on Prospect Ave. On the opposite side of the street, at 614 Superior NW, is the ornate John D. Rockefeller building, constructed in 1905 to house the oil magnate's shipping, coal, and iron offices. The 1888 Perry-Payne building, at 740 Superior Ave. NW, was recently restored and contains a great inner-lighted court, ringed by offices.

**8.** At the corner of Superior Ave. and Huron Rd. is *Terminal, 1979,* a painted steel sculpture by Gene Kangas that marks the boundary of the State Office Building.

Cross Superior to W. 9th St., then cross W. 9th.

**9.** Viaduct Gateway, on the left at Veterans Memorial Bridge, is a landscaped area commemorating a vital part of the city's history. This small park incorporates a bridge abutment for the old 1878 Superior Viaduct that carried people, wagons, and streetcars over the Cuyahoga River for 40 years. All that remains today are seven stone foundations; new curbs and sidewalks mark the old roadbed. In 1992 artists and landscape designers added a variety of wild plants in ornamental beds and aluminum markers to signify important events in the bridge's history.

**10.** Continue downhill on Huron to Settler's Landing, the first stop on the RTA's new waterfront line. Here enjoy a grand view of the Cuyahoga River and its colorful boats and buildings.

Walk down to the open grassy area west of the train stop. At Friendship Park, view a series of pillars embossed with tiles made by adults and children in celebration of Cleveland's 1996 Bicentennial.

Farther west is tiny Heritage Park with a replica of Lorenzo Carter's log cabin. Carter, Cleveland's first permanent resident, built his cabin at this strategic point in the bend of the river.

**11.** Walk back uphill (east) on Huron to W. 10th St. and turn left on W. 10th, going past River Bend Condominiums and Sammy's Restaurant, to W. St. Clair. Turn right (northeast) on St. Clair and go uphill past W. 9th St. and the Hoyt Block to W. 6th St., then turn left (north).

**12.** The Historic Warehouse District on W. 6th St. served as Cleveland's commercial center through the 19th century. In the 1840s the street was lined with warehouses and blocks of varied businesses, including clothiers and dry goods stores. The architecturally interesting facades of these old buildings range from cast iron to Italianate and Romanesque.

Pass Wolf's Gallery and turn right (east) on Lakeside and left at W. 3rd St. to Fort Huntington Park.

**13.** A stone plaque in Fort Huntington Park commemorates an 1813 skirmish here when General William Henry Harrison warded off the British fleet in the War of 1812.

William Walcutt's memorial to Commodore Oliver Hazard Perry commemorates another hero of that war, who made the memorable announcement, "We have met the enemy, and they are ours." At age 28, Commodore Perry was a national figure who turned the tide of the war in the Battle of Lake Erie. His monument has been moved many times—from its original site at Public Square to Wade Park, then to Gordon Park, and then finally taken out of storage and rededicated and placed here in 1991.

Toward the north end of the park is a statue of Jesse Owens, made in 1982 by William McVey to pay tribute to the African-American track star who brought four gold medals back to Cleveland from the 1936 Berlin Olympics.

Nearby stands the *Greater Cleveland Peace Officers Memorial*, a stunning new monument to law enforcement personnel who have died in the line of duty.

Cross W. Lakeside to the Justice Center.

**14.** Enter the Justice Center at the Lakeside doorway. Immediately to the right is award-winning artist George Segal's *Three Figures on Four Benches* (1981). This contemporary sculptor used plaster-soaked bandages wrapped around live models, then carefully cut away and reconstructed the work. These figures have been cast in bronze to withstand the weather, then coated in white to recapture the appearance of the original plaster.

Inside the lobby is *Edge, 1977* by Gene Kangas (see note #8), a five-figured steel sculpture placed on a multicolored steel floor. The bright mural painted on six panels is *Mondrian Linear/DIA, 1977* by John Pearson.

**15.** Walk to the W. 3rd St. exit to see two more contemporary sculptures. *Sentimental Scale*, on the right, is a 12-foot-high portrayal of the allegorical figure of Justice shown as a headless torso brandishing a shield. Along the outer wall on the left is *Wedge*, which serves as an architectural support device. These welded bronze works were created by the African-American sculptor Richard Hunt in 1977.

Return to the lobby and exit through the Ontario St. doorway.

**16.** Here is Japanese-American Isamu Noguchi's monumental work, *Portal*. This sculpture was Cleveland's first abstract public art placed in a prominent place downtown (1976) and drew considerable public reaction. Noguchi's 36-foot-high sculpture is of black-coated steel pipe that twists elegantly back upon itself to represent a modern Shinto gate or ceremonial entry to a shrine. (In this case, city and county courtrooms, jails, and police headquarters!) As you walk around the composition, look up to see surprising views framed by the steel tubes, and a continual transformation of the work.

Continue south along the sidewalk to the last Justice Center entryway near the corner of Ontario and W. St. Clair. The Cleveland Police Historical Society and Museum, Inc., is just inside the entrance and offers free admission during open hours, weekdays from 10 a.m. to 4 p.m. This small, interesting museum shows a 1926 jail cell, as well as a fingerprinting table, motorcycles, confiscated weapons, uniform displays, photographs, and other memorabilia of Cleveland's law enforcement history.

**17.** Continue south on Ontario, returning to Public Square and Tower City Center. Along the way note the ornate Standard Building at 1370 Ontario with its distinctive terra-cotta starburst design on the exterior panels.

This chapter prepared by the author with the assistance of Elinor Polster. Some information was adapted from the Committee for Public Art's booklet, *A Walking Tour and Guide to Public Art in Downtown Cleveland* (1995).

# 4 Ohio City

**Distance:** 4 miles

**Walking time:** 3 hours

**Description:** This walk is on sidewalks (with one hill to descend and ascend if the portion along the Cuyahoga River in the Flats area below Ohio City is toured).

**Directions:** I-90 eastbound to Exit 170A (W. 25th St.); north on W. 25th. OR, I-90 westbound to Exit 171C (Abbey Ave./W. 14th); left (west) on Abbey over bridge; right (north) on W. 20th St.; left (west) on Lorain Ave. to W. 25th. RTA trains (Red Line) and buses stop at W. 25th St. station.

**Parking & restrooms:** Park at the West Side Market lot, near the corner of West 25th and Lorain. Restrooms are located inside the market.

Ohio City, Franklin Circle, and Market Square together constitute a historic district of the city of Cleveland. Located on the west side of the Cuyahoga River along W. 25th St., this area was a bustling little town with many small homes and businesses in the mid-1800s. Originally a separate city (incorporated as such in 1836), Ohio City merged with Cleveland in 1854. It is now a culturally rich and diverse neighborhood, with many early homes and business buildings still surviving. There has been much restoration of homes and businesses in Ohio City in the past few years, the results of which can be seen on this walk. Improvements to the West Side Market and along W. 25th St. in the Market Square District are planned for the future.

**1.** Start the walk at 1979 West 25th St., the West Side Market. Built in 1912, this European-style market hall, centerpiece of the near West Side, is topped with the tall copper-domed Benjamin S. Hubbell clock tower, originally a water tower. It is open on Monday and Wednesday from 7 a.m. to 4 p.m. and Friday and Saturday from 7 a.m. to 6 p.m. (216-664-3386). It is interesting to view the food stalls inside the market and the open-air vegetable stands outside, many of which have been operated by the same families for generations. The facility (including its large, ornate western window) was restored in 1989. It is now a National Historic Landmark.

**2.** Opposite the market is Market Square Park. At the northwest end of the park is the Great Lakes Brewing Co. (2516 Market St.), an intriguing, multilevel restaurant with period decor and a brewery located inside the building. In the mid-19th century it was a seed and feed supply store.

**3.** Go west on the south side of Lorain. Athens Imported Foods at 2545 Lorain sells Greek foods and other imported Greek items both locally and all over the United States.

**4.** Hansa Import House, Inc., at 2701 Lorain, specializes in German goods and is a travel agency as well.

**5.** Next on Lorain is the imposing architecture of St. Ignatius High School (1888). The school was originally St. Ignatius College, which later became John Carroll University and moved to University Heights. The boys' high school remained, and in the 1970s new buildings, an athletic field house, and a track were added.

St. Ignatius High School

**6.** Turn right (north) on West 32nd to Carroll. Turn left (west) on Carroll to Fulton. Turn right (north) on Fulton to Bridge Ave. Turn right (east) on Bridge.

**7.** Carnegie West Branch Library (1910) is across the street. Restored in 1979, it was among the first branch libraries in Cleveland. It was built with money donated by Andrew Carnegie, who was impressed with Cleveland's progressive library system. This ornate building is triangularly shaped to conform to its three-sided lot.

**8.** St. Patrick's Church (1871) is north of the library at 3602 Bridge. It was built over a 10-year period by early Irish settlers who quarried the

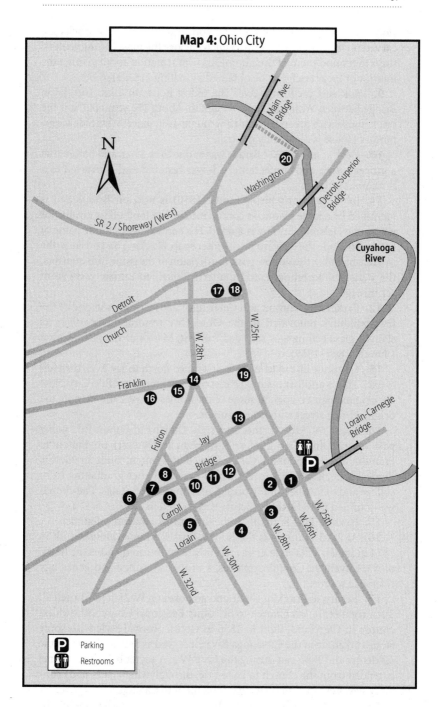

**Map 4:** Ohio City

stone in Sandusky for the building and tower. Inside, shamrocks are carved on the support columns, which enclose the masts of the settlers' ships to remind them of their homeland. Information about visiting the interior of the church can be obtained by calling 216-631-6872.

**9.** Walk east on Bridge Ave. The oldest house in Ohio City is on Bridge between West 32nd and West 30th. About 150 years old, it is the brick house with green trim and a wrought-iron fence. West Side Community House is diagonally opposite.

**10.** Heck's Cafe at 2927 Bridge was at one time a bar, and before that a grocery store and confectionary. It was restored and converted to a restaurant in 1974.

**11.** John Heisman's birthplace (c. 1850) is next on Bridge and is identified by a large plaque to commemorate the football innovator for whom the Heisman Trophy is named. His contributions to the game of football include the forward pass, center snap, blocking on end runs, the hidden-ball play, the double pass, the division of the game into quarters, the statistical scoreboard, and the term "hike!" to initiate plays from scrimmage.

**12.** Parker's Restaurant and Catering at 2801 Bridge is in one of the first buildings renovated in the Ohio City restoration of 1971. Its stained-glass ceiling was salvaged from St. Mary's of the Assumption Church (1865–1969).

**13.** Continue ahead to W. 25th St. and go north to Jay Ave.; turn left (west). This is another restored street of small homes in Ohio City. Note the original paint colors on some of the homes. At W. 29th Pl., note the original brick street with center gutters.

**14.** Reach W. 30th St. and turn right (north) to Fulton Rd., going past newer Ohio City homes. Turn right (northeast) on Fulton to Franklin Circle. Franklin Circle Christian Church, built in Gothic Revival style, is where James Garfield preached after graduating from college and before becoming president of the United States. The church was founded in 1842; the structure was erected in 1875.

**15.** Next, at 2831 Franklin, is the fortress-like Masonic Temple.

**16.** At 2905 Franklin is the Robert Russell Rhodes House, built in 1874 in Italian Villa style. It has recently been restored and is the home of the Cuyahoga County Archives, a property history and genealogy reference source.

**17.** Return to Franklin Circle and go north on W. 28th to Church St. Turn right (east) on Church to St. John's Episcopal Church, the oldest church in Cleveland. Built in 1836 in Gothic Revival style with some stones taken from the Cuyahoga River, it served as Station Hope on the Underground Railroad during the Civil War. A secret basement tunnel extended from the church to Lake Erie, through which (it is said) runaway slaves escaped to boats that took them to Canada.

**18.** The original home and office of Dr. George Crile, one of the founders of the Cleveland Clinic, still remains at 2516 Church St.

**19.** Turn right (south) on W. 25th St. and return to the West Side Market, passing Lutheran Medical Center on the right.

*Optional*

**20.** This walk can be extended by walking north from Franklin Ave. on W. 25th St. at point #18. Pass the Detroit-Superior Bridge and St. Malachi Church. Turn right at Washington Ave. (unmarked). Go downhill on Washington to the Flats area and the west bank of the Cuyahoga River. Start by exploring the Power House, a shopping mall converted from an old power station. You will recognize it by its tall smokestack. Walk north on the boardwalk, which is located just outside the Power House, along the river, to pass nightclubs, restaurants, and cruise and pleasure boats. Turn around at the end and traverse the always-fascinating boardwalk in the opposite direction. There may be large ore boats slowly navigating the sharply bending Cuyahoga River to the steel mills. Retrace your steps up Washington Ave. to W. 25th St. and the West Side Market.

Courtesy Ohio City Near West Development Corp.

Revitalized storefront, Market St.

# 5 Lakewood
## and Lake Erie Shore

**Distance:** 6 miles, with an optional mile extension
**Walking time:** 3½ hours
**Description:** This walk is flat and mainly on sidewalks.
**Directions:** I-90 to Exit 166 (W. 117th St.); north on W. 117th to Lake Ave.
  Left (west) on Lake to Lakewood Park; enter park at Belle Ave.
**Parking & restrooms:** At Lakewood Park.

This walk through parts of Cleveland and Lakewood reveals some fine old mansions, sweeping views of Lake Erie, and high-rise apartment buildings in the area along the lakefront's so-called "Gold Coast." Many lovely old homes built between 1900 and 1930 stand on tree-lined Edgewater Dr., Clifton Blvd., Lake Ave., and other wide avenues throughout the city. Many of the old mansions were built by well-known Clevelanders including Mark and Leonard Hanna, Robert Rhodes, Alexander Winton, and others. Most have been demolished now, but some of their former locations will be noted on this walk.

Lakewood, which celebrated its 100th anniversary in 1989, was settled by pioneers who were attracted by its abundant water, woods, and game. Later it became a farming community, known as East Rockport, and grew into a substantial town and an industrial city. Now Lakewood is an attractive suburb of about 60,000 residents, close to Cleveland's downtown.

The Oldest Stone House Museum, located at 14710 Lakewood Ave. in Lakewood Park (where this walk begins), is the home of the Lakewood Historical Society. The museum, just south of Foster Pool and the ballfield, houses period furnishings and memorabilia from the early 19th century. This pioneer home, built in 1838 by a Scotsman named John Honam, was moved to this site in 1952 and restored by the Lakewood Historical Society. Old gravestones grace the rear garden. The building is open 1–4 p.m. on Wednesday, and 2–5 p.m. on Sunday. Tours are free. The historical society office is open every weekday morning, but both the office and building are closed in December and January. Call 216-221-7343 for more information.

Nearby (but not on this walk) is the oldest surviving structure in Lakewood: Nicholson House, at 13335 Detroit Ave. James Nicholson, the first permanent settler in this area, built his attractive home in 1835. It is now used for special events and is not open for public viewing.

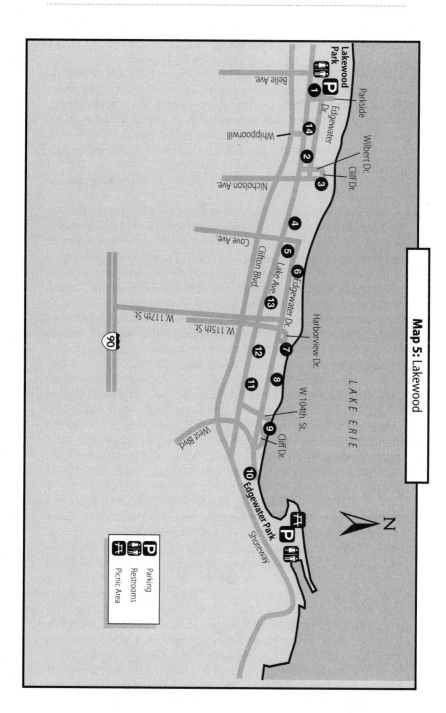

**Map 5:** Lakewood

Both the Oldest Stone House and Nicholson House are listed on the National Register of Historic Places.

**1.** Start the walk by viewing beautiful Lake Erie from behind the fence at Lakewood Park. In the open area, note the large purple-martin house that attracts these small purple-headed birds during the summer months. The 24-room summer home of Robert Rhodes, brother-in-law of businessman and U.S. senator Marcus A. Hanna, once occupied this site. The home, called The Hickories, built before 1880, served as Lakewood City Hall after 1918. It was torn down in 1959.

Walk out of the park on Edgewater Dr., east of the parking area and bandstand.

**2.** Follow Edgewater Dr. to Wilbert Dr. At 13823 Edgewater Dr. (east of Kirtland Ln.) is the location of the former Theodor Kundtz Castle, torn down in 1961. Kundtz was an inventor, manufacturer, financier, philanthropist, and patriarch of Cleveland's Hungarian community. He built his baronial mansion around the turn of the century on five beautifully landscaped acres between Lake Ave. and Edgewater Dr., including the present Kirtland Ln. Each room of the house was richly decorated with hand-carved woodwork and furniture. Kundtz was a skilled woodworker who founded the company that produced cabinets for the White Sewing Machine Co. The mansion featured an elevator, bowling alley, ballroom, and an atomic bomb shelter.

**3.** Turn left (north) to Cliff Dr. and another sweeping view of the lake. From Cliff Dr. turn right at Nicholson Ave. (Edgewater Dr. ends here.) Note the fancy stone wall on the left along the north side of Lake Ave.

**4.** Continue east on Lake Ave. to the series of tall high-rise apartment buildings. This residential area is called the "Gold Coast." Here stand The Carlyle (1968), Winton Place (1961), The Meridian (1971), Marine Towers West, and other structures of newer vintage.

At 12576 Lake once stood the Alexander Winton home, Roseneath, the 25-room residence of the inventor and pioneer automobile manufacturer. Tragedy hit the Wintons in 1903 just after they moved in, when Mrs. Winton was found floating in Lake Erie a half mile from their home, having apparently fallen from the cliff behind their house during a foggy night. Winton, who married three more times, founded Winton Bicycle Co., Winton Motor Carriage Co., and Winton Gas Engine & Mfg. Co.

Note the name Roseneath on the driveway pillars marking the entrance to the Winton estate. Again, note the beautifully crafted stone walls marking the Lake Ave. boundary of these homes.

**5.** At Cove Ave. turn left and walk to Edgewater Dr. Lake Shore Towers (1929) is straight ahead. It is one of several apartment buildings constructed in this area in the 1920s and '30s and later.

**6.** Turn right at Edgewater Dr. and continue going east. At 12000 Edgewater Dr. ("Twelve Thousand") once stood banker Lewis Murfey's 1903 home, Briarhurst.

Next on the left was Thornwood, William J. White's 52-room mansion. White, a chewing-gum manufacturer (American Chicle Co., the maker of Beeman's Pepsin Gum) and U.S. congressman, lost his fortune after business failures.

**7.** At W. 115th St. turn left. Then turn right to take the loop around Harborview Dr. Note the red-tile-roofed 1913 residence at 11320. This handsome Georgian sandstone home with its magnificent views of Lake Erie, the Cleveland skyline, and beautiful sunrises and sunsets, once belonged to Matthew F. Bramley, a businessman and owner of Cleveland Trinidad Paving Co., Templar Motors Co., Bramley Storage Co., and Luna Park (a famous local amusement park).

**8.** Continue east on Edgewater Dr. The home at 11212 Edgewater belonged to William F. Telling, president of the Telling-Belle Vernon Co., a dairy on Carnegie Ave. in Cleveland.

Between here and W. 103rd St. were three large lakeshore estates: Ednawood, at 10522 Edgewater (torn down in 1971), which belonged to the clothing manufacturer Julius Feiss; Urncliff, Leonard Hanna's home; and Glenmere, Marcus Hanna's home, designed by the well-known Cleveland architect Charles Schweinfurth. Leonard Hanna was a major Cleveland philanthropist, patron of the arts, and director of M. A. Hanna & Co. Marcus A. Hanna was president of the iron and coal company bearing his name, a national Republican leader, U. S. senator, and campaign organizer for President William McKinley.

**9.** Just past W. 104th St., turn left to Cliff Dr. and right (east) on Cliff Dr. for another sweeping view of Lake Erie and a stunning view of the Cleveland skyline.

At one time Jacob Perkins, friend of the Hannas and son of a wealthy railroad tycoon, owned farmland from W. 105th St. east to W. 76th St., including all of what is now Edgewater Park. His mansion, Twin Oaks, stood just east of Marcus Hanna's estate, high on the bluff near the present western edge of Edgewater Park.

**10.** Continue east on West Blvd. to enter Cleveland Lakefront State Park (Edgewater Park). In 1894, when Perkins sold his land to the city, Perkins Beach and Edgewater Park were created as two parks, Lower Edgewater and Upper Edgewater. The original pavilion on Upper Edgewater was renovated in 1982. (Restrooms are located here.) The 1902 monument to Conrad Mizar, father of concerts in the parks, is the oldest in the city of Cleveland.

A paved bicycle path connects the upper park to the lower park, which has a large grassy picnic area, a 900-foot-long beach (Perkins Beach), a bathhouse and beach concession, a 1.6-mile fitness trail, fishing platforms and a pier, and a boat launch.

NOTE: An optional walk through the park to the Edgewater Yacht Club and Marina is especially pleasant in the summer, when several hundred boats are moored here. This extension adds another mile to the walk.

**11.** Return through Edgewater Park to West Blvd. and Lake Ave. and walk west on Lake Ave. Finely designed homes are all along this wide street. The driveway pillars at 11100 Lake Ave., marked "Open Hearth," indicate the home of Charles Wellman, a partner in Wellman-Seaver Engineering Co.

**12.** At 11412-11416 Lake Ave. once stood a 22-room mansion called Westwood, belonging to millionaire Ralph Hickox, who frequently entertained financier J. Pierpont Morgan. Hickox was well known for his lavish entertaining.

**13.** Near 11732 Lake Ave., just past W. 117th St. and the Cleveland–Lakewood city line, was the J. C. Weideman home, Waldmere. Weideman, a German by birth, was a leading wholesale grocer and businessman. He established the Cleveland-based Weideman Co, initially a wine and liquor firm but later one of the largest wholesale groceries in the country.

The house with the long front stone wall at 12537 Lake Ave., marked "Shady Cove," was the home of Eva Kaber, Lakewood's so-called Lady Borgia, who engineered the murder of her husband. A fascinating account of this tale appears in John Stark Bellamy's true-crime compilation *They Died Crawling* (Gray & Co., 1995).

Stone driveway pillars at 12984 Lake Ave., marked "Lake Cliff," identify the home of a Cleveland funeral director, B. F. Harris.

At Nicholson and Lake Aves. are several fine homes.

**14.** Near Chase Ln. at 13900 Lake Ave. is a gas station discreetly hidden below street level to avoid disharmony with the residential surroundings of this handsome neighborhood.

Continue along Lake Ave., returning to Lakewood Park.

This chapter was prepared by the author with information from Tom Barensfeld, former *Cleveland Press* librarian and features writer.

# 6 Tremont

**Distance:** 2 miles

**Walking time:** 1 ½ hours

**Description:** The walk through Tremont is entirely on sidewalks and provides many stops for enjoyment of the community's historical, architectural, and gastronomic features. A weekday, when most of the shops are open, is a good time to visit Tremont. To enter some of the churches and other historic buildings it is necessary to telephone ahead. At the conclusion of the walk are several stops somewhat distant from the central community that are easier to visit by car. They are denoted on the map with square hike reference numbers.

**Directions:** I-90 westbound to Exit 171C (Abbey Ave./W. 14th); right (east) on Abbey; right (south) on W. 14th for three blocks to Lincoln Park. OR, I-90 eastbound to Exit 170A (W. 25th); cross W. 25th and proceed straight on marginal road (Wade Ave.); left (north) on Scranton Rd.; right (east) on Starkweather Ave. to Lincoln Park, on left after W. 14th. OR, I-77 north to I-490 west; exit at W. 7th St.; north on W. 7th; left on Literary to end at Lincoln Park, Kenilworth Ave., and W. 11th St.

**Parking & restrooms:** Free parking on Kenilworth Ave. at Lincoln Park; restrooms are available at the library.

This interesting walk will take you through 150 years of early settlement, decay, and renaissance.

Tremont is a small community located on an 80-foot-high plateau just south of downtown Cleveland above the Cuyahoga River. The small neighborhood is bounded by I-490, the Inner Belt (I-90), and the southwestern ridge above the flats. Residents enjoy an excellent view of the Cuyahoga River, the downtown skyline, and the steel mills in the industrial area below. This somewhat isolated area has a long and interesting history; it is home to 25 churches within one square mile—the greatest concentration of churches in the city. (A recent bequest by a generous benefactor ensured that many of Tremont's church steeples will be illuminated at night.) Its renaissance, celebrated in recent years, is due to local development efforts, community cohesion, and its successful, frequently offered art and architecture tours.

The first people to settle in Tremont came from New England in 1818. They were wealthy residents who wished to build their homes outside the city of Cleveland. Around the middle of the century, Cleveland

University was established in Tremont, but it was only in existence from 1851 to 1853. The area was then known as University Heights, and today several streets still bear the names given to them at that time: Literary Rd., Professor St., and College Ave. Because of Cleveland's industrial growth, this exclusive section lost many of its illustrious citizens to the eastern suburbs, but some of their attractive old homes still survive and can be seen on this walk.

When immigrants from Central and Eastern Europe flocked to the United States at the beginning of the 20th century, numerous families settled in Cleveland. Many lived in Tremont and built their churches there to be near the mills where they worked. After these residents had died or moved out, changes in the neighborhood caused the community to slide into decline in the 1950s and '60s.

In the last few years, Tremont has started to come back as a desirable place to live for young families and for people commuting to downtown Cleveland. It is a multicultural and multiracial community, with residents from Hispanic, Ukrainian, African-American, Russian, Greek, Polish, Slovak, and other ethnic backgrounds. The community is home to a number of artists and artisans.

**1.** Begin the walk at the northeast corner of Lincoln Park, at Kenilworth Ave. and W. 11th St. Lincoln Park, formerly Pelton Park, was originally part of a 275-acre parcel purchased by Mrs. Thirza Pelton and Mr. John Jennings for the campus of Cleveland University. When the university closed, the land continued to be used as a park. During the Civil War, President Abraham Lincoln sent troops here for an encampment; after that, residents changed the name to Lincoln Park.

At this intersection are several fine eating establishments.

**2.** At 2337 W. 11th St. stands a 1911 Romanesque building called Lemko Hall, formerly a Slavic social hall (Koreny's) with a saloon, gambling rooms, and a ballroom. Later the first floor housed a grocery store and, still later, in 1977, it was the site of the wedding reception in the film *The Deer Hunter*. Note how the building's shape conforms to its lot; note, also, its arched windows and striking corner tower with pointed dome. After extensive renovation several years ago, the upper level of Lemko Hall was converted to residential suites.

**3.** Continue to the right (northeast) up Literary Rd. to W. 10th St. You will pass an unusual old brick building at 2258 W. 10th St. Note the white decorative stars covering the building's bracings and the former stable doors in front.

On the right at 2280 Literary is a beautifully renovated home and studio whose owner practices the traditional religious art of iconography.

**4.** On the left at Literary Rd. and Professor St. is Lola, a fine eating establishment with a notable, contemporary interior design.

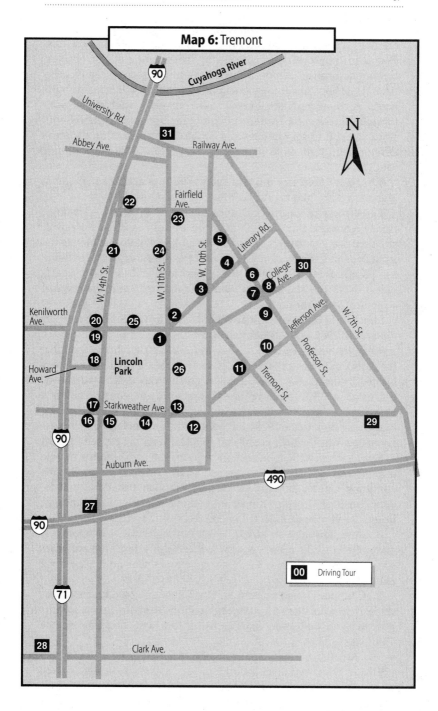

**Map 6:** Tremont

Cuyahoga River

University Rd.

Abbey Ave.

Railway Ave.

Fairfield Ave.

Literary Rd.

College Ave.

W. 10th St.

W. 11th St.

W. 14th St.

W. 7th St.

Jefferson Ave.

Professor St.

Kenilworth Ave.

Lincoln Park

Howard Ave.

Starkweather Ave.

Tremont St.

Auburn Ave.

Clark Ave.

N

00 Driving Tour

**5.** North of this intersection is Tremont West Development Corporation (TWDC), at 2190 Professor St. It is an organization whose mission is to "improve and maintain the living, cultural, and business conditions for all of Tremont." This community-based association helps rehabilitate housing for low- and middle-income families, assists businesses in commercial development, and organizes neighbors to work together on common issues to promote the Tremont neighborhood. You may wish to stop in for some updated information on the area's development. (For more information, call 216-575-0920.) Continue south on Professor St.

**6.** At 2247 Professor is Third Federal Savings and Loan, in one of Tremont's early-20th-century commercial buildings.

The owners of Raphael's Draperies, at 2253 Professor, have completely renovated this building to create a wholly new structure, with attention devoted to keeping its original look. With the exception of the front door and brick walls, everything in this once-dilapidated building has been replaced to create a shop, workroom, and three new apartments. Note the stained-glass window (retained from the original structure) above the door.

Matt Talbot Inn, a residential alcohol rehabilitation treatment center founded in 1965, is at 2270 Professor.

**7.** St. John Kantu (Cantius) Roman Catholic Church and School at the corner of Professor St. and College Ave. is a large building complex located in the heart of an old Polish neighborhood. The parish was organized in 1898, and it grew quickly, requiring the construction of a new combination church and school in 1913. A convent and parish house were built in the 1920s, followed by the present large and imposing yellow-brick church completed in 1925. With the capacity to seat 1,000 worshippers, St. John's has an inspiring interior. Beautiful marble angel friezes along the barrel-vaulted ceilings, stained-glass windows admitting natural light, and a magnificent altar installed from the demolished St. Joseph Franciscan Catholic Church all enhance its beauty. Services are conducted in Polish, English, and Spanish.

**8.** Note Edison's Pub at 2373 Professor. A favorite neighborhood establishment, Edison's was once a "five-and-dime store"; it now houses some interesting Thomas Alva Edison memorabilia and other offbeat antique items.

**9.** Continue along Professor St. The building at 2406 Professor was extensively rehabilitated in 1991 by Tremont West Development Corporation to create seven apartments for low- and moderate-income Tremont residents.

**10.** At Jefferson Ave. turn right (southwest). The Jefferson Branch (1918) of the Cleveland Public Library, at 850 Jefferson Ave., is well worth visiting to see how an old building has been converted for modern library use. This small limestone structure was modernized in 1981 by opening up interior space with skylight windows, yet the edifice still fits right in with its residential neighborhood. The renovation project won an Award of Excellence for Library Architecture in 1983. The library holds a large collection of historical materials on Tremont. Hours vary; call 216-623-7004.

**11.** Continue along Jefferson, past Iglesia De Dios Evangelica, a church serving the neighborhood's Hispanic population. On the right at Tremont and Jefferson is Tremont Elementary School. Continue southwest on Jefferson.

**12.** Cross W. 10th St. to Starkweather Ave. and walk west on Starkweather past several lovely old homes on the left. These Greek Revival double homes have all been renovated.

**13.** At the corner of Starkweather and W. 11th St. is the Merrick House Community Center, a social service agency offering diverse programs for Tremont residents. Named for Miss Mary Merrick, founder of the National Christ Child Society, the organization developed from a program begun in 1919 to aid new Cleveland residents. The current building was constructed in 1949.

Pulaski Post 30 at 1041 Starkweather is located in an architecturally interesting building with an unusual tower overhang above the entrance.

**14.** Beyond W. 11th on Starkweather are two grand examples of restored Victorian homes, at 1103 and 1107 Starkweather. The careful maintenance of these striking residences reflects this community's pride and respect for its heritage.

Dempsey's Oasis Tavern at 1109 Starkweather is another well-known Tremont landmark.

At the south end of Lincoln Park is the former Lincoln Park Bathhouse. This 1921 structure is a relic of the days when residents of Tremont lacked indoor plumbing and used this facility for bathing. Newly restored, it houses condominiums on two floors. Lincoln Pool is opposite on the right.

**15.** Reach W. 14th St. to start walking past a unique cluster of Tremont's churches. Many of these sacred landmarks date from the community's early, more populous days, but today these churches are still active and occupy a unique place in modern Tremont.

St. George Orthodox Church at 2587 W. 14th St. was built in 1892 as Lincoln Park Methodist Church. The massive exterior walls contain few windows, and the onion-shaped finials on the bell tower reflect the church's Syrian/Lebanese religious and cultural heritage. In 1933 St. George Church bought and refurbished the building only to have a fire destroy the interior. At the second rebuilding in 1935, a hand-cut crystal chandelier and handmade altar screen were added. The bishop's throne is of dark walnut inlaid with ebony, rosewood, and ivory. (Call 216-781-9020 for more information.)

**16.** Cross the street to the 1893 Pilgrim Congregational Church at 2592 W. 14th, the largest of the three churches on this corner. The rough, ashlar exterior features an impressive arched sandstone entrance with metal grillwork and heavy wooden doors on either side of wide stone steps. (Ashlar is rough-hewn stone that has been cut, squared, and laid in regular courses on a building's facade.)

Organized in 1859 as University Heights Congregational Church, its congregation first erected the building now occupied by St. Augustine's Roman Catholic Church, located a block north of here. Outgrowing that site, the members built the present structure, designed by church architect S. R. Badgley, to accommodate Pilgrim's many social, recreational, and educational programs. Its numerous multipurpose rooms enabled the church to open the first library on the west side of Cleveland, as well as the first kindergarten and first cooking school in the city. The building housed a kitchen, library, art museum, and gymnasium. Badgley was known for designing ceilings with intricate segments and coves unsupported by columns. His unique Akron Plan (originally used in Akron's First Methodist Church) allowed for sliding doors and interior windows that could open up to accommodate large groups of people. Tiffany glass windows and a Ferran-Votey organ restored in 1992 are among the treasures in this church. Pilgrim continues to be a very active force in the Tremont neighborhood and offers a wide variety of community programs, including musical and theatrical events. To visit the church, call 216-861-7388.

**17.** Although it has changed hands several times, services are still held in the handsome church at 2536 W. 14th St. Built in 1910 by German immigrants, this structure was originally known as Emmanuel Evangelical United Brethren Church. The building's Gothic and English architectural styles are evident in its large pointed windows with hood moldings (Gothic), and its two wide porch entryways and short steeple on the corner tower (English). Until World War I, services were conducted in German. In the 1930s, the church was well known for its missionary work in the Far East. In 1968, Cleveland Baptist Temple purchased the building. More recently it has become El Calvario, home to a Hispanic congregation.

Continue north on W. 14th St. On the left are more small, old Tremont homes, some of which have been carefully restored.

**18.** St. Augustine's Roman Catholic Parish at W. 14th St. and Howard began in 1860 as a mission church serving Irish parishioners living in Tremont. It was soon large enough to become a parish, and, with continued growth, members purchased the present building from Pilgrim Congregational Church in 1896. The Pilgrim congregation had built the simple red Victorian Gothic structure in 1870 with a high first floor to allow light to enter the basement Sunday School rooms (some of the windows are covered now). The attractive interior contains a raised marble altar at the end of a wide nave; the roof is supported by hammer-beam trusses and wrought-iron tie rods although no nails were used in the ceiling. The rectory is located in a restored Victorian home at 2486 W. 14th. St. Augustine's is a very active community church, serving as the Deaf Center of Cleveland, and providing free meals to hundreds of needy persons.

**19.** Holy Ghost Byzantine Catholic Church, west of Kenilworth Ave. and W. 14th St., was built in 1910 by the Ruthenian community, comprised of people who had emigrated from their homes in the western part of Ukraine. An impressive rose window is set above three small entry doors, and the towers are topped by Byzantine domes and crosses. Inside is a striking icon screen made in Budapest in 1924; with 48 icons, it is one of the most elaborate in Cleveland. Of the screen's three doors, the central, royal door is used only by the priest.

Continue north on W. 14th St.

**20.** Just beyond Kenilworth Ave. at 2346 W. 14th St. is St. Joseph-Our Lady of Angels School for the Mentally and Physically Handicapped. The program is run by the Catholic Diocese, and its principal is the Rector of St. Augustine's.

At 2363 W. 14th are the Pelton Apartments in a Romanesque-style building named for Mrs. Thirza Pelton, a founder of the original Cleveland University.

**21.** Continue north on W. 14th St., passing St. Andrew Kim Korean Catholic Church and a beautiful white "wedding cake" home at 2330. Opposite is Grace Hospital on the right, and north of it are a pair of attached Greek Revival homes that formerly housed the Olney Museum and its fine collection of art.

**22.** At the corner of Fairfield Ave. is the 1918 Greek Orthodox Church of the Annunciation with its familiar gold-topped twin towers and central dome that are seen daily by thousands from the freeway. As the mother church for the Greek Orthodox community in greater Cleveland, it reflects that country's culture both inside and outside the building. The impressive interior contains many frescoes and more than 80 icons.

**23.** Walk east on Fairfield Ave. to W. 11th St. On the northeast corner is a beautifully restored beige brick building that was formerly a grocery store. This Federal Italianate building with attractive windows and decorative stars covering the bracings has a sidewalk stepping stone that was used when horse-drawn carriages filled the streets.

Turn right (south) on W. 11th St. and note the three-story Stacey's Block building (2207 W. 11th) and next to it, a small, white brick Gothic cottage—one of the oldest in Tremont. All along this street are lovely small homes that have been or are in the process of being rehabilitated. As with many renovations in this neighborhood, owners have tried to preserve as much of the original architecture as possible.

**24.** The Byzantine-style yellow brick Iglesia Hispana (Asambleas de Dios, La Nueva Jerusalem) at 2280 W. 11th St. was formerly St. Vladimir Ukrainian Orthodox Church established in 1924.

Return to Lincoln Park.

**25.** Of note at 1202 Kenilworth Ave. (between W. 11th and W. 14th Sts.) is the converted home housing the Ukrainian Museum and Archives. This small museum contains a wealth of historical material of particular interest to those of Ukrainian heritage. The museum has collected hundreds of copies of *Svoboda* (Liberty), a Ukrainian-language newspaper published in Pennsylvania since 1893, and the *Ukrainian Weekly*, from the same publisher, printed for Ukrainians in English since 1933.

As the repository of the world's largest collection of Ukrainian literature produced in the displaced persons' camps of Germany and Austria following World War II, the museum is now cataloging hundreds of books and periodicals published by these refugees between 1945 and 1952. The museum also contains a collection of books, photographs, paintings, art objects, clothing, stamps, medals, currency, letters, leaflets, and historic records. Call 216-781-4329 for hours.

**26.** On W. 11th St. facing the park is the 1948 Our Lady of Mercy Roman Catholic Church, the newest of Tremont's churches. The variegated Tennessee crab-orchard stone exterior is unusual. It is the same building stone used in the Cathedral of St. John the Evangelist (see ch. 2, note #7). The interior has beautiful carved wooden statues, several shrines, marble altars, and Slovak folk painting.

*Optional Driving Tour*

To enjoy more of Tremont's treasures, here is a convenient driving tour to several more distant stops. As noted, it is important to telephone ahead for opening times and to make arrangements for tours.

**27.** Drive south on W. 14th St. to 2716. The 175-foot-tall octagonal spire of Zion United Church of Christ soars high above this Gothic-inspired church. The spire is a Tremont landmark visible for miles around. Organized in 1867 as the United German Evangelical Protestant Church serving German immigrants in Tremont, the congregation soon outgrew its quarters on College Ave. and moved into this new structure in 1884. The front exterior takes the form of a transept, with pointed arches over the windows and doors, and above the open belfry. Additions over the years included a parsonage, religious school, kitchen, and auditorium. Zion's Schule (Zion's School) next door is now a day-care center.

In 1934 Zion was the site of the historic vote to merge the Reformed Church in the United States and the Evangelical Synod of North America to form the Evangelical and Reformed Church. In 1957 another merger created the present Zion United Church of Christ. Call 216-861-2371 for information.

**28.** Continue driving south on W. 14th St. to Clark Ave. and turn right (west) on Clark to St. Michael Roman Catholic Church at Clark and Scranton (3114 Scranton Rd.). St. Michael's parish was founded in 1883 to serve German Catholics in the surrounding neighborhood. Today, St. Michael's is also the home of La Iglesia de San Miguel Archangel; services are regularly held here in Spanish.

When this magnificent Victorian Gothic-style church was built in 1892, it was the largest and most costly church in Cleveland. Its tall, graceful spires, reaching 232 and 180 feet, can be seen for miles around. Above the three arched doorways is a great pointed arch containing a large rose window with elaborate mullions.

The interior, seating 1,500 parishioners, is filled with a profusion of carved statuary, much of it from Germany. Behind the altar are polychrome statues of the 12 apostles, 9 angels, and the patron saint, St. Michael. A marble altar designed by Cleveland's John Winterick is modeled after the high altar of the Church of St. Francis, Borgo, Italy. The beautiful stained-glass windows, which permit natural light to enter, depict the infancy and childhood of Christ. Tennessee pink marble wainscoting contrasts with white marble flooring containing blue tile insets. Above the wainscoting in the entryway is a frieze of dragon heads. As the frieze continues into the sanctuary, the dragons change to angels, signifying that the power of Satan is broken within the church. Call 216-861-6297 for information.

**29.** Return to Tremont proper by driving east on Clark Ave. and north on W. 14th to Starkweather. Turn right (east) on Starkweather until just past Professor St., and on the right is St. Theodosius Russian Orthodox Cathedral at 733 Starkweather Ave. This magnificent Eastern Orthodox church, built in 1911 at the tremendous cost of $70,000, represents one of the best examples of Russian church architecture in this country. Located on a hill as a focal point for the Tremont neighborhood, its striking onion-shaped central dome and 12 smaller surrounding domes represent Christ and the apostles.

The cathedral, named after St. Theodosius, Bishop of Chernigov, is the center of Russian cultural activities in the Cleveland area. The building was patterned after Moscow's Church of Our Savior Jesus. The inspiring interior, shaped like a Greek cross with four limbs of equal length, contains a huge Czechoslovakian chandelier and a splendid icon screen from Kiev. A $100,000 renovation in 1953 added wall and ceiling murals created by Yugoslavian artist Andre Bicenko. In 1974 the church was placed on the National Register of Historic Places and, in 1977, wedding scenes for the movie *The Deer Hunter* were filmed here. St.

Theodosius's parishioners come from all parts of the city to worship here. An especially festive service is the Christmas choir concert, a tradition for many Clevelanders. Call 216-861-5363 for information.

Behind the church on St. Olga St. is an expansive view of Cleveland's industrial flats.

St. Theodosius Russian Orthodox Cathedral

**30.** From the cathedral drive east on Starkweather to W. 7th St. and turn left (northwest), proceeding to the southwest corner of W. 7th St. and College Ave. Saints Peter and Paul Ukrainian Catholic Church (Byzantine Rite) at 2280 W. 7th St. was originally built in 1910. The church was remodeled in 1956 and 1978, and is the mother parish of all the Ukrainian Catholic churches in the greater Cleveland area. The parish has a long history as a social center for Ukrainians arriving in Cleveland. In the past, it provided dramas, concerts, and classes in Ukrainian history, language, and dance. The Greek-style cross atop the tower reflects its Eastern Orthodox heritage. The interior retains the original pews, crystal chandeliers, icon screen with many religious images, and ceiling icon depicting Ukrainians in native dress. Call 216-861-2176 for information.

**31.** Continue on W. 7th St. to University Rd. Along the high embankment marking the northern edge of Tremont is a small park with a promenade enabling visitors to view the city of Cleveland from a unique vantage point. (TWDC is working with the Ohio Canal Corridor and the Trust for Public Land to develop a promenade park along Railway and University Rds.) At 1201 University Rd. is Sokolowski's University Inn, a well-known restaurant owned and operated by the same family since 1923, and now run by the third generation of Sokolowskis. It is open Monday through Friday, 11 a.m.–3 p.m. Its famous homemade lunches are served cafeteria-style.

From Sokolowski's, circle east one block on W. 11th St. to Fairfield Ave. and turn right (west) to the freeway entrance off Fairfield.

*Photo by Anthony Gray*

Edison's Pub

This walk reviewed and rewalked by the author, in consultation with Emily A. P. Lipovan, Director of Tremont West Development Corporation, and Laura McShane, TWDC Project Coordinator.

# 7 Brooklyn Centre
## Community in Renaissance

**Distance:** 2 miles

**Walking time:** 1 ½ hours

**Description:** This urban walk is on sidewalks and requires some street crossings at busy intersections. It includes a walk through tiny Brooklyn Centre Burying Ground (1835). To view the interiors of the churches on this tour, it is necessary to call ahead for appointments. Please respect the rights and privacy of homeowners by not trespassing onto lawns.

**Directions:** I-71 to Exit 245 (Pearl Rd./W. 25th St./US 42); right (south) on Pearl at the top of the exit ramp; follow Pearl two blocks to Brooklyn Centre shopping plaza on the right.

**Parking & restrooms:** At Brooklyn Centre shopping plaza.

Brooklyn Centre, a near West Side neighborhood, was one of Cleveland's oldest settlements. Forming a rough triangle enclosed by I-71 on the north, Riverside Cemetery and Jennings Rd. on the east, and Big Creek and railroad tracks on the south, Brooklyn Centre is listed on the National Register of Historic Places as a "multiple resource area." In 1997 it was named as a National Register Historic District. Brooklyn Centre also carries a landmarks designation by the city of Cleveland. The community's buildings are a mix of late-19th- to early-20th-century styles, including Italianate, Queen Anne, and Colonial Revival. This walk can be easily combined with the one featured in Chapter 8, Riverside Cemetery.

The village was first settled in 1812 by pioneer farmers from Connecticut, including members of the Fish and Brainard families. The settlement developed around the important rural crossroads of what is now Pearl Rd. and Denison Ave. This area was the center of old Brooklyn Township, a farming region west of Cleveland. In 1818 the first churches, now known as Brooklyn Memorial United Methodist Church and Archwood United Church of Christ, were founded. By 1867 the village of Brooklyn was incorporated and gradually developed into the residential community of large homes on spacious lots that you see today. Many of the new residents were from Germany.

As the population increased, the residents of Brooklyn voted in 1894 to be annexed to Cleveland to obtain such advantages as a better school system, fire and police protection, paved streets and sidewalks, and

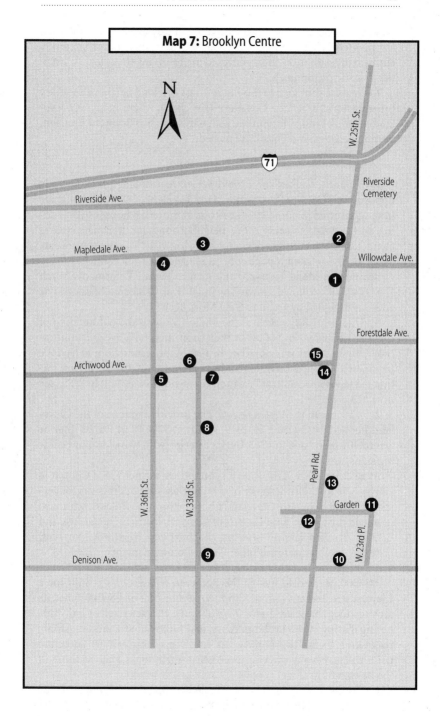

**Map 7:** Brooklyn Centre

other city services. Many of the homes and carriage houses built then are now enjoying a renaissance. Current homeowners are presently engaged in restoration efforts devoted to preserving the colorful past of this historic community.

To enhance your visit to this interesting Cleveland neighborhood, try to see historic Riverside Cemetery (see ch. 8), where many of Cleveland's earliest West Side families, with names such as Brainard, Lamson, Session, Rhodes, and Foster, are buried.

**1.** Begin the walk at the Brooklyn Centre shopping plaza. Directly opposite at 3731 Pearl Rd. is the Mallo House (c. 1880), an Italianate home converted to podiatry offices, one of the oldest houses still standing on Pearl Rd. As seen in this neighborhood, the Italianate style is characterized by tall arched windows, flaring eaves supported by ornate brackets, low-pitched hipped roofs, and ornate entrance porches.

Behind the Mallo House is the former Eighth Reformed Church (1909) at 2409 Willowdale Ave. The building is California Mission style and was designed by architect Paul Motzinger.

At 3723 Pearl Rd., north of the Mallo House, is the old building of Engine Company No. 24 (1894), built soon after the Cleveland annexation. Originally hay was stored in the rear of the second floor to feed the fire horses. This firehouse served the neighborhood until a new fire station—a few doors south at Pearl and Archwood—was built in 1985 (see note #13).

**2.** Walk north to Mapledale Ave. The Brooklyn branch of the Cleveland Public Library, built in 1919, stands at 3706 Pearl Rd. Its interior was totally renovated in 1985, but its exterior, with two old stone building signs, was preserved.

At 3648 Pearl Rd. is the stately, symmetrical former Third Church of Christ, Scientist. The designer of this neoclassical building was Frederick Striebinger, one of Cleveland's better-known architects, who also designed the former First Church of Christ, Scientist at Euclid Ave. and E. 77th St. Neoclassical style is characterized by sturdy cornices, columns, entablatures, and other Greco-Roman elements.

Turn left (west) on Mapledale Ave.

At 3000 Mapledale Ave. is the Bomante House (1910), built for a Cleveland restaurant owner. Although reminiscent of a Swiss chalet, its architecture is basically Tudor Revival, and is characterized by half-timbering, flaring eaves, broad porches, and multipaned windows. Home restoration in the community has emphasized historically authentic paint colors, usually three or more warm earth tones, such as those of the Bomante House.

**3.** Continue walking west on Mapledale. Many interesting restored homes are here. Note, for example, the Verona Apartments at 3127–31 and 3221 Mapledale.

At 3400 Mapledale is the three-story orange brick Karl F. Snow House (1909), originally built with a ballroom on the top floor.

**4.** At 3503 Mapledale is the former Emmaus Evangelical Lutheran Church, now Good News Ministries Church (1910). Note the beautiful Gothic window on the W. 36th St. side of this small religious structure.

Turn left on W. 36th St. past Virginia to Archwood Ave. and turn left again onto Archwood.

**5.** Along Archwood are more stunning examples of late-19th-century homes that have been carefully preserved by their owners and returned to their former architectural magnificence.

The Queen Anne–style home at 3515 Archwood is the Weldon Davis House (1895), constructed with an imposing three-story corner tower. Queen Anne–style homes are characterized by gables, broad porches, asymmetrical plans, steep roofs, and an occasional tower or turret. Again, authentic paint colors have enhanced this handsome home. A rear apartment addition to this home artfully blends the new with the old. Standing behind this house on W. 36th St. is a newly built carriage house that incorporates design elements matching the home and contains old windows from the demolished 1881 Brooklyn Methodist Church.

Return to Archwood. Next to the Davis House is a beautiful Italianate home at 3505 Archwood, the Charles Selzer House. Selzer, who was mayor of Brooklyn, a municipal judge, and founder of a weekly newspaper, built this colorful home around 1880.

**6.** Diagonally across the street at 3340 Archwood is the Doubleday House (ca. 1870), another noteworthy and finely restored Italianate home built by a family who owned much of the land in this area.

The William R. Coates House (1902) at 3304 Archwood was built by a man who was the mayor of Brooklyn when the village was annexed to Cleveland. Architect Frederick Striebinger designed this Colonial Revival–style home, as well as Third Church (see note #2). Colonial Revival homes are characterized by delicate detailing and classical ornaments inspired by early American architecture.

**7.** At 3101 Archwood is the Adam Poe House (ca. 1870), one of the finest brick Italianate-style houses in Cleveland. It has elaborate cast-metal hood moldings over its tall windows, porches, and distinctive brackets. Adam Poe was a storekeeper and lay minister at the Brooklyn Methodist Church.

Retrace your steps to W. 33rd St. On the corner of Archwood and W. 33rd are Archwood Manor and Brooklyn Manor, containing apartments that have recently been renovated by a Cleveland city housing program. Across the street at 3006 Archwood is the Frink-Pope House—a fine example of Queen Anne–style architecture and the former home of Washington Irving Pope, the mayor of Chagrin Falls from 1874 to 1878.

Turn left (south) on W. 33rd St.

**8.** Next to Denison Elementary School, the F. A. Shepherd House (1914) at 3785 W. 33rd St. is a Tudor Revival house that exemplifies the Arts and Crafts style of architecture. It is characterized by finely crafted yet simple oak woodwork, multipaned windows, and a massive gabled roof.

The home at 3800 W. 33rd St. is the Italianate Clayton Townes House (ca. 1865), whose front porch was added later. Townes was president of Cleveland's city council and mayor when William R. Hopkins, who initiated construction of the country's first municipal airport, was city manager.

**9.** On the corner of W. 33rd and Denison Ave. is St. Philip the Apostle Episcopal Church (erected in 1922); the congregation organized in 1894. This Neo-Gothic building is also home to St. Agnes Mission for the Deaf. This architectural style is characterized by lancet windows, steep roofs, and medieval-looking trim.

**10.** Turn left (east) on Denison Ave. Continue past Pearl Rd. to 2310 Denison to see the restored Kroehle House (1865). This large, beautiful Italianate structure was the home of the founder of Spang Bakery Co. (See ch. 8, note #21.) Note the long 10-car garage at the rear of the property where delivery trucks once were kept. Kroehle claimed to be the first baker in Cleveland to sell wrapped bread.

**11.** Turn left (north) for one block at W. 23rd Pl., to the small Brooklyn Centre Burying Ground (1835). Also known as Denison Cemetery, it was the site of the community's first burials. As early as 1823 some of Brooklyn's pioneer settlers were laid to rest here, including members of the Fish, Brainard, Storer, and Booth families. Just inside the cemetery and to the right, about halfway to the end, is the grave of the American Revolutionary War soldier, Ebenezer Fish (1757–1827) and his wife, Lydia, very early settlers of Brooklyn.

Turn left (west) on Garden St. to return to Pearl Rd.

**12.** The neoclassical Brooklyn Masonic Temple building straight ahead at 3804 Pearl was built in 1932 and remodeled in 1937 for the lodge that had been founded in 1871. Daniel Farnam, the architect of Archwood United Church of Christ (see note #15), also designed this structure.

**13.** Turn right (north) on Pearl Rd. The new Aldi's supermarket on the corner of Garden and Pearl is designed to conform to historic district standards, as was the next structure, Cleveland Fire Station No. 20 and EMS Unit No. 4 (1985) at 3765 Pearl Rd.

This handsome brick firehouse, designed by Ovington & Glaser and the City of Cleveland Division of Architecture, was the first new building in Brooklyn Centre to follow design review committee guidelines. The clock tower used for drying fire hoses is an attractive focal point for the neighborhood.

**14.** Opposite the new fire station at Archwood and Pearl, note the architecturally striking building on the southwest corner with unusual terra-cotta trim. It is the old Brooklyn Savings & Loan Co. (1904) designed by J. Milton Dyer, who was also the architect of Cleveland's magnificent City Hall (see ch. 1, note #19).

Just west of this corner at 2607 Archwood is Brooklyn Memorial United Methodist Church (1911), designed by architect Ray Fulton. The oldest Methodist congregation in greater Cleveland (founded in 1818), Brooklyn Memorial had occupied three different buildings before this unusual one was constructed. Of special interest is the wooden eight-sided tower with windows lighting an immense stained-glass dome over the sanctuary. The Gothic exterior features two square towers (with louvered belfries in one), lancet windows, pointed arches above the doors and windows, and elaborate stained-glass windows. The interior was built on the Akron Plan (see ch. 6, note #16) with sliding walls to provide flexible room arrangements.

**15.** Almost directly opposite is Archwood United Church of Christ, home of the oldest Congregational church in Cleveland, founded by New Englanders in 1819, only a few years after the first settlement. The original church was built in 1879, with a wing added on in 1912. Both were retained when the present Georgian Revival structure was built in 1929. Designed by architect Daniel Farnam to reflect 18th-century New England, its stately exterior includes Georgian details such as the tripartite doorway, front portico with a single round window, 12-paned windows, keystones and fanlights, and the tall copper steeple and weather vane.

Return to Brooklyn Centre shopping plaza next to the church.

This chapter, reviewed and rewalked by the author, was originally prepared with the generous assistance of building preservation consultant Steven McQuillin, a homeowner and resident of Brooklyn Centre Historic District. A walking tour prepared by the Brooklyn Centre Design Review Committee has been adapted for this chapter, using architectural designations from that source and additional material from Mr. McQuillin.

# 8 Riverside Cemetery
## Visiting Cleveland's History

**Distance:** 2 miles

**Walking time:** 2 to 2 ½ hours

**Description:** The walk is on cemetery roads that are generally flat, except for one hill. It is permissible to walk on the grassy areas of the cemetery.

**Directions:** I-71 to Exit 245 (W. 25th St./Pearl Rd./US 42); right (south) on Pearl Rd.; sharp left (just past the I-71 overpass) to enter main gate of Riverside Cemetery at 3607 Pearl Rd.

**Parking & restrooms:** Park along the road near the administration building and office; a restroom is available inside.

Riverside Cemetery is a 90-acre oasis of serene beauty in the midst of city and freeway traffic and nearby steel mills. It is the burial place of many early developers and wealthy businessmen of Cleveland's West Side. Planned by landscape architect E. O. Schwagerl and dedicated in 1876, the cemetery was created from land farmed by Titus N. Brainard high above the Cuyahoga River. The dedication ceremony was attended by many prominent Clevelanders, including Jeptha Wade, president of Lake View Cemetery Association (founded six years earlier, see ch. 10), and by Ohio governor and President-elect Rutherford B. Hayes. Originally the cemetery contained six acres of lakes with seven rustic wooden bridges spanning the waterways. The lakes are now drained and filled in. Occasionally tours are offered by the cemetery; one features local brewing history and is given annually on Father's Day.

Two of the cemetery's buildings are on the National Register of Historic Places: the 1896 Administration Building and the 1876 Stone Chapel, closed since 1953. Preservation plans are currently under way for full restoration of this building as a nondenominational chapel for persons buried at Riverside.

Along the front of the cemetery's property are a row of flowering crabapple trees that bloom magnificently each year in early May. Many lovely shrubs and trees grace Riverside Cemetery, as well as plantings by relatives, who have the unusual prerogative of doing their own landscaping on grave sites.

The cemetery is open from 7:30 a.m. to 5 p.m. daily, and the office is open from 8 a.m. to 4 p.m. Monday through Saturday. It is best to call ahead for this walk to ensure that a visit to Riverside will not interfere

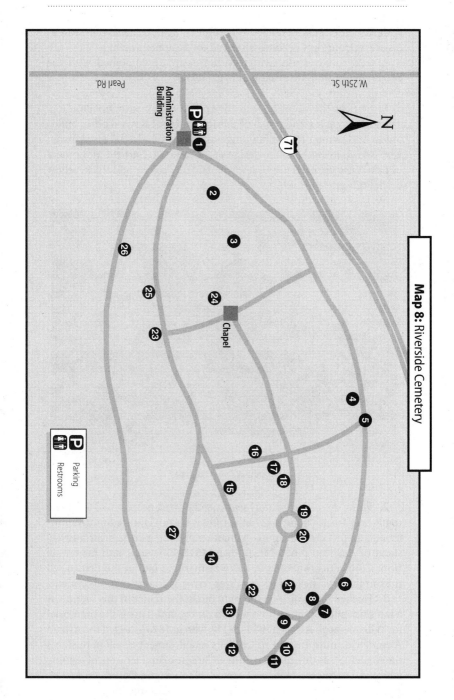

**Map 8:** Riverside Cemetery

with scheduled services that day (216-351-4800). Genealogy research-
ers are welcome but need to call ahead for an appointment.

A walk in Riverside Cemetery can easily be combined with the
Brooklyn Centre walk described in chapter 7.

**1.** Start at the beautiful, red-tile-roofed Administration Building.
The turrets, gables, and porch of this Romanesque Revival office building were designed by the building's architect, Charles W. Hopkinson,
who also contributed to the design of the James A. Garfield Monument
in Lake View Cemetery. A beautiful inlaid oak ceiling and thick, yellow
brick walls grace the interior.

Administration Building (1896)

**2.** From the office go northeast on the road nearest to I-71. (The
roads here are not named.) On the right is the tall Francis Branch monument, topped by a weeping woman embracing a cross, near a lovely
stand of Austrian pines. Mr. Branch (1812–77) came with his family
from Connecticut in 1818. A dairy farmer and one of the first to sell
milk in this area, he later served three terms as county commissioner.

**3.** Farther along, also on the right but in the center of this section, is
a tan stone monument with a wreath on the end. This is the memorial
for William Jacob Astrup (1845–1915), who in 1876 founded the Astrup
Awning Co., now the Astrup Co. This establishment is still in business
on W. 25th St. as one of the country's largest manufacturers of awning
fabric and hardware, tents, and canvas. Mr. Astrup, a Danish sailmaker,
started out by manufacturing sails for Great Lakes ships.

**4.** Toward the end of section 9 on the right near the road and just past the tall buckeye tree, is the unobtrusive grave of Linda Eastman (1867–1963). Miss Eastman was the fourth director of the Cleveland Public Library and the first woman in the world to head so large a library. She served when the present library on Superior and E. 6th St. was built in 1925, and she was nationally recognized for achievements, such as developing services for the visually and physically handicapped and establishing travel and business bureaus. Miss Eastman, who lived to be 95 years of age, served as president of the Ohio and American library associations. The Eastman Reading Garden adjacent to the Cleveland Public Library downtown and the Eastman Branch Library at Lorain and W. 115th St. were named in her honor.

**5.** As you continue along this drive, note the beautiful view of MetroHealth Medical Center on the left. On the right note the unusual carving that graces the 1901 Magdalene Fredericks Woehrle monument, especially the hairdo, dress collar, and exquisite folds and fringe of the grieving woman's shawl.

Although no one is buried inside the large casket-shaped, granite Humiston monument, also on the right, members of the family are buried all around it.

**6.** On the left is the Baggett monument, another beautiful stone carving of two grieving women, a common theme of late-19th- and early-20th-century cemetery art.

Next is the 1889 Brainard family mausoleum containing members of an early family of farmers. David S. Brainard owned many acres of farmland where MetroHealth Medical Center now stands. Also on the left is a small burial area for members of the Leisy family. Founded by Isaac Leisy (1838–92) in 1873, the Leisy Brewing Company was the oldest brewery in Cleveland and one of the longest surviving family-operated breweries in the country. A long view of the downtown Cleveland skyline and the Cuyahoga River valley can be seen next to this plot.

**7.** Farther along on the left is the Byelorussian Orthodox Church burial area maintained by members of this religious community.

**8.** Opposite on the right is a large boulder under a spreading evergreen tree. This is the burial place of Carlos Jones (1827–97), manufacturer of farm implements, real estate developer, mayor of Brooklyn, and founder in 1887 of Jones School & Home for Friendless Children, later Jones Home for Children. Several prominent businessmen, including James M. Coffinberry, Isaac Lamson, and Samuel Sessions, and Governor (later President) Rutherford B. Hayes served on the home's original corporate board.

Nearby, but not on this walk, is the three-story brick Jones building (1902) at 3518 W. 25th St. It was designed by the well-known architect Sidney R. Badgley, and is on the Register of Cleveland Landmarks.

To the east of Carlos Jones is a flat ground marker for James Milton Curtiss (1840–1916), a nurseryman and real estate developer who was the first superintendent of Riverside Cemetery. He conceived and promoted the idea for downtown Cleveland's Old Arcade (1890) between Euclid and Superior Aves. (see ch. 1, note #7) and for the Central Viaduct bridge (demolished in 1941, and later replaced by the Inner Belt Bridge).

**9.** A small burial area on the right, identified with a central stone for Emma Tamm, is used by members of Cleveland's Estonian community.

**10.** Opposite on the left is the grave of Titus N. Brainard (1825–1910) and his son-in-law Harry M. Farnsworth. Note their intertwined initials at the top. Titus Brainard's grandfather traveled from Connecticut by ox-drawn wagon in 1814 and purchased about 140 acres of land here for farming. In 1876 Titus sold 102.5 acres of his land to the Riverside Cemetery Association for development of a new burial ground.

Harry Farnsworth (1881–1955) was the secretary-treasurer of Brooklyn Savings & Loan. He was instrumental in the formation of Cleveland Metroparks and served on its first board of park commissioners. It was Farnsworth who first proposed the joining of parks to form what is now called the "Emerald Necklace."

**11.** More members of a single family are buried at the Meyer family plot with the small obelisk than in any other section of Riverside. The plot was chosen to overlook their farmland, now occupied by LTV Steel.

Standing alone on the edge of the embankment overlooking the Cuyahoga River valley and with its back to the road is a headstone with Chinese inscriptions. This memorial for a Chinese woman, Wai Wah Kwan, is situated to face the rising sun. Another more recently installed monument is dedicated to her son, Ray Don, a leading organizer and well-known activist in Cleveland's Chinese community.

**12.** Next on the left is a small ground marker for Diodate Clark (1798–1876), the first male schoolteacher in Brooklyn and later a large landowner and county commissioner, who came to Cleveland nearly penniless at the age of 19.

**13.** The tall, beautiful Lamson-Sessions monument—designed by an unknown artist—is the most noteworthy memorial in Riverside. Costing $10,000 when it was built in 1877, it was the most expensive monument in Cleveland at the time and quickly became a tourist attraction. The inscription (from 1 Cor. 15:52) reads: "The trumpet shall sound and the dead shall be raised incorruptible, and we shall be changed."

Samuel W. Sessions (1824–1902), Isaac P. Lamson (1832–1912), and Thomas H. Lamson (1827–82) all came to Cleveland from Connecticut with a group of skilled workers to establish the Cleveland Nut Company in 1872. Over the next 100 years their success enabled the business at W. 14th St. and Jennings Rd., later known as Lamson and Sessions Company, to become one of the country's leading fastener manufacturers with eight plants nationwide by 1930. Lamson and Sessions helped found the Visiting Nurse Association of Cleveland, Tremont's Pilgrim Congregational Church, and the Jones Home.

John Gould Jennings (1856–1937), who is also buried here, was Isaac Lamson's son-in-law, and a director at Lamson and Sessions.

Another artistic carving adorns the monument of Frederick Pelton (1827–1902) to the west of the Lamson-Sessions monument. Created by an unknown artist, this one was on display at the Chicago World's Fair (1894) before being transported here. Pelton, a founding trustee of Riverside Cemetery, was city council president (1866–69) and mayor of Cleveland (1871–73).

**14.** Toward the rear of section 20, identified by a monument with a seated woman, are Daniel P. Rhodes (1814–75) and his son James Ford Rhodes (1848–1927), members of a prominent West Side family who built the Robert Russell Rhodes family home (ca. 1874) at 2905 Franklin Circle. It now houses the Cuyahoga County Archives (see ch. 4, note #16). Daniel, a Vermonter, became wealthy as a coal mining entrepreneur and founder of Rhodes & Company. He also founded People's Savings and Loan and contributed greatly to the development of the Cuyahoga River's west bank.

James Rhodes joined the family business in 1870 and embarked on a study of the iron industry in Europe and the U.S. With his older brother, Robert, his brother-in-law, Marcus A. Hanna, and other partners, he reorganized the family's very successful iron, iron ore, and coal business in 1885 as M. A. Hanna Mining Co. James later became a prolific writer, winning many honorary degrees and awards, among them a Pulitzer Prize for his *History of the Civil War, 1861–1865.* A West Side Cleveland high school is named for James Ford Rhodes.

Note another beautiful carving adorning the Schuele burial site near the road. Christian Schuele was co-owner of Fries & Schuele Department Store, originally located in the structure that now houses the Great Lakes Brewing Co. (see ch. 4, note #2).

**15.** Down the road on the right is a polished granite memorial for George A. Tinnerman (1845–1925) and his son, Albert H. Tinnerman (1879–1961). George founded a stove manufacturing business in 1875 that became a diversified multimillion-dollar company. Albert originated the first all-porcelain enameled gas range with concealed fastenings in 1923. He also patented a spring tension speed nut fastener that revolutionized assembly lines.

**16.** Continue walking west to the next small road and turn right at the three cedar trees. On the left lies Charles W. Hopkinson (1865–1950), noted architect and two-time president of the American Institute of Architects whose well-known designs include Riverside's Administration Building, modifications to the Garfield Monument in Lake View Cemetery, Franklin Circle Masonic Temple, the Rockefeller

Building at Case Western Reserve University, and Hough Avenue United Church of Christ.

**17.** On the right is Claud H. Foster (1872–1965), automotive inventor of "Snubber" shock absorbers and the multitone Gabriel auto horn powered by exhaust gases. He was one of the first industrialists to develop an employee profit-sharing incentive program; he was also a philanthropist who made large gifts to hospitals, schools, and other agencies. Foster donated pipe organs to several churches and built the Brooklyn Branch of the Young Men's Christian Association (located just south of the cemetery) in memory of his mother. In 1952 he divided his fortune of almost four million dollars among 16 Cleveland educational and charitable institutions.

**18.** Turn right at the next corner. Some members of Cleveland's Ukrainian community, strongly represented in the city's history since the early 1900s, are buried in the Ukrainian section on the right. At the circle just ahead there was once a fountain and pool; here is where the 1876 cemetery dedication was held.

**19.** On the left, in the center of this section, is a small obelisk marking the grave of Stephen Buhrer (1825–1907), city councilman and mayor of Cleveland from 1867 to 1871. A cooper by trade, he was responsible for building the Cleveland House of Correction & Workhouse during his term as mayor.

On the left near the circle is the memorial monument for Josiah Barber Sr. (1771–1842), whose 1809 Western Reserve allotment encompassed land along the west side of the Cuyahoga River to W. 117th St. and north to the lake. He became a land developer and store owner who in 1840, with his partners, dedicated a large portion of acreage for an open-air market, later to become the West Side Market. Barber was also a circuit judge, the first mayor of Ohio City, and an incorporator of Trinity Parish in downtown Cleveland (Trinity Cathedral) and St. John's Parish at W. 28th and Church Sts. In 1834, Barber incorporated the Cuyahoga Steam Furnace Co., one of Cleveland's first manufacturing companies.

**20.** The tall obelisk to the left of the circle marks the grave of John B. Cowle (1826–1914). Cowle was the owner of Globe Iron Works (which later became part of Cleveland Shipbuilding), treasurer of Cleveland Drydock Co., and an associate of Universal Machine & Boiler Co. Two Lake Erie ore freighters were named for him.

Exquisite carving on James M. Coffinberry's nearby monument depicts a woman raising her left arm to heaven—note, particularly, the folds of the woman's dress. Coffinberry, an attorney, journal editor, and common pleas court judge, was a Union supporter in the Civil War and, later, legal counsel for the founding of Riverside Cemetery.

**21.** Past the circle on the left is a large black granite block marking the final resting place of Julius Spang (1852–1950), co-founder, with his wife, Fredericka, of the J. Spang Baking Co. Spang, a German immi-grant, managed the baking operations, and his wife supervised the financial affairs of the company, which remained at the same site, 2911 Barber Ave., for 70 years and employed 433 persons in three plants before it closed in 1958. Spang served as president of the company until his death at age 98 (see ch. 7, note #10).

Opposite, gracing the grave of John B. Koelges (1833–99), is another artistic monument carving depicting a woman with raised arm.

**22.** Turn right at the next corner. Shaded by the large evergreen shrubs on the right are playwright Avery Hopwood (1883–1928) and his mother, Julia Hopwood. Mr. Hopwood was a well-known early-20th-century playwright who wrote such Broadway plays as *Streets of New York* and *The French Doll.* He died in a drowning accident in Nice, France. His mother had the monument erected and died herself just eight months later.

Turn right again and continue west on this road past section 20 and past the road going downhill, to near the end of section 11.

**23.** On the left is the 1879 J. J. Cartright mausoleum built to resem-ble a small chapel.

Next is the Ruetenik family plot. Rev. Herman J. Ruetenik (1826–1914), an educator, author, and editor, came from Germany in 1848 as a political refugee. He became a minister and missionary in Cleveland, establishing the First through Ninth German Reformed Churches and Calvin College on W. 25th St. for German-speaking men. Ruetenik's Fourth Reformed Church founded what is now Fairview General Hospital. Herman's son, Martin (1868–1947), founded Ruetenik Greenhouses and Gardens on Schaaf Rd. in Brooklyn in 1885, Cleveland's first greenhouse that used scientific methods. The three-and-a-half-acre greenhouse became a leading national producer of hothouse vegetables.

**24.** To the right (north) is the 1876 Stone Chapel, closed since 1953 because of deterioration. Exterior restoration of this beautiful little structure was completed in 1997. Completion of the interior restoration is expected by the year 2000.

**25.** Back on the road beyond the Ruetenik plot and on the left in the small mausoleum is Leonard Schlather (1835–1918). A German immi-grant, Schlather founded the L. Schlather Brewing Co. and operated it from 1857 to 1902 at Carroll and York (W. 28th) Aves., in a building still standing. It was one of the three largest breweries in Cleveland. Later Schlather became active in financial affairs, banking, and philanthropy. He built this small family mausoleum in 1882.

**26.** Continue walking to the Administration Building, turn left (east) at the end of section 5 and follow this road downhill. In former times a large lake was situated in this depression with several north–south bridges spanning the water. On the left are two small, above-ground columbaria. Next on the left and right are burial plots for infants and young children, poignantly decorated with toys, flowers, mementos, and touching inscriptions—very special memorial plots.

**27.** Continue to the next intersection and turn left. About halfway uphill on the left is the second (1966) Case Western Reserve University Medical School memorial headstone containing the cremated remains of persons who have chosen to donate their bodies upon death for the advancement of science. The first lot, begun in 1947, is southeast of this one and has an identical monument. This stone, donated by a monument company in 1967, reads: "In Memoriam . . . they gave in Death for Those In Life . . ." Since 1947, the medical school has held a yearly burial service, to which their families are invited.

Follow this road uphill, staying left at the top and left at the next intersection, and follow the road back to the Administration Building.

*Courtesy Riverside Cemetery Association*

Stone Chapel (1876)

This chapter was originally prepared with the generous assistance of William R. Halley, general manager of Riverside Cemetery and the secretary-treasurer of the Riverside Cemetery Foundation. It was reviewed and rewalked by Emily Gregor with the assistance of Jean Znamenek.

# 9  University Circle

**Distance:** 5 miles

**Walking time:** 3 hours

**Description:** This easy walk is flat but has many busy street crossings.

**Directions:** I-90 to Exit 177 (Martin Luther King, Jr., Dr.); south on MLK across E. 105th St.; bear left around traffic circle; right on East Blvd. (goes uphill, past VA Hospital). OR, from the eastern suburbs, Mayfield Rd. (US 322) west to Euclid Ave. (US 6/US 20); left (west) on Euclid to East Blvd., right (north) on East Blvd. to the museum, on the left.

**Parking & restrooms:** At the Cleveland Museum of Art, 11150 East Blvd., for which an hourly parking fee is charged (except Thursdays for senior citizens, when parking is free). Street parking (metered) available.

University Circle, five miles east of downtown Cleveland, is home to more than 70 cultural, educational, health care, social, religious, and other institutions. Information about activities here can be obtained from University Circle, Inc., 10831 Magnolia Dr., Cleveland, Ohio 44106 (216-791-3900). A University Circle walk is not complete without visiting at least one of the many cultural institutions, such as the Cleveland Museum of Art, Cleveland Museum of Natural History, Western Reserve Historical Society, or Cleveland Botanical Garden. Although many charge an admission fee, some have free admission at certain times.

**1.** Start the walk at the Cleveland Museum of Art and stroll through the galleries to the south entrance. (If closed during winter months, exit at the north entrance and take the sidewalk around to the south side of the museum and its Fine Arts Garden.) The museum is open Tuesdays, Thursdays, and weekends from 10 a.m. to 5 p.m., and on Wednesdays and Fridays from 10 a.m. to 9 p.m. It holds one of the world's great collections of art and provides extensive educational programs, as well as films, concerts, and lectures.

From the Fine Arts Garden on the south side of the museum, walk around the Wade Park Lagoon, which has beautiful flowering trees in the spring. Take the Delia Holden White marble steps at the south end of the lagoon up to the terrace and sidewalk along Martin Luther King,

Jr., Drive (MLK). Cross MLK at the traffic light at Chester Ave.; on this corner note the striking Epworth Euclid United Methodist Church. This Gothic Revival church was built in 1928 and has magnificent stained-glass windows. Continue one short block west on Chester to E. 107th St. and turn right (north).

**2.** Opposite the church, at 1890 E. 107th St., is Judson Manor. Built in 1923 as Wade Park Manor, an elegant residential hotel, it was renovated in the 1980s to become part of Judson Retirement Community.

**3.** Follow E. 107th St. (it becomes Park Lane) west to E. 105th St. and turn right (north). Below on the right is the Chinese Cultural Garden.

**4.** On E. 105th St. is The Temple Tifereth Israel (Reform) in Silver Park. The Temple Museum of Religious Art is here; it can be viewed by appointment (216-791-7755), as can the very large temple itself. The museum is dedicated to Judaic cultural, religious, and ceremonial art objects, and artifacts of ancient Israel. The new Lee and Dolores Hartzmark Library, opened in 1997, features adult and children's titles, computer workstations, an aquarium, and a puppet theater in the children's section. Another area houses the Abba Hillel Silver Study and Memorial Archives.

**5.** Next to The Temple, at E. 105th St. and Mt. Sinai Dr., is the Mt. Sinai Medical Center, a 450-bed hospital.

**6.** On the right is the new Cancer Survivors Plaza. Carefully cross several traffic islands heading northeast. Continue uphill on East Blvd., passing the Veterans Administration Hospital on the left (north) side.

**7.** To reach the Cleveland Museum of Natural History, turn right (south) on Oval Dr. The front entrance is on the right (west) side of Oval Dr.; it is open Monday–Saturday, 10 a.m.–5 p.m. and Sunday, noon–5:30 p.m. (216-231-4600).

**8.** Turn left (north) from East Blvd. onto E. 108th Street. The buildings of the Western Reserve Historical Society (WRHS) dominate the northeast corner of East Blvd. and E. 108th St.; the complex consists of the Crawford Auto-Aviation Museum, the Hay Mansion (1910), and the Hanna Mansion (1918), joined together into one building, with the WRHS Library at the rear of the facility. In the museums you can see the oldest closed automobile, Cleveland's first airplane and horseless carriages, a replica 1890s Street of Shops, and topical local history exhibits. In the mansions are fine collections of American furniture, period musical instruments, art, and apparel. The historical society is open Monday through Saturday from 10 a.m. to 5 p.m. and Sundays noon to 5 p.m. (216-721-5722).

**9.** Turn right at Magnolia Dr. Along this street are once-elegant homes that today house a variety of institutions. The ornate window at the brick Historical Society Library was once the entrance to downtown's Cuyahoga Building (demolished to make room for the BP America Building).

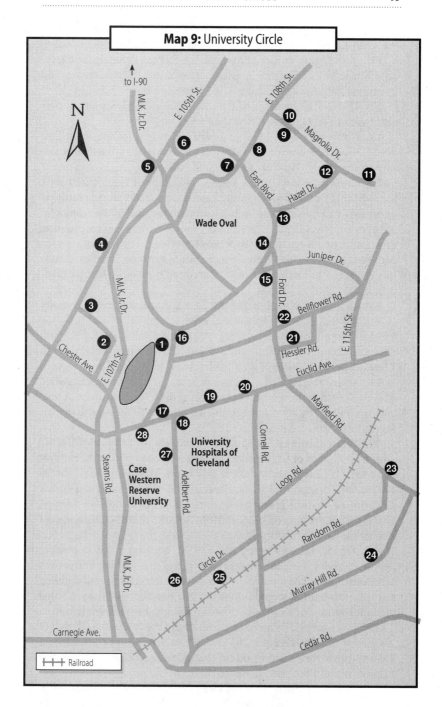

**Map 9:** University Circle

**10.** At 10831 Magnolia are the offices of University Circle, Inc. (216-791-3900), where more information about the area can be obtained.

**11.** At the north corner of Magnolia and Hazel drives is the Cleveland Music School Settlement, which offers music lessons, classes, and programs for persons of all ages and income levels.

**12.** The Gestalt Institute, to the south, holds a wide variety of personal growth workshops and courses year round.

**13.** Go west on Hazel to the Cleveland Institute of Music on East Blvd. This prestigious conservatory offers many free student and faculty concerts. Call 216-791-5000 for information.

**14.** Cross East Blvd. to the Cleveland Botanical Garden and walk through this facility and its lovely gardens. Educational programs on gardening and horticulture, lectures, workshops, and outstanding seasonal exhibits are featured here. Short wooded trails and an exquisite Japanese garden lie in the ravine, below street level. The building is open Monday through Friday 9 a.m.–5 p.m., Saturday noon–5 p.m., and Sunday 1–5 p.m. The gardens are open year round from dawn to dusk (216-721-1600).

**15.** The Gund School of Law at Case Western Reserve University (CWRU) is opposite the Botanical Garden.

**16.** Proceed southwest on East Blvd., passing Bellflower Rd. You will pass the Cleveland Institute of Art and CWRU's new Kelvin Smith Library. (Its main entrance is on Euclid Ave.)

**17.** Severance Hall, the beautiful home of the world-renowned Cleveland Orchestra, is at the corner of East Blvd. and Euclid Ave. A tour can be arranged by appointment, and it is well worth the time to see this lovely 1930 Art Deco building (216-231-7300).

**18.** Walking east up Euclid Ave. you will see the campus of CWRU and the buildings of University Hospitals of Cleveland. On the right, at the corner of Euclid and Adelbert Rd., is the Allen Memorial Library (1926), with its medical library, special collections, and the Dittrick Museum of Medical History. The museum is open Monday through Friday 10 a.m.–5 p.m. (216-368-3648). The library is open daily except during the summer; hours vary.

**19.** On the left is Thwing Hall (1913), housing CWRU's student center and bookstore, the Mather gallery, and many of the university's large event halls. The interior integrates the older Thwing Hall building with the contemporary addition; the two are connected by a small atrium. Food service and public bathrooms are also available here.

**20.** The Mary C. Painter Memorial Arch (1904) and the Church of the Covenant (1909) are at 11205 Euclid. The Neo-Gothic church has an elegant interior with rich wood carvings. Organ concerts and a diverse array of lectures are often presented here.

Continue along Euclid for one block to Ford Dr. and turn left (north).

**21.** Hessler Rd. and Hessler Ct., off Ford Dr., were chosen as Cleveland's first historic district. The individual 1900-era homes here were saved from demolition in the 1970s, as was the street itself—the only remaining street in the city paved with wooden blocks.

**22.** Continue out Hessler to Bellflower Rd. and go left (west) past the Mandel School of Applied Social Sciences (1991) and the George S. Dively Executive Education Center (1995), both new facilities of CWRU.

**23.** Turn left (south) on Ford Dr. and cross Euclid Ave. to Mayfield Rd. Follow Mayfield to Cleveland's Little Italy Historic District. This Italian neighborhood was developed in the late 19th and early 20th centuries by immigrants who worked nearby in the stone-cutting business and carved monuments for use in Lake View Cemetery. Along Mayfield Rd. are Holy Rosary Church and Montessori School, Italian shops, art galleries, restaurants, and the Little Italy Historical Museum, located at 12026 Mayfield Rd. (It's open only one day a week; call 216-231-8915.) Alta House, a community center named after the daughter of John D. Rockefeller (who helped finance the original structure), is on the south side of Mayfield at E. 125th. The original building, destroyed in a 1981 fire, stood where two bocce courts now reside. The building's cornerstone lies adjacent to the courts.

**24.** Walk back through Little Italy and turn west on Murray Hill Rd. Many artists and craftspeople have located their shops and galleries along this street. At the renovated Murray Hill School (closed in 1978), several artisans have established their businesses and they welcome visitors.

**25.** From Murray Hill Rd. turn north onto Cornell Rd. and west on Circle Dr. Walking behind the CWRU Medical School, Health Sciences Library, and Power Plant, you will reach Adelbert Rd. Walk north on Adelbert a short distance to the One-To-One Fitness Center.

**26.** Walk past the south side of the fitness center to enter the Case quadrangle on the right, with its classroom buildings on either side of this quiet enclave.

**27.** Adelbert Hall, at the end of the quad, built in 1881, is the location of the university's administrative offices and office of the president. A devastating fire in 1991 gutted this landmark building, but it has been handsomely rebuilt.

**28.** Amasa Stone Chapel (1911) is a lovely, small Gothic Revival church with a 121-foot tower topped by three angels and a gargoyle.

Cross Euclid Ave. to East Blvd. and walk along the east side of the Wade Lagoon back to the Cleveland Museum of Art. The Delia Holden White Terrace, connecting Euclid Ave. with Wade Lagoon, was renovated in 1997.

This chapter was reviewed and rewalked by LaFronza Hardy.

# 10 Lake View Cemetery

**Distance:** 4 miles

**Walking time:** 3 hours

**Description:** The cemetery is on a hill, the last remnant of the Appalachian Plateau before it descends to Lake Erie. The hills in Lake View are steep but short.

**Directions:** I-90 to Exit 173B (Chester Ave./US 322); east on Chester to Euclid Ave. (US 20) in University Circle; left (east) on Euclid to the main entrance, on right after railroad/RTA underpass. OR, from eastern suburbs, take Mayfield Rd. (US 322) west to where Kenilworth splits off from Mayfield; enter cemetery through the Mayfield Rd. gate, at the Mayfield/Kenilworth intersection.

**Parking & restrooms:** At the Garfield Monument on Garfield Rd.; follow the signs toward the left just inside the gate.

Lake View Cemetery, founded in 1869, contains the final resting places of some of Cleveland's most illustrious and industrious citizens in a most beautiful horticultural park of 285 acres. The President James A. Garfield Monument and the Jeptha Wade Memorial Chapel are two of the cemetery's most famous and significant buildings. Both are in the National Register of Historic Places. An interesting note: Lake View lies in three cities—Cleveland, Cleveland Heights, and East Cleveland. Please call the cemetery at 216-421-2665 to reserve a time for this walk in order to avoid scheduled services. Walking on the grassy areas of the cemetery is permitted. The cemetery is open daily from 7:30 a. m. to 5 p. m.; a small gift shop is located within the Garfield Monument.

**1.** Start your walk at the gate. To your right is the award-winning new (1990) Memorial Chapel mausoleum. It is open during the day and can be visited now or later in the tour. Near the gate are two very old Japanese pagoda trees, not usually found in this climate, which bloom gloriously in August. Note that many trees in the park have been identified by small attached plaques.

**2.** Walk left, following signs to the Garfield Monument. Directly ahead is the Upson Memorial with its distinguished Ionic columns. Behind it are several graceful paper birch trees.

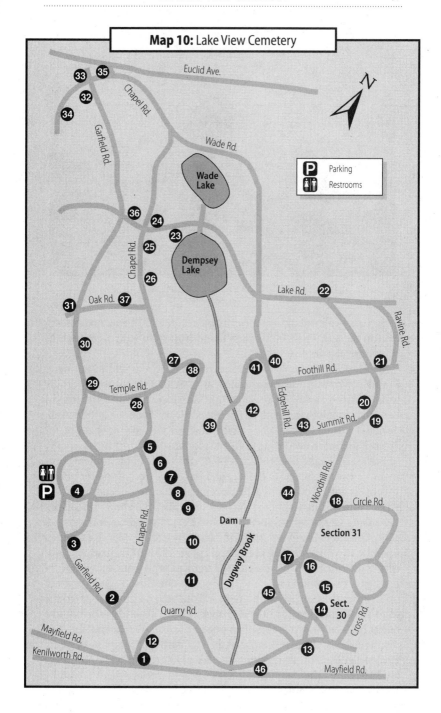

**Map 10:** Lake View Cemetery

Photo by Bill Baughman

President James A. Garfield Monument

**3.** Pass beautiful old Japanese maples on the right and a hackberry tree on the left. The Coulby monument is next on your right with its symmetrical columns.

**4.** Ahead is the imposing President James A. Garfield Monument. President Garfield was inaugurated in March 1881, but was mortally wounded by an assassin's bullet in July of that year; he died in September. A large ginkgo tree with its fan-shaped leaves is on the left sidewalk near the entrance. (Ginkgoes have remained virtually unchanged for 200 million years, according to fossil records.)

Built in 1890 and restored in 1984–85, the Garfield Monument commands a sweeping view of the city and Lake Erie from its upper porch. It is open daily from April 1 to November 15 with a docent who will guide you through the magnificent interior and show videotapes describing Garfield's life and the cemetery's outstanding horticultural collection. Note the five-part frieze carved by Casper Buberl, a talented sculptor, to depict scenes from Garfield's life (1831–81) as a teacher, legislator, and president. Note also the gargoyles projecting outward from just below the conical tower and the rose window directly over the door.

**5.** From the Garfield Monument walk north and up the steps to the John D. Rockefeller (1839–1937) memorial. This white obelisk, the tallest in Lake View, memorializes one of Cleveland's most notable and distinguished citizens. Founder of the Standard Oil Company of Ohio, Rockefeller lived on a large estate in Forest Hills (East Cleveland/Cleveland Heights). The monument's upper acanthus leaves were carved by Joseph Carabelli. Carabelli was one of the early settlers of Little Italy and founder of a company specializing in cemetery memorials that still bears his name. Many Carabelli carvings can be seen in Lake View.

**6.** Beyond to the east is the Dr. Harvey Cushing (1869–1939) memorial to the pioneer brain surgeon and organizer of the historical medical library at Yale University.

**7.** Next is the monument to John Milton Hay (1838–1905), a poet, journalist, historian, and statesman who was secretary to Abraham Lincoln. The angel that guards his grave was sculpted by James E. Fraser.

**8.** Continue eastward on the grass among the old monuments. A large European beech tree with its purple leaves is near the Amasa Stone grave. Beyond the Corning obelisk on the left and behind the fence can be seen an immense dam spanning the ravine below. Constructed in 1977 to hold back potential flood waters of tiny Dugway Brook, it has left exposed layers of very ancient rock on both sides.

**9.** Next are the graves of members of the Severance family, major Cleveland philanthropists. Nearby Severance Hall in University Circle was built in 1931 with funds donated by John L. Severance, whose home (Longwood) once stood on the present site of Severance Town Center (see ch. 11, note #17).

**10.** Carabelli designed the imposing pair of 35-foot-tall Corinthian columns with a cap to represent the portal to an early Greek temple. This monument to Charles F. Brush (1849–1929) commemorates the inventor of the arc lamp (1879), the first flicker-free lamp to light any city electrically. Brush, a prolific inventor, also perfected a device to power the first electric street railway. The monument reads: "Death is but a portal to eternal life."

**11.** Beyond is the architecturally significant Stevenson Burke family mausoleum. Herman N. Matzen (1861–1938), a noted Danish sculptor and teacher, was engaged by Burke's widow to design and construct this small building with its four carved allegorical figures representing Law, Art, Commerce, and Benevolence. The bronze door handles are finely sculpted heads wreathed with poppies.

**12.** Continue south to Quarry Rd. to the Memorial Chapel mausoleum. Take a moment to enter this quiet building of granite and glass if you did not do so at the start of this walk. Return east down Quarry Rd. and you will see (on the right) layers of exposed Euclid Bluestone, a buff-colored sandstone that is about 360 million years old (see appendix A). This stone was quarried here until the 1930s and, among other purposes, was used for some construction in the cemetery. The massive stone wall along Mayfield Rd. going downhill to Little Italy is composed of these stones. Across Dugway Brook on the left side of Quarry Rd. are the unusually fragrant white lacy flowers of white fringe trees that bloom in May.

Continue eastward on Quarry Rd.

**13.** On the right are the Garden Crypts. From here on, note the cemetery sections marked with small signs.

**14.** Directly ahead in the center of section 30 are the graves of Mantis J. (1881–1935) and Oris P. Van Sweringen (1879–1936), bachelor brothers who were railroad magnates and real estate developers of downtown's Terminal Tower, the suburban rapid transit system, and much of the community of Shaker Heights.

**15.** The magnificent bald cypress tree near the Lucas mausoleum in section 30 is a rare specimen that loses its foliage in winter. Scattered throughout the cemetery are very old and extremely slow-growing Japanese threadleaf maples, also called laceleaf maples. Several of these graceful reddish trees can be seen in section 31 near the Mitchell monument and across the way in section 35 near the Stone mausoleum.

**16.** Just around the corner on the left (section 30), and surrounded by ivy, is the flat gravestone of Dr. George Crile (1864–1943), one of the founders of the world-renowned Cleveland Clinic Foundation.

**17.** In section 8 toward the west (left) is one of four Moses Cleaveland trees still growing in Lake View. They were so named because it is thought that they were growing here at the time of the arrival of Cleaveland, the Connecticut Land Co. surveyor who founded the city in 1796. This tree is a magnificent white oak, about 75 feet tall with a spread of 90 feet.

**18.** Walk past the Liberty Emery Holden Mausoleum at Woodhill and Circle roads. Holden (1833–1913) was the publisher of *The Plain Dealer* around the turn of the century (see ch. 16, note #5). This 1917 building is another of Herman Matzen's masterpieces. Its open-work bronze door contrasts with the solid granite building atop the wide steps. Note again the lovely Japanese threadleaf maples.

**19.** Walk down Daffodil Hill on Woodhill Rd. In April more than 100,000 yellow daffodils are in bloom, a gorgeous spring sight.

**20.** On the left in section 3 is one of the nation's largest Sargent's weeping hemlock trees. Although it was damaged by a recent storm, its umbrella-like shape is striking.

**21.** Near the corner of Foothill and Woodhill roads stands a huge, beautiful fernleaf European beech. Also at this corner is a small building with public restrooms. Turn left at Ravine Rd. in section 42 and left again at Lake Rd.

**22.** All along Lake Rd. in section 4 are flowering crabapples that are magnificent in the spring. The row of small houses behind the wall on the right are homes on Forest Hill Ave. in East Cleveland.

**23.** Lake Rd. bears right and passes between two lakes usually populated with a variety of waterfowl. Bordering the south side of the lake on the left are more very tall bald cypress trees with unusual feathery green foliage that disappears in the winter. The Eliot Ness marker (dedicated in 1997) is on Lake Rd. near Edgehill. It memorializes Ness (1903–57), the nationally known law enforcement official who served as Cleveland's public safety director from 1935 to 1942. Turn next to the small granite building on the right resembling a Greek temple, Wade Chapel.

ELIOT NESS
APRIL 19, 1903 · MAY 16, 1957
DEPARTMENT OF THE TREASURY
1928 · 1935
SAFETY DIRECTOR OF CLEVELAND
1935 · 1942

LOVING WIFE
ELISABETH ANDERSEN
NESS
APRIL 9, 1906 · NOVEMBER 4, 1977

LOVING SON
ROBERT ELIOT
NESS
JULY 10, 1946 · AUGUST 31, 1976

*Courtesy Lake View Cemetery Association*

Eliot Ness Memorial

**24.** The Jeptha Wade Memorial Chapel (1900) is one of the gems of Lake View Cemetery and is listed on the National Register of Historic Places. It was built in memory of the founder of the Western Union Telegraph Company, who also donated land for Wade Park in University Circle. The entire chapel interior was designed by Louis Comfort Tiffany. A priceless Tiffany stained-glass window depicting the Resurrection is one of the artist's most important works. The walls, depicting Old and New Testament figures in gold leaf and glass mosaics, were Tiffany-designed, as were the marble ceiling, floor, chancel rail, and lighting stands. The wooden pews are made of cedar. The exterior stonework is by Joseph Carabelli. A small booklet that describes the figures and wall inscriptions is available within the chapel.

**25.** After exiting the chapel, turn left on Chapel Rd. In section 6 there is a memorial to Samuel L. Mather (1817–90), a mining and shipping industrialist who contributed greatly to Cleveland's growth. The sculpted Mather cross is typical of the fine stone masonry of the Italian craftsmen who lived in nearby Little Italy. Throughout this older section of the cemetery are examples of their finest work, carved into these elaborate monuments and considered necessary for prominent and wealthy Clevelanders of the 19th century.

**26.** Nearby is the memorial to Leonard Case, Jr. (1820–80), a benefactor of Case School of Applied Science (later Case Institute of Technology), of the Cleveland Public Library, and of the Western Reserve Historical Society.

**27.** At the end of section 6 is an 80-foot-tall dawn redwood tree with its short symmetrical branches. This tree and others like it were cultivated from trees growing in China and are thought to have been living at the time of the dinosaurs.

**28.** At this intersection and to the right in section 12 is the unusual Lemen Monument with its Doric columns preserved from the demolished Lemen family home, formerly located on Public Square. Directly in front of it is a stately Kentucky coffee tree.

**29.** Turn right at Temple Rd. and right again at Garfield Rd. At this intersection take note of the beautiful purple leaf European beech standing alone in its own triangle.

**30.** As you walk down Garfield Rd. heading west, again note the opulence of these remarkable 19th-century monuments to Cleveland's oldest and wealthiest families. Lake View contains one of the country's most significant collections of Victorian cemetery monuments.

**31.** Follow the signs pointing toward the business office and Euclid Ave. gate. In section 23 on the left, enclosing the Kunz headstone, are Lake View's finest specimens of the incredibly beautiful Japanese threadleaf maples. Some of these delicate-looking trees are more than 80 years old, yet they are still quite small. Their gracefully curving trunks show evidence of careful pruning. Their vivid bright red, orange-red, or variegated foliage is especially spectacular in the fall.

**32.** Follow Garfield Rd. toward the office. You will pass an enormous double-trunked black oak tree on the left.

**33.** Soon reach the business office of Lake View where you may pick up a free brochure describing the monuments of members of the Early Settlers Association Hall of Fame. Opposite the office are two large, rare American elms.

**34.** Just beyond the office to the south is another Herman Matzen–designed monument, this one commemorating the disastrous 1908 school fire in Collinwood in which 172 students and 3 teachers lost their lives. Nearby are two large, beautiful star magnolias, among the first of the hundreds of flowering trees to bloom in Lake View in the spring. A beautiful Scotch pine stands across Office Rd.

**35.** Walk north now on Chapel Rd. to the flagpole. The Shaw High School Memorial is just behind it. Busy Euclid Ave. is on your left, as is a lovely Siberian elm tree. Continue along past the Wade Garden on the right. Two more Moses Cleaveland trees are on the right—a beech and a tulip tree.

**36.** Next is a row of small ornate family crypts. Farther along Chapel Rd. on the right is the Beach Mausoleum; take a peek inside to see the beautiful Tiffany stained-glass window installed by this family. There are other Tiffany-designed windows in many family crypts.

**37.** Go past the Wade Chapel again and continue on Chapel Rd. At Oak Rd. in section 22 is a Herman Matzen–designed monument to Thomas White, the inventor of the White sewing machine, and his wife. The words "Courage" and "Love" are engraved on the woman's side, with "Diligence" and "Judgment" adorning the man's.

**38.** When you reach the dawn redwood tree again (see note #27), turn left this time, taking a narrow lane downhill past the vehicle barrier to an open, grassy area below the dam. The old wall on the right was constructed of native Euclid Bluestone from the cemetery's quarry. Along the right are more small family crypts.

**39.** Cross the small bridge spanning Dugway Brook and continue uphill to Edgehill Rd. and turn right.

**40.** On the left is the Herman Matzen–designed John S. Newberry Memorial for Ohio's most prominent geologist (1822–92).

**41.** A little farther uphill on the right is another Herman Matzen–designed monument—for Frances Haserot. The 6-foot-high seated winged figure, cast in bronze and weighing 1,500 pounds, required over two months of foundry labor to produce.

**42.** At the top of Edgehill is the Marcus A. Hanna (1837–1904) mausoleum, complete with its own sidewalk doormat. On the hill below it is another Sargent's weeping hemlock with its straight trunk under weeping evergreen branches.

**43.** The Jeptha H. Wade (1811–90) monument is in section 3 on the left. The tall angel-crowned Corinthian column overlooking Lake View is a fitting memorial to the cemetery's organizer and first president.

**44.** Continue up Edgehill, noting another ginkgo tree on the left and the dam below on the right. This structure is 114 feet tall and 520 feet wide, and exposes 360-million-year-old Chagrin and Cleveland shales topped by the younger Euclid Bluestone (see appendix A).

**45.** The magnificent miniature classic Greek temple for members of the Andrews family lies to the right in section 9. Samuel Andrews became a multimillionaire through his early partnership with John D. Rockefeller in 1865. This imposing structure, reflecting the grace and elegance of another age, contains 36 handcrafted, fluted columns and exquisitely carved molding on the entablature.

**46.** Return to the starting point by retracing your steps on Quarry Rd. to the gate.

This chapter was reviewed and rewalked by Michael and Lidia Murphy.

# 11 Cleveland Heights
## History Walk

**Distance:** 5 miles

**Walking time:** 2 ½ to 3 hours

**Description:** This walk will introduce you to some landmarks in the city of Cleveland Heights, from the very old (Superior Schoolhouse) to new construction at Severance Town Center.

**Directions:** From east or west take Mayfield Rd. (US 322) to the Jewish Community Center near Taylor Rd. in Cleveland Heights.

**Parking & restrooms:** Jewish Community Center, 3505 Mayfield Rd.

Cleveland Heights, incorporated as a city in 1921, was begun as a pioneer settlement of Connecticut's Western Reserve in the early 1800s. It is a well-preserved city with many old, gracious homes still beautifully cared for. Its proximity to the city of Cleveland and University Circle's cultural institutions, its thorough building and housing inspection program, strong schools and libraries, and cultural and recreational programs make it a sought-after place to live.

**1.** Start your walk at the Jewish Community Center (JCC) at 3505 Mayfield Rd. This JCC (1960) and the Mandel JCC (1987) at 26001 South Woodland Rd. in Beachwood serve the 81,000+ Jewish population of Cleveland, as well as other area residents, with a wide variety of cultural, social, educational, recreational, and physical and health activities for all ages.

**2.** Across Mayfield Rd. is the Cleveland Heights City Hall (1986) at 40 Severance Circle.

**3.** Walk west on Mayfield Rd. past the Cleveland Heights Fire Station (1982) at 3445 Mayfield.

**4.** Continuing west, at 3352 Mayfield Rd. reach the Sts. Constantine and Helen Greek Orthodox Cathedral (1957). A popular summertime Greek festival is held at this beautiful church. Tours can be arranged by calling 216-932-3300.

**5.** Park Synagogue occupies 33 acres of land with a large complex of buildings at 3300 Mayfield Rd. Built in 1950 by architect Eric Mendelsohn, this synagogue is widely recognized as one of Cleveland's most significant landmarks. Landscaping the site was challenging because a

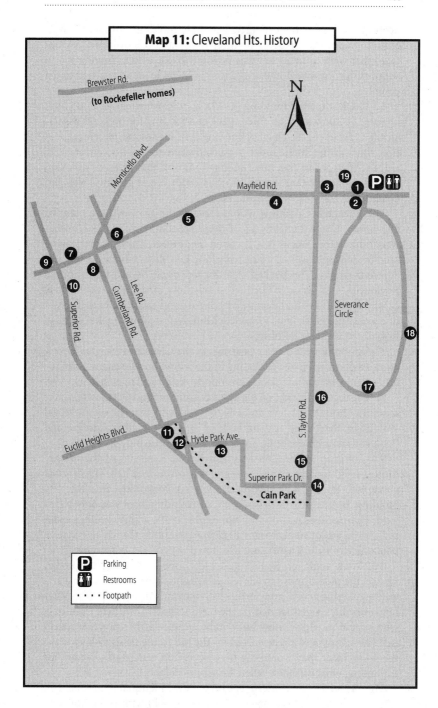

**Map 11:** Cleveland Hts. History

deep ravine bisects the property. The main building, with its 65-foot-high dome, was constructed on three different levels over rock formations that were difficult to excavate but provide a solid foundation to support this massive dome. Call 216-371–2244 to arrange a visit to the complex.

**6.** The Rockefeller Building (1930), at 3099 Mayfield Rd., was built by John D. Rockefeller as office space and lodging for business associates. The facade of the Heights Building is Romanesque, its central portion four stories high under a peaked slate roof with dormers. Its entrance facade features stone quoins (long and short masonry blocks) and an exposed beam design. Various shops are at ground level, and apartments and offices are upstairs.

The Rockefeller Building was to serve as the gateway for a planned 600-home village, but only 81 of these French Norman brick homes were built before World War II ended the project. These homes can be seen by driving north on a side trip along Lee Blvd. to Brewster Rd. and adjacent streets. The peaked slate-roofed brick homes once housed Rockefeller's employees. Of interest on these structures are the steel casement windows and decorative trim around the doorways. This set of homes and the Heights Rockefeller Building are both on the National Register of Historic Buildings.

**7.** Continue west on Mayfield Rd. to the Cleveland Heights Recreation Pavilion, used for ice skating in the winter and for many community events year round. A new community center will open here in 1999.

**8.** On the south side of the road is Cumberland Park, with a war memorial honoring Cleveland Heights residents who served in World War II. Farther south in Cumberland Park is the city's Cumberland Pool, with its architecturally interesting bathhouse built in 1927.

**9.** Continue walking on Mayfield Rd. to Superior. At the corner, Motorcars Honda occupies the site of the former city hall. The original entry with its city hall identification was incorporated into the new building. In the early days when the surrounding area was only farmland, Phare's Store was on this site. In the 1870s a blacksmith, a cider mill, and a wagon-maker were all clustered around this corner. Later a post office came to Phare's, and this "town" was called Fairmount, Ohio.

**10.** Walk south on Superior to 14299, the location of the Preyer House, the oldest house in Cleveland Heights. John Peter Preyer was a wealthy German who grew extensive vineyards in the Superior-Mayfield area after he emigrated in 1864. He imported workers from Italy who settled in what is now Little Italy, located farther down Mayfield Rd. These Italian workers walked up the hill to the fields to help make the wine. Later they would dig the sewers and water lines needed for expanding what was then called "Mayfield Heights."

The Preyer House is considered the oldest identifiable residence in Cleveland Heights. Built between 1820 and 1840 with stone quarried from the property, it has two-foot-thick walls. Preyer purchased the property in 1864; it originally occupied 70 acres, with a barn, stables, pond, and gardens. Dugway Brook still runs through the deep ravine behind the house. Notice the unusual dormers on the second story resembling Oriental helmets. These were added to introduce much-needed light into the upper rooms.

Continue south on Superior.

**11.** At 14391 Superior Rd. is the Superior Schoolhouse. Its two rooms once served six grades (the first floor was built in 1882, the second in 1915). Town meetings were also held here. There has been a school building on this site since 1853. Virtually unchanged from the way it appeared in the 19th century, it was last used as an educational building in 1963. It's now the home of the Cleveland Heights Historical Society.

**12.** Turning left (east) on Euclid Heights Blvd., go a few steps to enter a green park on the right and walk diagonally through this grassy area to Lee Rd. and the main entrance to Cain Park.

**13.** The idea for a park, community theater, and recreation area in the ravine along Superior Rd. came from Cleveland Heights mayor Frank Cain in the 1930s. Cain Park is a steeply graded 20-acre ravine used for music, art, theater, dance, tennis, and other recreational activities. It was built by veterans, the Works Progress Administration (WPA), and philanthropists in 1934–38. John D. Rockefeller donated hundreds of trees to beautify the area. Both the Alma Theater and the Evans Amphitheater were refurbished for the park's 50th anniversary in 1988. Owned by the city of Cleveland Heights, the brick office and administrative buildings, the arcade above the amphitheater, with its Tuscan-style columns, and the two brick light towers were designed to fit into the surroundings and to create a village-like atmosphere.

**14.** Emerging from Cain Park onto Taylor Rd., turn left (north) on Taylor.

**15.** The Hebrew Academy of Cleveland at 1860 South Taylor Rd. is Cleveland's oldest Jewish day school (founded in Glenville in 1943). With an Orthodox orientation, it serves 700 students from preschool through high school.

**16.** Along Taylor Rd. are kosher butcher stores, bakeries, grocery stores, and restaurants. At Taylor and Euclid Hts. Blvd. is Mosdos Ohr Hatorah (1994), an Orthodox Jewish day school, synagogue, and mikveh (ritual bath).

**17.** When you reach Severance Town Center you will be on the former site of the John L. Severance estate. Transformed by recent renovations and new store construction, this shopping complex (already remodeled several times) was one of the first suburban malls constructed in Cleveland. Opposite 7 Severance Circle is an alabaster statuary fountain (nonfunctioning) at the edge of the parking lot. It is the only reminder of the grandiose formal gardens surrounding Long-wood, the Severance estate, which was razed in 1961.

**18.** To the east are the new Cleveland Heights Medical Center (still under construction) and the recently opened Cleveland Heights Post Office. The post office was built on the site of the original stables of the Severance estate.

**19.** Continue around Severance Circle and emerge onto Mayfield Rd. once again at the Jewish Community Center. The JCC site was once a large estate called Glenallen, the home of John L. Severance's sister, Elizabeth. Her estate and gardens, considered as elegant as Longwood, were demolished in 1945.

On the northeast corner of Mayfield and Taylor Rds. stood another baronial mansion called Ben-Brae, the home of Julia Severance Millikin, a Severance cousin. It was demolished in 1951. Today there is hardly a trace of the opulence that existed in this area where three elegant mansions once stood.

*Courtesy City of Cleveland Heights*

Cain Park Amphitheater

This chapter was reviewed and rewalked by LaFronza Hardy.

# 12 Cleveland Heights
Architecture Walk

**Distance:** 5.8 miles

**Walking time:** 3 hours

**Description:** This generally flat walk is mostly on sidewalks. The city's early residences exemplify a variety of architectural styles. Please respect the rights and privacy of homeowners by not trespassing onto lawns. Call the individual churches on this walk to arrange tours.

**Directions:** From the east or west take Mayfield Rd. (US 322) to Coventry Rd. and turn south to the parking garage on the east side of the 1800 block of Coventry.

**Parking & restrooms:** Park in the metered Coventry parking garage, 1800 block of Coventry Rd. Restrooms are available at Coventry Library or at public restaurants.

The city of Cleveland Heights was established in 1921, but its history goes back to pioneer days in the early 1800s when it was part of Connecticut's Western Reserve. It is a fine, enduring city with many old, gracious homes of varying architectural styles, still very well cared for. Cleveland Heights is an aesthetic delight to walk (or drive) through because of its wonderful collection of lovely old homes.

This walk begins at the Coventry Library at the corner of Coventry Rd. and Euclid Heights Blvd.

**1.** From the parking garage, walk south on Coventry Rd. to Euclid Hts. Blvd. On the southeast corner is Coventry Village Library. It was built in 1926 by the John H. Graham Company in Tudor Revival style, of red brick with stone trim. Inside are friendly librarians and a wealth of information. Large northern and western windows provide perfect light for reading in this comfortable, heavily used branch library. The library's nighttime exterior appearance has been enhanced by the addition of floodlights.

**2.** From the library go west on Euclid Heights Blvd. On the north side of Euclid Heights Blvd. are large, stylish apartment buildings, many now converted to condominiums. Most were constructed in the 1920s and 1930s and remain in fine condition.

**3.** Turn right (west) at Edgehill Rd. and note the hand-painted Italian tiles on the front of the home at 2555 Edgehill.

On the left is the 1993 St. Alban's Episcopal Church and Temple Etz Chayyim, whose congregations built this interesting house of worship, containing both common areas and separate spaces for worship on different days, in the Episcopal and Reform Jewish traditions. The building, with its many projections, just fits its triangular corner lot.

**4.** At 2463 Edgehill is an English-style home. Around the turn of the century, this part of Cleveland Heights was laid out by an English landscape engineer who favored homes reminiscent of his native land. He also named the streets after towns in England—Derbyshire, Berkshire, Lancashire, Hampshire, and Coventry.

Opposite at 2460 Edgehill is the Patrick Calhoun House, designed by architects Alfred Hoyt Granger and Frank B. Meade and built in 1898 on 200 acres of land. This very large wood-frame residence was constructed by the grandson of Vice President John C. Calhoun (who served under presidents Adams and Jackson), who wished to be able to view the lush, green landscape of Lake View Cemetery and the newly constructed Garfield Monument. Calhoun was a wealthy attorney and developer who envisioned a noble English village in this setting, featuring mansions and boulevards that would attract wealthy Clevelanders moving out from the city. It was his landscape engineer who gave English names to the streets in this vicinity.

The George Grieble home (1919) at 2432 Edgehill has an interesting multilevel terrace and employs stone decoration over its unusually wide first-floor windows.

The Charles Farnsworth House (1916) at 2416 Edgehill was one of the first in the Calhoun development. The arched garage door is balanced by an arched window on the opposite side and an ornate stone arch over the entrance.

**5.** At the corner of Edgehill and Overlook Rds. is the baronial three-story sandstone John Hartness Brown House at 2380 Overlook. Built in 1896, it is one of the earliest homes in Cleveland Heights and was designed by Alfred Hoyt Granger in a Tudor Gothic style. There are handsome window bays in this dark house of weathered sandstone with two main entrances: a pedestrian entrance and a porte cochere on the Overlook side. An inside stairway rises to the third floor. The former carriage house at 2405 Edgehill is now a separate home.

**6.** Turn left (southwest) onto Overlook Rd. The D. B. Alexander house at 2348 Overlook is now the College Club, a social, philanthropic, and literary organization. It was designed by Abram Garfield (President James A. Garfield's son) in 1904, of handsome hand-crafted materials. Despite additions, it still has a somewhat Victorian look with its tall, narrow front gables, now hidden behind trees.

Farther ahead is Alfred Hoyt Granger's home at 2141 Overlook, now the home of the Cerebral Palsy Association. It is the only surviving building of eight houses on Overlook designed by Granger and Frank B. Meade in the late 1890s.

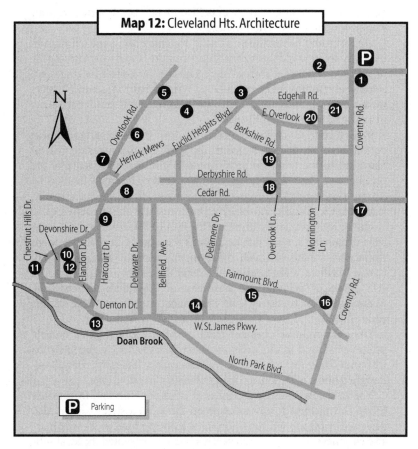

**Map 12:** Cleveland Hts. Architecture

Waldorf Towers, at 2300 Overlook, was once the site of a magnificent pillared mansion called Lowe Ridge. It was built in the mid-1890s by William Lowe Rice, a wealthy Cleveland attorney and businessman. Rice's 1910 murder at the corner of Euclid Heights Blvd. and Derbyshire Rd. remains unsolved. The grisly event is recounted in John Stark Bellamy's *They Died Crawling* (Gray & Co., 1995).

**7.** At 2200 Overlook is the striking First Church of Christ, Scientist, opened in 1931. Its octagonal, domed interior sanctuary and beautiful woodwork are well worth viewing. Its tall tower, majestically lighted at night, is a landmark in this area. For tour information please call 216-721-7766. Across the road are the buildings of Overlook House, a Christian Science sanatorium, at 2187 Overlook.

Just beyond on the left is a cul-de-sac called Herrick Mews, where several charming carriage houses and stables that once belonged to the huge mansions are located. Most of the mansions have been razed, and the remaining carriage houses have been converted to private homes.

**8.** Near Overlook and Cedar Rds. is the elegant Buckingham Condominiums at 2330 Euclid Heights Blvd., a handsome structure with stonework on the roof and facade.

Opposite and farther east on Euclid Heights Blvd. is the tall Braverman apartment building at 2378. This structure is well worth noting for its excellent 1930s Art Deco design. The angular corner balconies are somewhat reminiscent of Frank Lloyd Wright's work. Sigmund Braverman, a noted architect and synagogue designer, built these apartments in 1937 and lived here until 1960.

**9.** Return to Cedar Rd. and carefully cross this busy intersection at pedestrian crosswalks to Harcourt Dr. The Georgian mansion at 2163 Harcourt, formerly the home of Samuel Halle, is the residence of the president of Case Western Reserve University. Designed in 1906 by Abram Garfield, it was occupied for many years by the Halle family, leaders in Cleveland's cultural, civic, business, and musical activities.

On the right is a steep cliff, part of the Portage Escarpment. This slope runs diagonally across Ohio and marks the edge of the 900-foot-high Appalachian Plateau. Uphill roads in this vicinity such as Fairhill, Cedar, Mayfield, and Superior all ascend the escarpment. Euclid Ave. (US 20/US 6) delineates its base east of Cleveland. Ancient Lake Maumee, which predated Lake Erie, once reached the edge of this escarpment.

**10.** Turn right at Chestnut Hills Dr. off Harcourt. Some notable homes are found in this quiet enclave of Cleveland Heights. At 2025 Chestnut Hills Dr. is a Frank B. Meade and James M. Hamilton–designed home with unusual window shapes and divisions.

The 1917 Joseph O. Eaton House at Chestnut Hills and Devonshire (2207 Devonshire) forms an angle on the curved street corner. Also designed by Meade and Hamilton, it has a sloping roof, wide eaves, massive chimneys, and bay windows. This house represented the ideal suburban home of the early 20th century.

**11.** Judson Retirement Community, at 1801 Chestnut Hills Dr., is a multibuilding complex perched on a hillside. The entrance to the main building at this level is on the seventh floor; another entrance is several floors below on Ambleside Rd.

Adjacent to the main building is the 1919 Warren Bicknell Mansion, designed and built by Meade and Hamilton and now converted to seven independent-living units called The Mansion Courts. Take a look at the newly landscaped gardens in the front courtyard with a small waterfall for the residents to enjoy.

As a complete retirement community, Judson maintains independent living apartments, assisted living facilities, and a nursing care center. The newest building, Bruening Center, was completed in 1992 and houses acute-care beds, a health center, pool, and large parking garage.

**12.** Continue along Chestnut Hills Dr. as it bends around the edge of the escarpment. In the fall and winter one can see a beautiful view of the city of Cleveland.

On the left is Denton Dr. and two blocks over is Elandon. Two Frank Lloyd Wright–style homes are notable on this street. The George Canfield house at 2232 Elandon (1913) and another at 2236 Elandon (1914) were designed by William Bohnard and Raymond Parsson.

Continue on Denton to Harcourt and turn right (south) to North Park Blvd.

**13.** At North Park Blvd. turn left (east). Watch for fast traffic when crossing North Park Blvd. to the south side above Doan Brook, or, optionally, remain on the north side of the street.

The cliffs along the sides of Doan Brook gorge are composed of very old, dark Cleveland Shale (see appendix A) interspersed with manmade stone walls erected to protect the banks from erosion. Here and there above the brook are short woodland trails that can be found winding in and out of the trees. Opposite Delaware Dr. a small trail descends to a rocky ledge on old stone steps. The huge rocky outcrop here is Berea Sandstone, a very resistant and hard sedimentary rock that was formed about 360 million years ago out of the sand and silt laid down by an ancient inland sea that covered Ohio (see ch. 15, Berea).

The ravine below has been carved over the ages by water in the brook running downhill from Shaker Lakes. It flows through a culvert under University Circle, then runs along Martin Luther King, Jr., Dr., and empties into Lake Erie at Gordon Park.

**14.** Continue along North Park Blvd. to Bellfield and West St. James Pkwy. All along North Park Blvd. are beautiful old mansions, many built in the 1920s and designed by Meade and Hamilton.

Near Bellfield bear left (east) on West St. James Pkwy. to Delamere Dr. and follow Delamere north past lovely homes to Fairmount Blvd.

**15.** Turn right (east) at Fairmount. All along beautiful Fairmount Blvd., a National Historic District, are lovely mansions built mostly between 1908 and 1929 as country homes for those who wished to get away from the grand baronial mansions of Cleveland's Euclid Avenue to the rural highlands of Cleveland Heights. At one time this wide thoroughfare carried trolley tracks to take citizens to and from some of the finest homes in the Heights. All architectural styles are represented here: New England Colonial, Dutch Colonial, Tudor, Cotswold, and others.

**16.** At the broad intersection of Coventry and Fairmount are two beautiful old churches: St. Paul's Episcopal at 2747 Fairmount and Fairmount Presbyterian Church at 2757 Fairmount Blvd. Fairmount Presbyterian is a splendid house of worship graced with detailed wood chancel carvings and a magnificent new organ. For information about the interior call 216-321-5800.

St. Paul's Episcopal Church at 2747 Fairmount is a large Gothic Revival structure built in several stages, the most recent addition being a 1990 south wing containing classrooms, an art gallery, and an enclosed patio garden. An outstanding wooden choir screen in the chancel was completed by master woodcarver Edward Fillous, and a sculpture, *Hands of the Risen Christ*, was done by Sir Jacob Epstein. Exquisite needlepoint tapestries in both the chancel and chapel were done by members of the parish. For information call 216-932-5815.

**17.** Continue north on Coventry. At the intersection of Coventry and Cedar Rds. is another significant religious building, St. Ann Church. This imposing church complex was dedicated in 1952 but has a long and interesting history predating that.

In 1925 the Reverend John M. Powers took advantage of the fact that historic First National Bank on Public Square in downtown Cleveland was being torn down. From the bank he bought 10 pillars, marble slabs for the sanctuary walls, chandeliers, two bronze balcony rails, a clock, 14 tellers' lamps (now used to illuminate the 14 Stations of the Cross), and marble drinking fountains (now serving as holy water fonts). These were all put into storage for what turned out to be more than 25 years.

Powers then found and purchased a Steere-Skinner organ and a set of carillon bells from a Presbyterian church in Massachusetts. Ever resourceful, he acquired oak paneling from the Dan Hanna house for the confessionals and wood paneling for the priest's sacristy. He also got hold of more marble for the private chapel walls from the razed Ritz-Carlton Hotel in New York City, bricks from Cleveland's old Murray Hill School, and the sanctuary rug from Cleveland's Midland Building. Finally, he purchased two bronze sanctuary doors, a wood and bronze communion railing, and marble altar steps from the Central National Bank Building. Lastly, Powers acquired Oriental rugs from the C & O Railroad! Irish goldsmiths crafted the monstrance and the tabernacle on the main altar. Then, amazingly, this eclectic collection was all unified into the present St. Ann Church in 1952. Information regarding a viewing of the sanctuary is available by calling 216-321-0024. The church is open at varying hours.

**18.** Continue north on Coventry Rd. One block north of Cedar Rd., turn left at Derbyshire Rd. and follow Derbyshire west two blocks to Overlook Ln. On the left is the rear of Cedar Hill Baptist Church. On this site at the turn of the century was the immense mansion of Dr. George Crile, one of the founders of the Cleveland Clinic; the home was demolished in the 1940s.

Turn right (north) onto charming, brick-paved Overlook Ln., one of several hidden lanes in Cleveland Heights, and walk one block to Berkshire Rd.

**19.** The home on the southwest corner (2648 Berkshire) is an 1898 Victorian-style home with a magnificent wraparound porch, another home designed by architects Frank B. Meade and Alfred Hoyt Granger.

On the right at 2656 Berkshire Rd. is a beautiful 1910 Meade and James Hamilton home once called the "Henn House," after the large family who lived there. It has a sloping roof with wide eaves. Note the beautifully designed chimneys and arched windows.

Continue north on Overlook Ln. one more block to E. Overlook and turn right (east). All along E. Overlook are lovely homes with eclectic architecture. Many of these houses were designed by Meade and Abram Garfield. These remarkable early-20th-century architects always found a way to relate a splendid house to its spacious land and garden.

**20.** The William H. Warner House at 2689 E. Overlook was built in 1908 by Meade and Garfield. The east wing of this charming home has its gabled end toward the street. Note the way the chimney rises through three stories: first as a projecting bay and then as a blank wall. The west wing is turned at a slight angle to rest of the house, and at this angle is a splendid projecting staircase modeled after the famous 16th-century spiral-staircase tower on the Chateau du Blois.

**21.** Turn left at Mornington Ln. The handsome garden condominiums at Mornington Lane between Overlook and Edgehill Rds. were built in 1963 on land belonging to the Dr. Charles E. Briggs estate. The original iron gateway, iron fencing, brick walls, stables, and coach house all remain from the original estate. Around the corner on Edgehill Rd. can be seen the tiny children's playhouse still standing behind the blue door in the brick wall. It was designed by Charles Schneider in the 1920s.

Continue up Edgehill Rd. to Coventry, turning left (north) on Coventry past Coventry Library to the parking garage.

*Courtesy of the College Club*

The College Club

This chapter reviewed and rewalked by LaFronza Hardy.

# 13 Shaker Heights
### and Shaker Lakes

**Distance:** 8 ½ miles
**Walking time:** 3 ½ hours
**Description:** This tour will introduce you to the Shaker Lakes and to the grand residential architecture of Shaker Heights's most beautiful streets. It is a flat walk on sidewalks.
**Directions:** I-271 to Exit 29 (Chagrin Blvd./US 422); west on Chagrin; north on Warrensville Center Rd.; right on Fayette Rd. (SR 87) to Bertram Woods Branch of Shaker Heights library (at corner of Warrensville Center and Fayette).
**Parking & restrooms:** At the library.

Shaker Heights was named for a communal religious sect that lived here from 1822 to 1888. Many artifacts from that period are preserved in the Shaker Historical Museum on South Park Blvd. (see note #5). Shaker Lakes offers an outstanding recreational area for walking, biking, cross-country skiing, and bird-watching within a residential area.

**1.** Starting at the busy intersection of Warrensville Center Rd. and Shaker Blvd. East, cross at the light to the west side of Warrensville above the Rapid Transit station. Across from the fire station, turn left (west) on South Park Blvd. Many of these large homes were built in the prime of Shaker Heights's development by real estate entrepreneurs Oris P. and Mantis J. Van Sweringen. These brothers were men of vision and taste who conceived the idea of planning an ideal residential community joined to downtown Cleveland by a rapid transit line. They had control over all the buildings erected here through restrictive covenants in each deed that could dictate the location, size, type, cost, and use of every structure. These specifications included the proportion of a home's width to its depth, its building lines, additions, driveways, and outbuildings. By planning curving roadways, preserving areas of natural beauty, and rebuilding the Shaker Lakes dams and enlarging the lakes, the Van Sweringens created exquisite and valuable home sites.

**2.** One outstanding example of residential architecture is the Motch House at 19000 South Park Blvd. It is a Classical Revival mansion designed by Charles Schneider in 1924.

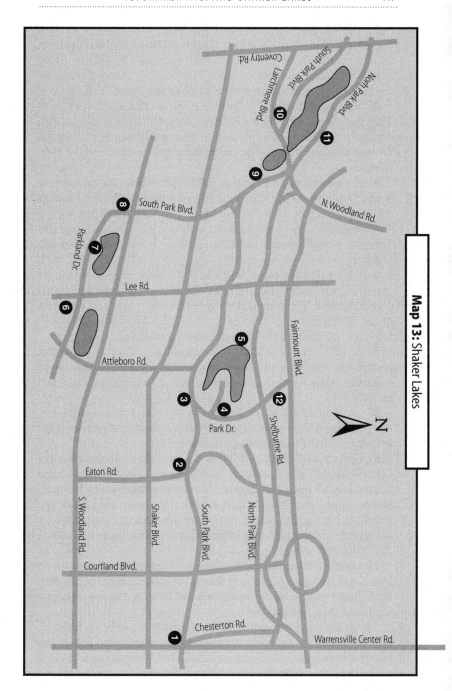

**Map 13:** Shaker Lakes

**3.** The Van Sweringen brothers' own home is at 17400 South Park Blvd. overlooking Horseshoe Lake. This magnificent mansion was originally designed in 1912 but extensively remodeled in 1924 by Philip Small into a more fashionable Tudor Revival. It has a steep all-embracing roof, half-timbered dormers, and a three-story tower in front.

**4.** Turn right (north) at the head of Horseshoe Lake onto Park Dr. At 2701 Park Dr. is the Salmon P. Halle estate, a French provincial villa designed by the firm of Corbusier, Lenski, and Foster in 1927 for the brother of Samuel Halle. The Halles were prominent Cleveland merchants.

**5.** A path will take you around lovely Horseshoe Lake to return to South Park Blvd. At 16740 South Park is the Shaker Historical Society and Museum. Open from 2 p.m. to 5 p.m. Tuesday through Sunday, this Van Sweringen–era mansion houses a library, gift shop, and large collection of Shaker artifacts, including furniture, household goods, tools, and farm implements. A tour can be arranged by calling 216-921-1201.

**6.** Walk east back along South Park to Attleboro and turn right (south). Cross Shaker Blvd. and South Woodland, and turn right (west) on Parkland Dr. There are many fine homes along here, and two more of the Shaker Lakes—Green Lake (the "Duck Pond") and Marshall Lake, the latter hidden behind homes just past Lee Rd.

**7.** At 16111 Parkland Dr. is an outstanding example of residential architecture, the Alfred Fritzsche House. This beautiful Tudor house was designed by architects Frank Meade and James Hamilton and built in 1923.

**8.** Cross South Woodland Rd. leaving Woodbury School on the left, and continue north on South Park Blvd. Southerly Park will be on the left with its fitness trail just visible inside the park.

**9.** Cross Shaker Blvd. and follow South Park Blvd. to the Shaker Lakes Regional Nature Center at 2600 South Park Blvd. The center and its gift shop are open Monday through Saturday from 9 a.m. to 5 p.m. and on Sunday from 1 to 5 p.m. A variety of trails surround the center, including some boardwalks; they are open from 6 a.m. to 9 p.m. A map for exploring this area can be obtained inside the center or by calling 321-5935.

**10.** Leaving the nature center driveway, turn left, then left again on North Woodland Rd. Cross over the end of Lower Lake to South Park Blvd. Turn right (west) on South Park to Coventry Rd. (or walk on a small trail alongside the lake).

**11.** At Coventry turn north to North Park Blvd. and follow it east on the paved walkway to Shelburne. Enjoy the many pleasant homes and tranquil views of the lakes on North Park Blvd. The plaques at the foot of the large old maple trees along North Park honor servicemen who died in World War I.

**12.** North Park enters Shelburne Rd. Follow Shelburne Rd. east to Chesterton. Turn right (south) onto Chesterton to South Park Blvd. and follow South Park to the start of the walk at Warrensville Center Rd.

*Courtesy of The Nature Center at Shaker Lakes/Photo by Bob Baillie*

The Nature Center at Shaker Lakes

# 14 Chagrin Falls
## Victorian Village

**Distance:** 2 miles

**Walking time:** 2 hours

**Description:** This walk is almost entirely on sidewalks and includes a 58-step stairway to view the falls under the North Main St. bridge.

**Directions:** I-271 to Exit 29 (Chagrin Blvd.); east on Chagrin Blvd. into Chagrin Falls.

**Parking & restrooms:** Park at the free municipal lot on the north side of W. Washington St. at S. Franklin St. Public restrooms not available here.

The picturesque Victorian village of Chagrin Falls has often been featured in magazine and newspaper articles as the quintessential American small town. Located at the far eastern edge of Cuyahoga County only 18 miles east of Cleveland, lovely Chagrin Falls is an old settlement with an interesting history. Noah Graves traveled here from New England in 1833 and was the first visitor to grasp this territory's potential for settlement. Virgin forests supplied tall trees that could be used for buildings, and a clear, flowing river provided waterfalls that could be harnessed to power mills. Soon a few families from New England settled here, and by 1844 Chagrin Falls was incorporated as a town.

During the 19th century, the village grew into a bustling metropolis with dozens of mills, factories, foundries, stores, shops, and homes. Today many beautiful Victorian homes built by prosperous mill owners and businessmen still survive and have been lovingly restored to lend this quiet community its charm. Of the many mills here, only the Ivex Paper Mill on Cleveland St. remains and is still in operation. The Popcorn Shop on N. Main St., in the original office building adjacent to the Gates Grist Mill site, dates from 1868. The oldest business buildings remaining in the shopping district are Millside (1846) at 98 N. Main St. (now the Ohio Bank), and Chagrin Hardware at 82 N. Main St., built in 1857. Many of the old buildings in downtown Chagrin Falls have undergone various transformations, but the town has managed to maintain the look of a Victorian village.

Far from being any kind of disappointment, successful Chagrin Falls truly belies its name, whose origin has raised much speculation. According to an 1874 historian, C. T. Blakeslee, Chagrin might have been a corruption of the Indian word *shaguin,* meaning clear river.

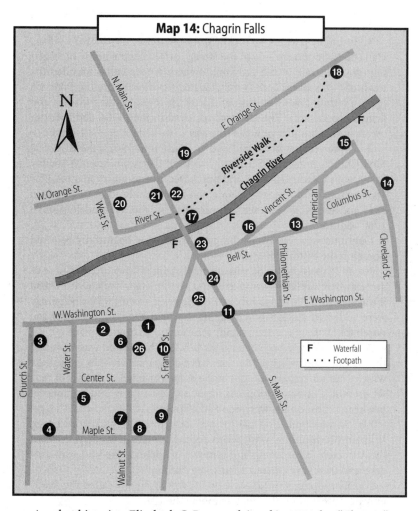

**Map 14:** Chagrin Falls

Another historian, Elizabeth G. Rogers, claimed in 1976 that "Chagrin" derived from an Anglicized and corrupted version of the name of a French trader, Francois Seguin, who operated a trading post on the Cuyahoga River in 1742. Subsequently his name was attached to the river that flows through this town.

Though the true source of its name may be unknown, the source of the Chagrin River itself is known. It arises north of here in Geauga County, gathers several smaller streams along the way, then flows over hard shale and sandstone to form successively larger and larger waterfalls as it approaches Chagrin Falls. The largest waterfall, in the center of town, drops 25 feet. It can be viewed by taking the stairway to the falls next to the Popcorn Shop at the bridge on N. Main St.

**1.** From the parking lot on W. Washington St., note the 1874 Village Hall (on the opposite side of the street), originally the home of Washington Gates, one of the early mill owners, whose father founded the town of Gates Mills. Gates's mill, located next to the present Popcorn Shop, produced flour and ground feed for many of the villagers and farmers in the area. The mill was removed in the 1930s, and the spot where it once stood is now the stairway to the falls.

**2.** On the corner of Walnut and W. Washington Sts. is the attractive First Church of Christ, Scientist. The local Christian Science Society first met as a group in 1931 and purchased this property in 1944. The 1836 saltbox built by Seth Henderson was remodeled as a church in 1945 and achieved its present appearance after more remodeling and a 1960 addition.

Continue west on W. Washington St. to view beautifully restored homes in the historic district.

*No. 44 W. Washington St.* was originally built in 1845 on a bed of rock and clay that was later excavated to add a basement to the house. In 1850 it was sold for $500 to a family named Hewes. The west wing and garage were added in 1982; a porch railing that had been stored under the porch for 50 years was then finally returned to its original place.

*No. 49* began as a barn behind the house at *No. 44* and was moved to this plot in 1866 to house Mrs. Hewes's elderly mother. In its early years wings were added to both sides of the home's original peaked-roof center section. The restoration has included landscaping and an unusual brick lamp post on the west side of the house.

*No. 54* was built in 1850 for the local druggist and storekeeper, William Waldron, who was a relative of the families living at *Nos. 44 and 49.* Attractive landscaping and removal of some of the Victorian gingerbread trim have created a charming home.

*No. 55,* a Greek Revival–style home, was originally called the Academy because it housed a small school in the 1840s.

*No. 64,* now a private home, was until recently the Federated Church parsonage. It was once the magnificent home of the John Bullard family, which operated a thriving wooden ware factory at the rear of the property. This important business produced butter molds, kitchen utensils, and rolling pins for the general population. Examples of the Bullards' products can be seen at the Chagrin Falls Historical Society Museum. In the early 1870s, Mr. Bullard, the first mayor of Chagrin Falls, moved the house that originally stood on this site to *86 W. Washington,* in order to build this much larger and grander home.

This impressive building is said to be a prime example of Chagrin Falls's Victorian architecture. Homes in this style had all sorts of projections, wings, and bays that were designed to accommodate each family's individual needs. Decorative embellishment or gingerbread on these homes included brackets, scrollwork, bargeboards on the gables, cornices, finials, fretwork, and other ornamentation. The Bullard house is noted for its belvedere, the open-roofed gallery that crowns this striking dwelling.

Note the different styles of roof braces that adorn these beautiful Victorian homes.

*No. 86*, the original home of the Bullard family, was moved to this site from *64 W. Washington* and has been remodeled by various owners, who have added a garage and screened porch.

On the ground at the corner of Water and W. Washington Sts. is a large millstone from a local mill, twin to one located at Triangle Park in the center of town. Continue west to Church St.

**3.** Now turn south on Church St., but first note *No. 4 Church St.*, with its solid sandstone foundation and 40 cornice boards on the roofline. These decorations were common in 1874, when this home was constructed. Recent renovation has restored the original lines of the home except for the screened porch, shutters, and front door.

Many beautiful homes line Church St.

**4.** Continue two blocks down Church St. to Maple St. and here turn left (east).

*No. 93 Maple St.* is a modest 1880 home whose additions include a 1920s-era front porch and a rear two-story projection built in the 1980s.

*No. 83* is another of this district's beautifully restored Victorians built in Italianate style. Its two-story rear addition was constructed in the 1960s.

**5.** Turn left (north) on Water St. to view more charming Victorian homes:

*No. 68 Water St.* and its mirror-image twin next door at *No. 56* were both built by a Mr. O'Malley, a Chagrin Falls lumberyard owner, in 1876 and 1875 respectively. *No. 68* originally had an iron grille over each window; they were removed to discourage roosting pigeons. Its west wing was added in 1920.

*No. 56* (1865) retains most of its early construction details in the exterior trim, front door with iron grillwork, and window casings.

*No. 51*'s original section dates from 1835–40 and features solid rock cellar walls that are two feet thick, hand-hewn log floor and roof joists, and mortised and pegged joinings. In the 1870s, Dr. J. E. Phelps, a Chagrin Falls dentist, raised the house onto a brick foundation and built an addition containing a dental office, kitchen and pantry, and wood storage area. In the 1960s, a garage and another addition were built. This home's two chapel windows, one of which is in the facade and the other on the north side, are considered to be fine examples of Western Reserve Gothic architecture.

*No. 44* is one of the first brick homes in Chagrin Falls, built before

1848 by William Hutchings, a master builder and brick maker from England. Several additions have been made to the house over the years.

*No. 29* was built in 1864 on W. Washington St. and moved here in 1883, when a bay window and single-story rear section were added. Some of the original work includes the cut-stone foundation and hand-hewn beams.

*No. 23* was owned from the 1850s to the 1950s by the Porter family. At one time they rented a room to future U.S. president James A. Garfield, who was then employed as a construction worker at the Disciple Church, originally located nearby on Walnut St. A small north wing was added early in the home's life, and a 1960 two-story rear wing doubled the size of the original home.

**6.** Turn right (east) on W. Washington St. one block to Walnut St. and then turn right (south) on Walnut.

**7.** Here are several more of Chagrin Falls's National Historic District homes and the home of the Chagrin Falls Historical Society (see note #26).

*No. 24 Walnut St.* originally stood on the site of the old post office on W. Washington St. (now an office building) when it was constructed in 1883 by Orin Frazer. At that time a gazebo stood in front of this stylish Victorian home. Although it has lost its large imposing entrance and two-story bay windows, it retains its typical ornamental cutwork and spindles over the doorway, and has lovely landscaping.

*No. 32* features small front gardens and a brick walkway reminiscent of Williamsburg, Virginia. Although the brick portions of this lovely house date from before 1860, frame additions over the years have enlarged it to accommodate two families, though presently it has reverted to a single-family home.

*No. 54* is a beautiful stately home built in the 1840s by J.W. Williams and is one of several remaining mill owners' or businessmen's homes in Chagrin Falls. Mr. Williams, a foundry operator, gave this house to his son, A. C. Williams, and had it moved here in 1873 from its original site. Still retaining its original wood trim under the eaves and the iron work on its roof, it was lovingly restored in 1963, and a downstairs wing was added in the 1970s.

*No. 65 Walnut St.* was J.W. Williams's original brick stable and carriage house constructed in 1872–3 at the rear of his handsome new brick home (at 60 S. Franklin St.). Converted to an attractive home in 1971, its front bow window was once the carriage entrance; the kitchen is the former stable area.

**8.** Walk east (left) one block on Maple St. and turn left again (north) on S. Franklin St. Underfoot you will occasionally notice ripple marks in the sandstone sidewalk blocks. These were made by underwater currents during the Devonian era—360 million years ago—when Ohio was covered by a warm and shallow inland sea. Over the millennia the sand hardened into rock and was quarried from many places in Northeast Ohio (see appendix A).

**9.** *60 S. Franklin St.*, the graceful J. W. Williams home, was owned by this illustrious family whose iron foundry was located on the Chagrin River near W. Washington St. The foundry was internationally known for its iron products, especially cast-iron toys and sadirons, the implements used in many homes to press fancy Victorian clothing.

This gorgeous house stayed in the Williams family until 1918. Remodeling in the 1940s, 1950s, and 1970s has restored the home to much of its former splendor. The brick is original on all but the north wing addition, and the wrought-iron trim in the 10-foot-high front doors remains from the early building.

**10.** Continue north on S. Franklin St. to the United Methodist Church (1884) on the left, whose congregation first gathered in 1833–34. The church originally was located in a brick and frame building directly across the street from its present site.

**11.** At W. Washington St. turn right (east). On the northeast corner of N. Main and E. Washington Sts., where Key Bank now stands, try to imagine a famous Chagrin Falls landmark first built in 1852: Irving House Hotel. In its heyday it was notable for its fifty-cent oyster suppers, ballroom dances, and many private parties and testimonial dinners. In 1875 the Women's Christian Temperance Union picketed the saloon in this hotel and nine other Chagrin Falls saloons in one epic day! A grand remodeling in 1892 added Victorian towers, ornate trim, electric lights, and central heating. Unfortunately, however, a fire destroyed the famous Irving House on January 13, 1897, when firehoses froze, an event that prompted the town to establish a central water system. Photographs of this well-known establishment are on exhibit at the historical society.

The building owned by Brewster and Stroud on the southwest corner of S. Main and E. Washington Sts. has an interesting history. This small white building with red shutters opened as the Falls Hotel in 1897 with central heating, electricity, and plumbing; guests were charged the high price of $2.00 a day for these then very modern conveniences.

Continue walking east on E. Washington St. to Philomethian St. All along here are many lovely restored homes, some dating from the 19th century.

At *87 E. Washington* is the Reed-Nichols-Brown Funeral Home in a building once owned by one of the members of the Ober family. The Obers, inventors of the Ober lathe, operated a large sawmill at 210 Bell St., of which the main building (1873) is still standing.

**12.** At Philomethian St. (this name means both love of learning and love of methodism) turn left (north). Here are smaller homes once owned by workers in the various mills of Chagrin Falls.

The large school building complex on the left houses Chagrin Falls Middle School. The center section of the building is the oldest part—

the 1914 high school facing E. Washington St. It is surrounded by additions built in 1940 and later. As the town and school populations grew, many of the elementary and high school grades were moved to a campus on E. Washington St. on the former East Cuyahoga County Fairgrounds.

**13.** Continue north to Bell St. and turn right (east). On the left is the Valley Art Center at 155 Bell St., open 10 a.m.–4 p.m. Monday through Friday and 10 a.m.–2 p.m. on Saturday. The structure was built in 1922 as a service garage.

**14.** Turn left (north) on American St., where there are no sidewalks, and right onto Columbus St. to Cleveland St. Please use caution along here because Cleveland St. also has no sidewalks. However, pedestrians may walk on the grassy area just above street level.

The entrance to Hamlet Retirement Communities at 150 Cleveland St. is opposite on the right. This extensive community was constructed on land originally belonging to Dr. Justus H. Vincent, who in 1837 built the large white frame home to the north at 170 Cleveland St. The Hutchings family added on to the home and lived in it in the 1870s, and the Crawford family occupied it in the 1890s.

Established in 1965, Hamlet offers retirees a variety of beautiful rental accommodations and common areas at Hillside Garden Homes, Atrium Apartments, and Hamlet HealthCare. You may wish to stroll through the attractive grounds. For information and a tour of the facilities, please call ahead at 440-247-4201.

**15.** Continue north on Cleveland St. past Vincent St., using great care on this busy road with no sidewalk. Arrive at a bridge overlooking a beautiful, wide waterfall on the Chagrin River. Here is the last remaining mill building in Chagrin Falls, which has seen service under several different names (and served several purposes) since the 1840s; most recently, it was the Ivex Paper Mill. The Chagrin River becomes a beautiful pond behind this magnificent waterfall, called the Upper Dam. As you look east beyond the falls and the dam, you will see the site of the once thriving community of Whitesburg. In the 1840s, Whitesburg supported a woolen mill, an axe factory, and small workshops. Later the town was incorporated into the Village of Chagrin Falls.

**16.** Retrace your steps to Vincent St. and turn right to follow Vincent west to Bell St., noting the river below on the right. At Bell St. is the landmark Federated Church, whose spire can be seen for miles around. Its congregation first worshiped in 1846 in a frame church on Bell St. as the Bible Christian Church. In 1884, Bible Christian merged with the Congregational Church and, in another merger, the Disciple and Congregational Churches formed the present Federated Church.

**17.** Continue to N. Main St., turn right, cross the bridge, and turn right again into pretty Riverside Park and the brick-paved Riverside Walk. This pleasant walk alongside the Chagrin River affords a magnificent view of another of the town's waterfalls, Upper Falls. Riverside Park was once the site of the mills of Chagrin Falls Paper Company, established by Noah Graves in 1841, but the buildings were razed in the 1930s to create this lovely park. Follow the brick walk eastward past the children's play area to its end, and go up the steps to reach the Chagrin Falls Library, a branch of Cuyahoga County Public Library. Among the treasures in the library are microfiche copies of the well-loved *Chagrin Falls Exponent*, published from 1874 to 1964. This acclaimed newspaper contained national as well as local news, vital statistics, industrial information, and advertising. Original copies of the *Exponent* are preserved at the Historical Society Museum.

**18.** From the library, walk westward on E. Orange St. passing the Valley Lutheran Church on the right. This congregation started meeting in the town hall in 1932 and built on this property in 1946, adding a sunday school and church offices in 1954 and other additions in the 1960s.

More turn-of-the-century homes line E. Orange St.

**19.** At the corner of E. Orange and N. Main Sts. is a shopping center called Stepnorth, housing a variety of shops.

On the southeast corner is Millside, the oldest building still in use in Chagrin Falls, now housing the Ohio Bank. It was built in 1846 and has had various uses in its approximately 150-year existence.

**20.** Continue across N. Main St. onto W. Orange St. and turn left at one-block-long West St. On both sides of this small street is a dense cluster of historic and commercial buildings. To the south of Hearthside Clothing is the newly and beautifully restored Inn of Chagrin Falls at 87 West St., and next to it is the old Gamekeeper's Taverne. All three of these yellow buildings once made up Crane's Canary Cottage, an inn offering dining rooms, reception and card rooms, and living quarters. Owned by the family of poet Hart Crane, who occasionally visited here, the establishment opened in 1928 and closed in 1942 because of the difficulty of obtaining food and supplies during World War II.

The Village Exchange at 79 West St., the former Joseph O'Malley residence, is an interesting consignment shop that is well worth visiting.

Turn right onto River St. Near the west end of River St. is Chagrin Valley Little Theatre, which opened in 1949 and began presenting legitimate plays after the decline of the Opera House (see note #21).

On the south side of River St. is a new restaurant overlooking the magnificent Lower Falls. Next to it is a small frame structure at 9 River St. that was originally a Chagrin Falls shoe store owned by W.H. Caley. In 1910 it was moved to W. Orange St. and later to this location. For many years it was a barber shop, but at present this quaint historic building houses a deli.

**21.** Walk back to N. Main St. and note Township Hall on the left at mid-block. The original portion was built in 1848 to house a library. In

1874 the town purchased the building and added a stage to the second floor, and the building became known as the Opera House. In 1875, Henry Church, Jr.—the sculptor of Squaw Rock in South Chagrin Reservation (see ch. 29)—designed and made the weather vane that sits atop the cupola.

In its heyday the Opera House provided the town with minstrel and vaudeville shows, drama and musical performances, and an arena for political activities. The Chagrin Valley Little Theatre used this building from 1930 until 1943, when a fire destroyed the upper half of the building. When it was rebuilt in 1944 it became Chagrin Falls Township Hall, and it now consists of a large one-story room that is rented out for public and private gatherings.

**22.** Across the street is Chagrin Hardware at 82 N. Main St., another old store worth visiting because it remains in virtually the same condition as when it was built in 1857.

**23.** All along N. Main and S. Franklin Sts. are commercial buildings with long histories. The two-story brick building at the southwest corner of River and N. Main Sts. was where the *Exponent* was published from the 1880s to 1964.

At the Popcorn Shop, take the 58-step stairway to the falls alongside the shop down to the foot of the 25-foot lower falls for a glorious view of this turbulent waterfall. Imagine how this river must have looked over 150 years ago when many busy mills lined both sides of the embankment! By looking up under the bridge you can still see some of the original stonework done by William Hutchings, one of the occupants of the home at 170 Cleveland St. (see note #14).

**24.** Return up the stairs and continue on S. Main through the central shopping district of Chagrin Falls to note some of the interesting commercial buildings.

The 1882 McClentic Building, on the west side of the street, was once considered the finest building in town; it had 54 gas jets to light the lower-story dry goods store and a modern basement furnace. It was completed at the then-high cost of $20,000.

The 1891 sandstone building marked "Bank"—above the women's clothing store on S. Franklin St.—once housed the Chagrin Falls Banking Company.

The I.O.O.F. (International Order of Odd Fellows) building on N. Main St. above Dink's Restaurant once housed City Hall and the Fire Department.

**25.** The 1877 Bandstand in Triangle Park was the site of the Buckeye Carriage Shop until the city decided to create a new park here in 1875. It was and still is the location of the "Concerts in the Park" series of Thursday evening summer band concerts sponsored by the chamber of commerce. An honor roll dedicated to the memory of those who died serving their country in World War I is here, as is an old millstone and a 1983 time capsule to be opened in 2033.

**26.** Before returning to the starting point at W. Washington St., it is well worth your time to view interesting relics of an earlier time at the Chagrin Falls Historical Society and Museum at 21 Walnut St. Please call ahead (440-247-4695) or plan to visit on a Thursday afternoon when the Historical Society is open. (You might then want to stay in Chagrin Falls for dinner and a summertime Thursday evening band concert, at 7 p.m. in June and July.) The museum has many photographs on display, and in its collections, that show how Chagrin Falls looked in earlier times during its industrial era, before it became a quaint Victorian village. Also on display are many fine examples of items made in Chagrin Falls during this time.

This walk prepared by the author with the generous assistance of the Chagrin Falls Historical Society's volunteer curator, Pat Zalba, and its president, Scrap Zalba, with additional valuable contributions by Annie Gumprecht. The Historical Society is located in the 1965 Shute Memorial Building at 21 Walnut St. Its interesting museum is open on Thursdays from 2 to 4 p.m. and by appointment, by calling 440-247-4695. Jonathan Cameron assisted the author with the rewalking of this chapter.

# 15 BEREA
## and Baldwin-Wallace College

**Distance:** 5.5 miles

**Walking time:** 3 hours

**Description:** This walk is primarily on sidewalks and some trails in the Mill Stream Run Reservation of Cleveland Metroparks.

**Directions:** I-71 south to SR 237 south, past the airport; south on Front St. into Berea, bear left past the I-X Center to remain on Front St.; bear right past center of town Triangle; left after the Berea Police Dept. into the municipal parking lot.

**Parking & restrooms:** Park at the south end of the municipal parking lot near Coe Lake Park and the gazebo overlooking the lake. Public restrooms are in the adjacent library, city hall, or pool area.

The city of Berea, a mostly residential community of about 20,000, could today be considered just another one of Cleveland's older southwest suburbs. Yet its early history is that of an important independent community, primarily because a layer of high-quality sandstone was discovered lying near the surface of its soil. The earliest products of this sandstone (subsequently named Berea Sandstone) were world-famous Berea grindstones and whetstones for tool sharpening. At first sandstone was removed from the bed of the Rocky River, but when important new uses were found for this excellent stone, Berea's first quarry opened in the early 1840s. The stone was subsequently used in constructing buildings, bridges, curbs, and sidewalks in the developing city of Cleveland and elsewhere. During the next hundred years, thousands of trainloads of Berea Sandstone were shipped from here, enabling Berea to be called the sandstone capital of the world.

John Baldwin was one of Berea's early grindstone entrepreneurs and a devout Methodist who felt he needed to repay God for the abundant prosperity that had come to him as a result of his business success. He gave the village land and an income-producing quarry that resulted in the inception of what would eventually become the highly respected Baldwin-Wallace College.

The name of the village was selected by the toss of a coin. Given two choices by the town's leaders, Baldwin called "heads" and the end result was the name—Berea. In the biblical Book of Acts, Berea was a community where people studied the scriptures and were governed by

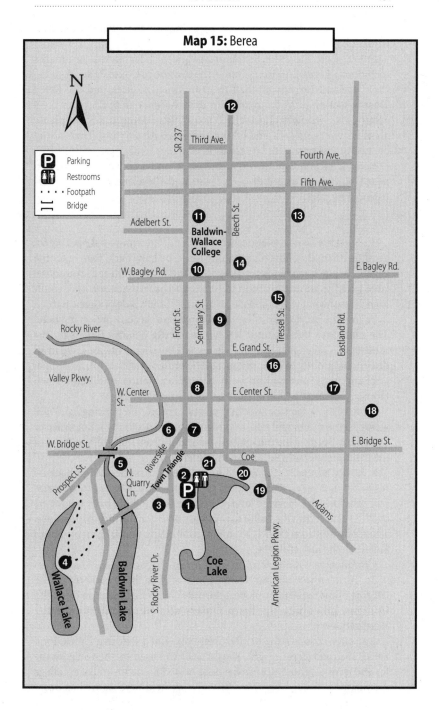

Map 15: Berea

them. The founders of modern Berea hoped that their population would do likewise.

Other than the college, important present-day Berea landmarks include the Berea Children's Home, the Cuyahoga County Fairgrounds, the Cleveland Browns football team training facilities, and the Berea Quarry section of Mill Stream Run Reservation, one of Cleveland's 14 Metroparks. Baldwin and Wallace lakes, Music Mound, several picnic areas, a swimming area, and hiking and paved All-Purpose Trails are all located in this part of the reservation.

Berea is 14 miles southwest of Cleveland and is conveniently located near I-80 (Ohio Turnpike), I-71, I-480, and Cleveland Hopkins International Airport.

**1.** Start the walk at the southeast corner of the municipal parking lot heading down the short path leading into Coe Lake Park, then enter the gazebo. Many large blocks of Berea Sandstone are scattered around the lawn area. As an introduction to sandstone quarry history, look south for a view of what was called the fashionable South Side of Berea, named by many "the Lord's side of town," before there was any quarrying here. The same area later became known as the Big Quarry, Berea's largest sandstone quarry. It extended well beyond the shores of Coe Lake in all directions and north to E. Bridge St. The present parking lot, municipal pool and playground, library, city hall, police station, and Berea Town House Apartments were all built on filled-in quarry pits.

**2.** Return to the sidewalk at the south end of the parking lot. Walk west past the municipal pool and turn right (north) onto S. Rocky River Dr., which borders the parking lot. Carefully cross the street in front of the eight-story Baldwin House Apartments.

S. Rocky River Dr. (formerly Elm St., and nicknamed Hog's Back by residents) is a survivor of the quarrying operation. Isolated by quarries on both sides, this elevated land served as a dam to hold back the waters of Mill Pond (now Coe Lake) to provide power for turning grindstones. The roadway also served as a last link connecting the fashionable South Side with the rest of Berea.

Continue past the apartment building to N. Quarry Ln.

**3.** Turn left (west) onto N. Quarry Ln. Stay on the grassy area on the left side of the lane and walk past the water treatment plant on the right. Continue down into the Berea Quarry section of Mill Stream Run Reservation.

Just after crossing the bridge over stone-lined Baldwin Creek, look across the road to your right. The area with a raised earthen stage at the far end is Music Mound. This site once hosted Baldwin-Wallace College graduations. Today May Day festivities are held here, as well as occasional summer weddings.

Continue to the top of the concrete arched bridge over Rocky River to view the pretty waterfall. The water to the left is Baldwin Lake. Cleveland Metroparks periodically dredges the lake to maintain an open body of water by preventing the river from filling with silt.

You are now in the western section of Berea's former fashionable South Side. Here John Baldwin's Old Red House and the original Baldwin University (an outgrowth of Baldwin Institute) were located on five acres. Later these buildings were either razed or moved when the sandstone quarry was extended into this area. When quarrying operations were over, the area became a vast wasteland. Due to the efforts of Cleveland Metroparks and the federal Works Progress Administration (WPA), however, this space was beautifully transformed into the lovely park you see today.

**4.** After crossing the bridge, turn left onto the paved All-Purpose (Walk/Bike) Trail and walk south until you reach the short spur on the right that crosses the park road at the entrance to the Wallace Lake area. (Optionally, you may wish to continue a short distance farther to the observation tower on the left, overlooking Baldwin Lake.)

Carefully cross Valley Parkway and walk toward the concrete bathhouse and cafe. There is a lifeguard-protected swimming area at Wallace Lake. The lake is also used in winter for ice fishing and ice-skating.

Walk diagonally right (northwest) at the end of the parking area onto a small gravel road. Pass the cafe and follow the gravel path north along the lake past picnic and playing areas, and fishing platforms. Continue beyond the small parking lot and walk on the grass along the tree line on the left to a paved access trail alongside Valley Parkway. Follow this path (with the railing) uphill to Prospect St.

**5.** Walk to the right (north) a short distance on Prospect St., then turn right (east) onto W. Bridge St. Cross the bridge over Valley Parkway. Across the street on the left is Parkway Shopping Center, originally built in 1951 and extensively renovated in 1995. Although at first it was a major competitor to the Triangle business district, the center has now become an integral part of downtown Berea.

Walk across the bridge spanning the Rocky River to Riverside Dr. and the traffic light.

**6.** Turn left (north) and cross W. Bridge St. at the traffic light. Walk north on Riverside Dr. along the west side of the Town Triangle. Within the Triangle are memorials to area soldiers and sailors who served in the Civil and Spanish-American wars, both world wars, and the Korean and Vietnam wars. Continue ahead to the bell tower. The names on the tower honor outstanding Berea citizens for their contributions to the community.

The Triangle area was for many years a hub for business and shopping in southwest Cuyahoga County, but structural deterioration and parking problems led to a major urban renewal project in the early

1970s. The buildings on the east side of the Triangle were spared, but those on the south side were replaced by the present Berea Commons. The area along Riverside Dr. was left open to enable residents and visitors to enjoy the river and overlook.

**7.** Cross Front St. and walk north past the bakery to a unique clock shop with an interesting collection of grandfather, cuckoo, and many other clocks. This 1953 store specializes in repair and restoration of all kinds of timepieces.

Continue ahead to the Kulas Musical Arts building, the home of the Baldwin-Wallace Conservatory of Music. Directly behind it is Merner-Pfeiffer Hall, where the Riemenschneider Bach Institute and Bach Memorial Library are located. An annual two-day Bach festival held in May celebrates various aspects of the composer's repertoire and attracts music lovers from all over the world.

**8.** Turn right at the Kulas Musical Arts Building and walk up the short flight of concrete steps leading to the south campus of Baldwin-Wallace College. Across the street and directly ahead is Marting Hall, housing the humanities division and writing laboratory. Turn left at Seminary St. and head north. The white sandstone structure on the left is Kohler Hall, the oldest (1867) building on the campus. Across the street is Lindsay-Crossman Chapel, the center of the college's religious activities.

This area was originally selected by John Baldwin and two Methodist ministers as the location for Lyceum Village and Seminary, which might have become Berea's town center had it not failed in 1842. Despite near bankruptcy, Baldwin persisted in his efforts and, due to his financial success in the grindstone industry, was able to establish Baldwin Institute at this location. The institute became Baldwin University in 1855 (see note #3) and also became the nucleus of Baldwin-Wallace College.

In 1863, James Wallace, another financially successful quarryman, established German Wallace College to serve the large population of German immigrants who had settled in the area. Although neither the university nor the college duplicated each other's courses, they continued as separate organizations administratively until 1913. As the German population gradually became more Americanized, the two schools merged to become Baldwin-Wallace College.

**9.** Continue north on Seminary St. past the United Methodist Church (on the east) to Bagley Rd. St. Thomas Episcopal Church is on the southeast corner. Cross at the traffic light at the college's Ritter Library; turn left and reach the four-way intersection at Bagley Rd. and Front St.

**10.** The building on the northeast corner of Bagley Rd. and Front St. is Philura Gould Baldwin Library, the college's original (1893) library, built in memory of John Baldwin, Jr.'s daughter, and now the home of special collections.

The buildings on the southwest corner housed South West Hospital from 1925 to the mid-1970s, when the hospital was relocated two miles east on E. Bagley Rd. This much enlarged and modernized facility continues to serve Berea and surrounding communities.

The large Victorian-style house on the northwest corner was designed by the well-known architect Stanford White. It is now a residence hall for Baldwin-Wallace College women.

Walk north on Front St. The next sandstone building on the right is Wheeler Hall. Mrs. John Baldwin, affectionately called "Grandma Baldwin," was given the honor of turning the first shovelful of dirt at the groundbreaking ceremony for the construction of this building in 1891.

**11.** Continue north on Front St. to Adelbert St. (on the left). The northwest section of Berea (to the west) began as a settlement of Polish immigrants who came to Berea to work in the quarries. This region still retains some vestiges of its Polish heritage. (As an option, you may wish to walk west a short distance on Adelbert to view St. Adelbert's Church, school, and convent.)

Still heading north on Front St., reach Third Ave. Opposite is the Berea Recreation Center, originally a 1942 roller-skating rink and bowling alley. This building was taken over by the city of Berea in the mid-1990s and converted into a municipal recreation center, with swimming pool, track, and other facilities.

**12.** Cross Third Ave. and turn right (east) to Beech St. Walk north on Beech to the fence enclosing the Cleveland Browns football practice and training complex. Here is a good view of the outdoor practice field and, beyond it, buildings holding an enclosed indoor football field, workout and training suites, offices, and other spaces.

**13.** Double back and return south on Beech St. along its left (east) side. Just south of Fifth Ave. is a large brick, Colonial Revival home on the right that once housed the president of Baldwin-Wallace College. It now serves as Alumni House. Beyond this manse are a series of residence halls. Behind 296 Beech St. is a brick building used by the Cleveland Browns football organization before their new complex was constructed.

Continue south to Bagley Rd. and turn left (east).

**14.** The Kleist Center for Art and Drama on the corner accommodates several college departments and two theaters, one of which is home to the nationally acclaimed Berea Summer Theater.

Continue east on E. Bagley a short distance to George Finnie Stadium. Use the angled sidewalk to obtain a better view of the artificial-turf football field surrounded by a quarter-mile track.

Finnie Stadium is where the Baldwin-Wallace Yellow Jackets and Berea High School Braves play football. (The high school is on E. Bagley Rd. just beyond here.) This field was also formerly used by the Cleveland Browns football team.

**15.** Cross E. Bagley Rd. at the traffic light and walk south on the west side of Tressel St., named for Lee Tressel, a legendary football coach at Baldwin-Wallace. The large structure on the southwest corner of Bagley and Tressel is the Baldwin-Wallace Recreation Center. This building houses Ursprung Gymnasium, a 200-meter track, a six-lane swimming pool, and many other facilities.

Directly across Tressel St. is the Berea Children's Home, built in 1864 as the German Methodist Orphan Asylum. According to one version of its early history, it was founded to provide shelter for children who were orphaned at the end of the Civil War. Although no longer housing orphans, the home continues to provide help to troubled children and their families through a continuing relationship with the United Methodist Church.

**16.** Continue south on Tressel St., crossing Jacob St. Turn right at the next street past the Mathematics and Computer Science Center, turn right (E. Grand). The large brick building on the left (south) is Strosacker, the college union, an activity center for both the Baldwin-Wallace and Berea communities. It is the site of a restaurant, snack bar, bookstore, lounges, restrooms, and various recreational activities.

**17.** Continue west on E. Grand to Beech St. and turn left (south). Walk past the tennis courts on Beech St. to E. Center St. and turn left again. Continue east on E. Center St., past several residence halls, to Eastland Rd. On the left is the Brian Bonds, Jr., Administration Building, housing B-W's principal administrative offices.

**18.** Turn right (south) on Eastland. On the opposite side of the street and just beyond the homes that front Eastland are the Cuyahoga County Fairgrounds. The first fair was held on this land in the 1890s when a festival was organized to serve the western part of Cuyahoga County, just as the Chagrin Falls annual fair served the eastern part of the county. In 1914, the commissioners of Cuyahoga County consolidated both fairs into one at the Berea location.

Continue walking south on Eastland and cross E. Bridge St. Look to the left to see the ornamental steel arch over the fairground's main entrance, identifying this as the Cuyahoga County Fair. Much of the time the entrance is open and one may enter the grounds to see the exhibit buildings, racetrack, and grandstand. The large and fascinating fair is held annually in August.

**19.** Continue walking south, past the Eastland Inn, to Adams St. and make a hairpin turn to the right. The houses on the southwest side of Adams are located on what was originally the edge of the Big Quarry. Continue along Adams St. to American Legion Parkway and turn left. Walk down the short hill on the road past the Albert E. Baesel American Legion Post 91, named for a World War I lieutenant who was killed in France in 1918 and posthumously awarded the Congressional Medal of Honor.

Turn right into the parking lot for a lovely view of Coe Lake. Circle the building clockwise and walk up the short road between the hall and Adams St. Cemetery, Berea's second and oldest remaining burial site, which contains gravestones dating from the mid-1800s. During quarrying operations at this location, the Cleveland Stone Co. generated landslides at the edge of the cemetery, but strong public reaction halted further destruction. In contrast, Berea's first cemetery was lost without any records of its burials when quarry excavators dug up coffins and human remains and left them piled in heaps.

**20.** Turn left (north) on Adams St. and left again onto Coe St. (northwest), passing Coe Lake on the left. Reach the Mahler Museum and History Center (Berea Area Historical Society) at a point just after Coe St. turns right. Optionally, you may stop at this center for more information about Berea's fascinating history.

**21.** Continue a short distance to E. Bridge St. and turn left (west) past Berea Townhouse Apartments. These units, built on filled-in quarry land, proved the feasibility of this type of construction.

Walk to the four-way intersection just past the apartments and turn left on the S. Seminary St. extension to reach the beginning of the walk. Before making this final turn, however, look in both directions down the length of E. Bridge St. This road marks the northernmost extent of Berea's quarrying operations. It is intriguing to consider how changing markets and technology shaped the future of Berea by leading to the decline of the sandstone industry. Had artificial carborundum not made the grinding wheel obsolete and growing use of concrete for construction not made sandstone obsolete, Berea might have remained a quarry town, never becoming the fine city it is, with its vibrant intellectual activity, scenic lakes and river, and beautiful parks.

This hike prepared in its entirety by Bill Manthey with some assistance from the author.

# 16 Bratenahl
## A Lakeshore History Walk

**Distance:** 7.3 miles

**Walking time:** 4 hours

**Description:** This walk is mostly on sidewalks along Lake Shore Blvd. and has several side-street detours. In general, you will follow the sidewalk on the north side of Lake Shore Blvd.

**Directions:** I-90 to Exit 177 for Martin Luther King, Jr., Dr. (MLK); north on MLK, follow signs to Bratenahl; left at sign into Cleveland Lakefront State Park.

**Parking & restrooms:** Park in Cleveland Lakefront State Park (Gordon Park). Public restrooms are available at the park entrance.

Bratenahl is a residential community on Lake Erie, about six miles east of downtown Cleveland and just north of I-90. It is about four miles long and less than half a mile wide, occupying 552 acres (less then a square mile). This interesting community has a long and distinguished history, and its palatial mansions along or near the Lake Erie shoreline were built for and occupied by many of Cleveland's most prominent citizens.

Until the 1850s about two dozen families farmed Cleveland's rural area, which extended to the community of Glenville. In 1865 William J. Gordon, a wealthy Clevelander, began to buy up rural land along Lake Erie, and in 1892 Liberty Emery Holden purchased the Charles Bratenahl farm (see also ch. 10, note #18). Other prominent Clevelanders also began buying up land in the area, primarily for summer recreational use.

In 1903, when Cleveland's annexation of Glenville was planned, the independent community of Bratenahl was formed. Named for the Bratenahl farming family, it continues today as a community separate from Cleveland. In 1906, when Collinwood, another nearby community, was annexed to Cleveland, the land from Coit Rd. to E. 140th St. was also added to Bratenahl.

During the last part of the 19th century and for several decades into the 20th, many prominent Clevelanders built mansions on large parcels of land along the lake, particularly along the north side of Lake Shore Blvd. The largest estates (50 to 100 acres) were owned by the Holden, Clark, Corning, and Coit families.

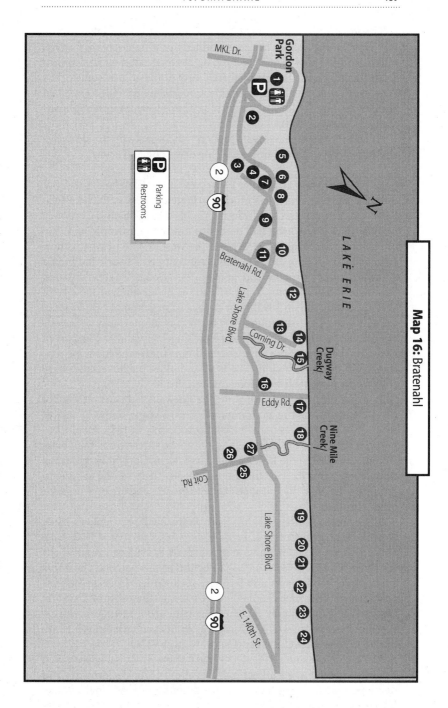

**Map 16:** Bratenahl

This walk focuses on those homes that remain today and that are visible from the sidewalks. They are identified by the names of the families for whom they were originally built, or, in some cases, by well-known subsequent owners. The original architects of the homes, some of the sources of family wealth, and pertinent interrelationships of Bratenahl families are noted. Most of Bratenahl's citizens were important philanthropic leaders of Cleveland.

NOTE: Please respect private property and remain on the sidewalks and public ways to avoid trespassing on driveways and lawns.

**1.** Start the walk at Gordon Park, part of the Cleveland Lakefront State Park group, which also includes Edgewater Park, Euclid Beach Park, Villa Angela, and Wildwood Park. In 1865 William J. Gordon, a wealthy Clevelander who had made his fortune in groceries and iron ore shipping, purchased 123 acres at the western end of what is now Bratenahl. He developed it into a magnificent private park and built a sprawling home called the Cottage at its eastern edge. He stipulated that his estate should become a public park at his death, and the city of Cleveland took title in 1893. Prior to the construction of I-90 in 1952, the park was a city playground with many recreational facilities including fishing, boating, bathing, and picnicking. This land is now part of Cleveland Lakefront State Park where administrative functions are centralized in the main building. Boating and other public facilities have recently been reestablished along the waterfront.

**2.** From the park walk east along the sidewalk and pause in front of the Defense Management Command. This was the home of one of seven Nike missile sites built in Cuyahoga County in 1955. All of these bases, constructed to counteract an airborne threat from the Soviet Union, were part of the U. S. Air Defense System. Gordon Park was the control area, and the launch base was located here on the command grounds. The Nike sites became obsolete in 1971 and are now used for other purposes.

**3.** Continue northeast along Lake Shore Blvd. past Holden Lane. Note the Georgian/Cotswold brick house with slate roof at 9448 Lake Shore Blvd. (south side). It was originally built in 1925 as a wedding gift for Delia White and Herman L. Vail by the bride's parents. The home overlooks a wooded area and Japanese rock garden. Herman Vail was an attorney whose son, Thomas Vail, became the publisher of *The Plain Dealer*. The White family fortune was made from sewing machines, automobiles, and trucks. Delia's parents, Thomas and Almira White, are buried in Lake View Cemetery (see ch. 10, note #37).

**4.** Also on the south side, at 9534 Lake Shore Blvd., is a house called Brightwood built as a summer home in about 1876. The property was developed as a farm and subsequent additions were made to the home. Edward P. Williams, the original owner, was a co-developer of the Sherwin-Williams Paint Co. in Cleveland.

**5.** The property at 9511 Lake Shore Blvd. on the northwest side of the road represents what remains today of the Liberty Emery Holden estate. The 34-room Tudor manor house belonging to Liberty Holden was razed to accommodate the Nike missile site. The home remaining, barely visible from the street, was the last residence of Mrs. R. Henry Norweb, granddaughter of Liberty Holden. Mr. Holden was a teacher, college professor, and school superintendent. He moved to Cleveland in 1862 and began investing first in real estate and then, in 1873, in iron ore and silver mining properties. In 1885 he purchased and then launched the morning edition of *The Cleveland Plain Dealer.* As president of the Cleveland Museum of Art's building committee, Holden was largely responsible for the construction of this magnificent building in University Circle and the Wade and Rockefeller parks adjacent to it. He became mayor of Bratenahl in 1903. Emery May Holden Norweb (Mrs. R. Henry) was the first female president of the Cleveland Museum of Art and a private art collector herself. Her acquisitions of Oriental and pre-Columbian art formed the nucleus of the museum's collections. Holden Arboretum was established in 1912 through the philanthropy of Albert Fairchild Holden, Emery May's brother.

**6.** Breezy Bluff, at 9619 Lake Shore Blvd., was named and first owned by George A. Benedict in the 1870s when he built a summer cottage on this site. That cottage burned, and in 1905 Jay Pickands built the current house designed by J. Milton Dyer. It is considered one of Dyer's most outstanding residential homes in Renaissance Revival style. The house is of stucco masonry with tall, hipped roofs, four high chimneys, and 12 gables. The loggia and balustrade terrace overlooking the lake boast one of the most spectacular views in Bratenahl.

Jay M. Pickands was the son of James Pickands, one of the founders of Pickands Mather and Co. The younger Pickands died at age 33 in 1913, and the house was purchased in 1916 by Dr. Edward F. Cushing. Dr. Cushing was the son of Dr. Henry K. Cushing, a founder of the Cleveland branch of the American Medical Association, and brother of Dr. Harvey Cushing, a well-known brain surgeon at Yale University (see ch. 10, note #6).

The home is now owned by Richard Fleischman and Helen Moss. Mr. Fleischman, a prominent architect, has designed the nearby residences as part of his Breezy Bluff development.

**7.** On the south side of the street, at 9718 Lake Shore Blvd., was the home of Abram Garfield, son of President James A. Garfield, and a prominent Cleveland architect. He designed this impressive brick and stucco Tudor house in 1897 for his bride, Sarah Williams. The east wing was completed in 1928; it features a magnificent two-story drawing room and a fireplace said to be "large enough to roast an ox." The property was given to the couple by Sarah's father, Edward Williams, who lived next door at Brightwood (see note #4). Mr. Garfield, who designed many early-20th-century Cleveland homes, was often called the dean of

Cleveland architecture. Some of his homes in Cleveland Heights and Shaker Heights are described in chapters 12 and 13.

**8.** The home at 9913 Lake Shore Blvd., called Wayside, is of chateau-like design, constructed in 1923 by Walter Cottingham as a wedding present for his daughter, Alicia, bride of Frank B. Dangler. Cottingham came to Cleveland in 1866 to become plant manager of the Sherwin-Williams Co. The Danglers founded the Dangler Stove Co., which merged with eight other companies in 1902 to form the American Stove Co. In 1929 this company produced the revolutionary and popular Magic Chef stove.

**9.** On the south side of the road at 10024 Lake Shore Blvd. is a brown-shingled house that was originally located across the street in a pasture on the Goff estate. Frederick H. Goff, president of the Cleveland Trust Co. from 1908 to 1923, helped to establish the Cleveland Foundation in 1914. As mayor of Glenville in 1903, Goff was successful in ending gambling at the Glenville Racetrack. He endorsed Glenville's annexation to Cleveland and was a leader in establishing Bratenahl as an independent community.

This house was the home of the first nursery school in Bratenahl. Margaret Hamilton, who starred as the witch in *The Wizard of Oz,* was a teacher here.

**10.** Haysmar, the estate comprising the four stucco houses at 10221, 10229, 10305, and 10311 Lake Shore Blvd., was designed by architects Frank B. Meade and James M. Hamilton. Although the homes were occupied in 1911, they were not finished nor the grounds completed until 1913. The estate was built by Kaufman Hays as an enclave for his family. Hays married the daughter of Simson Thorman, the first permanent Jewish resident of Cleveland (1837). Hays later lived in one of the two front houses with his daughter, Belle, and her husband, Martin A. Marks. Haysmar was derived from the last two names—Hays and Marks. Both men were prominent in banking and insurance in Cleveland and were leading philanthropists.

Nettie Hays Richman occupied the residence to the west. Her son, George Richman, ultimately became president of Richman Brothers Co., a leading Cleveland clothing store. The house to the east was built for Rabbi Moses Gries and his wife, Fanny Hays Gries. Gries was rabbi of University Circle's Temple Tifereth Israel from 1892 to 1917 (see ch. 9, note #4). His successor, Rabbi Abba Hillel Silver, and Silver's wife, Virginia, later lived in the home.

Later occupants of the Gries home were William F. McDermott, a well-known theater critic for *The Plain Dealer,* and his wife, Eva. Their guests included actors Helen Hayes, Charles Laughton, Tallulah Bankhead, John Barrymore, Alfred Lunt, and Lynn Fontanne, and the composer and librettist of many popular Broadway musical shows—Richard Rodgers and Oscar Hammerstein. The actors Sir Cedric Hard-

wick and Katherine Cornell once gave a private performance for the ail-
ing McDermott in his living room.

**11.** The Victorian house on the south side of Lake Shore Blvd., at
10322, was the home of Charles Pratt, who came to Cleveland from
Boston in 1893 and became chief engineer of the city's parks board. In
1900 he went into private practice and received a commission for park
designs in Ambler Heights and Euclid Heights, now part of present-day
Cleveland Heights. Turn left at Bratenahl Rd. and walk almost to the
end.

**12.** The Georgian brick mansion at 193 Bratenahl Rd. replaced a
home built by the H.F. Clark family. The current mansion was owned by
Sophia Strong Taylor until her death in 1938. She was heir to the
William Taylor Son & Co. department store. This 26-room residence
was then bought for Archbishop Edward F. Hoban of the Cleveland
Catholic Diocese. Bishop James A. Hickey, who followed Bishop
Clarence G. Issenman in 1974, did not wish to live in such palatial sur-
roundings, so the mansion was sold in 1977, raising an estimated
$400,000 for the Catholic Diocese.

Return to Lake Shore Blvd. Private condominiums are located at
10501. Continue east to Corning Dr. and walk nearly to the end of it.

**13.** The Tudor mansion at 298 Corning Dr. was the home of Clai-
borne Pirtle, who was founder and president of the Electric Controller
and Manufacturing Co. After Mrs. Pirtle's death in 1957, the home was
purchased by Abram Garfield, who died in 1958 after living there only
a year. Abram was the son of James A. Garfield, the assassinated U. S.
president, whose impressive monument is the centerpiece of Lake View
Cemetery (see ch. 10, note #4).

**14.** The 20-room tan stucco house at 282 Corning Dr., called Drift-
wood, is at the northwest end of the street, adjacent to the lake. It was
originally owned by U.S. senator and Mrs. Robert Jones Bulkley. In
1973, it was purchased by E. Mandell De Windt, chairman of Cleveland's Eaton Corporation. England's Prince Charles stayed in this home
on October 20, 1977.

**15.** The 70 acres that make up Corning Dr. were originally owned by
the Warren H. Corning family, Cleveland manufacturers and investors.
In the late 19th century, they used the grounds as their summer camping site for parties and for entertainment of other wealthy Clevelanders,
including industrialist Mark Hanna and President Garfield. They set up
drawing-room-sized tents with Oriental rugs and antique furniture,
and hired orchestras for their extravaganzas. Frank B. Meade and James
M. Hamilton were the architects of the Corning home at 281 Corning
Dr., which is barely visible behind the late-20th-century home nearby.

Return on Corning Dr. to Lake Shore Blvd. and continue east.

**16.** The high-rise condominiums at One and Two Bratenahl Place
were built in the late 1960s and early 1970s. In 1870 this land was the site

of Coit House, a summer hotel and tavern owned by land-rich Charles Coit, grandson of Daniel Coit, an original Connecticut Land Co. investor. The hotel was famous for its oyster suppers in those days.

Formerly the Bit and Bridle Club, the first country club west of the Alleghenies was founded here in 1889. The club opened in 1895 with property extending south from Lake Erie and Dugway Creek to the railroad tracks beyond Lake Shore Blvd., and east to Coit Rd. After merger with and then separation from the Cleveland Golf Club, and after several fires, a new clubhouse designed by Abram Garfield was built in 1908. In 1928, Mantis J. and Oris P. Van Sweringen, the developers of Shaker Heights and the Shaker Rapid Transit, persuaded the club to relocate to Pepper Pike as The Country Club. The old building remained as the Lake Shore Country Club and was torn down in 1964 to be replaced by Bratenahl Place in 1967.

Turn left and go to the end of Eddy Rd.

CAUTION: Watch for traffic entering and leaving Bratenahl Place.

**17.** The brick, stone, and reinforced concrete Jacobean-style mansion at the northeast end of Eddy Rd. was built for Howard Melville Hanna, Jr., in 1910. Designed by the New York architectural firm of McKim, Meade and White, this is the only house left in this area that was designed by that firm. The owner was the son of Howard Melville Hanna, a founder of the M. A. Hanna Co., a Cleveland iron and coal company. Hanna's two sisters lived in houses just east of this one, now demolished.

Return south to Lake Shore Blvd., turn left, and continue east. Note the "H" for Hanna carved in stone on all four sides of the tall brick fence posts at the driveways to the Hanna mansion.

**18.** Stop walking at the fire hydrant at Nine Mile Creek and look north toward the marina. Depending upon the season, it may be possible to glimpse imposing Shoreby, Samuel Mather's Bratenahl home. Samuel, a descendant of New England's Cotton Mather, came to Cleveland in 1843 to manage his father's Western Reserve of Connecticut land purchases. He was a founder of Pickands Mather and Co. and made his fortune in shipping and steel. In 1881 he married Flora Stone, daughter of Amasa Stone, a benefactor of Western Reserve University.

The mansion faces Lake Erie just west of Nine Mile Creek. The exterior stone is identical to that used in the construction of bridges spanning Martin Luther King, Jr., Blvd. The 25-room Romanesque-Revival home was built in 1890 by Charles Schweinfurth, Mather's favorite architect, who was also the designer of Trinity Cathedral, where Mather was senior warden and vestryman. (Schweinfurth designed the interior of Old Stone Church, the Union Club, and other Cleveland landmarks.)

When Shoreby was renovated in the 1970s, a quotation, probably from a Cotton Mather sermon, was found carved into a wooden mantelpiece in a child's bedroom: "Sleep not 'til u hath considered how thou hast spent ye day past. If thou hast well done, thank God. Other wise repent ye."

The Mathers were the most influential leaders and philanthropists of their generation in Cleveland. At the time of his death in 1931, Samuel Mather was the richest man in Ohio. Shoreby is now Shoreby Club, part of the 75-acre Newport Harbor development.

**19.** The magnificent Gwinn, at 12407 Lake Shore Blvd., is named for William Gwinn Mather's mother, Elizabeth Gwinn, and is probably the most publicized and most distinguished of Bratenahl's mansions and gardens. Built for Mather in 1908, the home was designed by Charles Platt and the gardens by Warren Manning, costing one million dollars.

Much thought was given to gracious outdoor living when planning the estate. Off the library is a lovely terrace facing the wide expanse of lawn to the south. A Renaissance balcony overlooks Lake Erie and the geometric Italian gardens by the lake. The formal gardens on the west are flanked on the north by a pagoda and on the south by a teahouse with colorful hand-painted ceilings and walls. In the center of the garden is a reflecting pool and fountain.

Front view of Gwinn

William Gwinn Mather was a half brother of Samuel Mather who made his fortune through Cleveland-Cliffs Iron Co. He was 72 when he married the widow next door, Elizabeth Ring Ireland, in 1929. Both Mathers were avid gardeners and offered Gwinn as a meeting place for the founders of the Garden Center of Cleveland, now Cleveland

Botanical Garden. The Mathers, leading Cleveland philanthropists, bequeathed Gwinn as a conference center for nonprofit organizations. The estate is now maintained by University Circle, Inc.

**20.** The home at 12611 Lake Shore Blvd., called Edgewater, was designed in 1910 by Abram Garfield for Henry G. Dalton. This Georgian mansion originally was surrounded by five acres of gardens. The ground floor contains a replica of a bar found on the luxury liner Queen Mary. Ten private underground telephone cables were installed for Dalton's business transactions when the home was built. Samuel Mather had brought Dalton into Pickands Mather and Co. in 1883. The estate was used as a backdrop for scenes from the 1960s television series, *Route 66.*

**21.** The residence at 12717 Lake Shore Blvd., also designed by Abram Garfield, was built for Alvah Stone Chisholm in 1910. Chisholm was a founder of the company that later became American Steel and Wire Co. He married Adele Corning, daughter of Warren H. and Mary Helen Wick Corning.

**22.** Moyenage, at 12725 Lake Shore Blvd., was originally designed by James Hunt and later redesigned by Charles Schweinfurth. Jay Morse of Pickands Mather and Co. lived here from 1905 to 1928. The center hall is an enclosed courtyard with massive beams and a breathtaking stairway. Spectacular cut-glass leaded windows were installed throughout the first floor.

**23.** At 13003 Lake Shore Blvd. is a Georgian mansion designed by Meade and Hamilton for attorney Henry E. Sheffield.

**24.** James Hamilton, of the Meade and Hamilton architectural firm, designed the French chateau at 13303 Lake Shore Blvd. This stucco and brick home with slate roof and copper gutters and downspouts was built for Ralph Coe in 1923. Coe, an executive in the family business, Cleveland City Forge, was a Francophile and an internationally known collector of modern French impressionist and post-impressionist paintings. Both Coe and his wife were leaders in Cleveland's arts community. Their living room facing the lake contains a large and unusual fireplace made in France, a replica of a 13th-century fireplace in the Cluny Museum near Paris.

Return west on Lake Shore Blvd. and turn left on Coit Rd.

**25.** The sprawling eclectic home at 12401 Coit Rd. called North Acres was designed in 1911 by Arthur Oviatt for millionaire Oliver P. Clay. Clay was a stock investor, sportsman, and active member of the Republican party. Clay's son, L. Joseph Clay, went to Nicaragua in 1926 for Standard Oil Co. of Ohio and was actively involved in quelling a revolution in that country.

In 1916 the estate was purchased by Edward Grasselli, a descendant of Caesar Grasselli, who founded the Grasselli Chemical Co. in 1867. He incorporated some of the paneling and fireplaces from the 19th-century

Grasselli home at E. 6th St. and St. Clair Ave. in downtown Cleveland.

**26.** On the opposite side of the street, at 12304 Coit Rd., is Badby, a Newport shingle summer home designed by architect Alfred Hoyt Granger for Frederick Payne Root in 1890. Root was an owner of Root and McBride, which was the largest wholesale dry goods company in the Midwest until the mid-1920s.

The residence was originally located on Lake Erie, 200 yards east of Eddy Rd., and was moved across the old country club golf course (see note #16) to this site in 1910 by its new purchaser, T. P. Howell. Mrs. Howell, one of the founders of the Garden Center of Cleveland (now the Cleveland Botanical Garden), maintained award-winning formal gardens behind the property.

**27.** On the southwest corner of Coit Rd. and Lake Shore Blvd. is a mansion built early in the 20th century by Charles Coit as a small Italian villa for his second wife. In 1923 the next owner hired the firm of Philip Small and Associates to enlarge the home. (Small also designed Shaker Square, Moreland Courts, mansions along S. Park Blvd. in Shaker Heights, and The Country Club on Lander Rd.)

The Coit family originally owned all the land in this part of Bratenahl, having purchased it from the Connecticut Land Co. in the early 1800s.

Return to Lake Shore Blvd. and walk west to the parking lot at Gordon Park.

This hike prepared by Earl Waltz with assistance from the author.

# 17 Rocky River
## Lakefront and Residential Walk

> **Distance:** 4.5 miles
>
> **Walking time:** 2.5 hours
>
> **Description:** This hike is almost exclusively on sidewalks and is generally flat but has some mildly hilly sections when you are close to Lake Erie and the Rocky River. Rocky River's Lake Erie shoreline—like most of the shoreline west of Downtown Cleveland—is notable for its high cliffs on which many fine homes perch. There are many views of the lake on the hike's first half. The hike for Rocky River Reservation (North) is accessible from the midpoint of this walk (see also ch. 26).
>
> **Directions:** I-90 westbound to exit for Clague Rd.; right (north) on Clague; right (east) at dead-end on Lake Rd./US 6 for 1 mile to Bradstreet's Landing, on left (marked). OR, I-90 eastbound to exit for Detroit Rd./SR 254; left (east) on Detroit, cross over I-90; left (north) on Elmwood Rd.; left (west) on Lake Rd./(US 6 to Bradstreet's Landing, on right (marked).
>
> **Parking & restrooms:** At Bradstreet's Landing and Rocky River Park.

The small but historic shoreline community of Rocky River is nestled among its former Rockport Township neighbors of Lakewood (on its eastern boundary) and Fairview Park (southern boundary), as well as Bay Village and Westlake, which lie at Rocky River's western and southwestern boundaries, respectively (and which both grew out of Dover Township). Considered among the most affluent of Cleveland's West Side suburbs, Rocky River is named for the river that flows along its eastern border. The city is known for its picturesque streets and fine homes. The handsome architecture of its residences can also be seen in a number of its older nonresidential structures. Rocky River also has many fine shops and restaurants, and a surprising number of manufacturing businesses.

This walk reveals all of these distinct features as you travel east along beautiful lakeside residential streets, from historic Bradstreet's Landing (the site of the municipal fishing pier) to the Lake Erie outlet of the Rocky River gorge, and then journey south and west through the community's upscale shopping and manufacturing district (in the Detroit Rd. area) before cutting north and west for the return to Bradstreet's Landing. This hike stops at Rocky River Park, which has a small beach but is posted for no swimming. Dogs are allowed at the beach, something to bear in mind if your pooch happens to be a hiking companion.

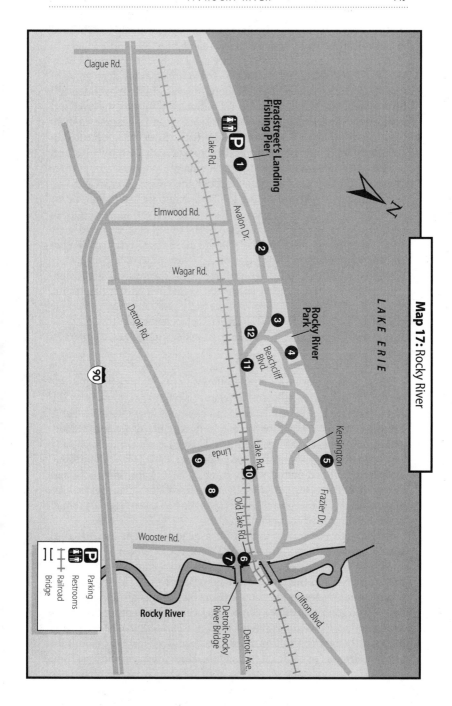

**Map 17:** Rocky River

LAKE ERIE

Clague Rd.

Lake Rd.

Elmwood Rd.

Avalon Dr.

Wagar Rd.

Detroit Rd.

Bradstreet's Landing
Fishing Pier

**1**

**2**

Rocky River
Park

**3**

**12**

**4**

Beachcliff Blvd.

**11**

90

Linda

**9**

**8**

Lake Rd.

**10**

Old Lake Rd.

Kensington

**5**

Frazier Dr.

Wooster Rd.

**7** **6**

Detroit-Rocky
River Bridge

Clifton Blvd.

Detroit Ave.

**Rocky River**

][

Parking
Restrooms
Railroad
Bridge

Rocky River was originally part of Rockport Township (established in 1819), subsequently re-formed as a hamlet in 1891 and a village in 1903, then incorporated itself as a city in 1930. Bridges played an early and important role in Rocky River's development, as the deep gorge of the Rocky River impeded travel along the lakeshore. A wooden toll bridge constructed in 1821 eased the difficulty of fording the river and made ferry service obsolete. It was replaced by an iron bridge in 1890 (see note #6). The original Detroit Rd.–Rocky River Bridge, erected in 1890, was the longest unreinforced concrete arch in the world and increased traffic through the area substantially.

Even with the increased traffic through the village, Rocky River was still primarily rural prior to the 1920s. Greenhouses and small farms remained profitable businesses as Rocky River grew into a suburban residential area by the 1940s. Bisected by the Nickel Plate Railroad (now operated as the Norfolk & Western Railroad), Rocky River's small retail and commercial district along Detroit Rd.—as well as on the surrounding streets and, later, along Center Ridge Rd.—grew substantially during this period with the easy access to freight lines and bridge traffic. The area continues to thrive commercially with an array of unique small retail shops, plazas, and specialized craft manufacturers.

(See also Rocky River Reservation, North & South hikes, chapters 26 and 33.)

**1.** Begin the hike with a stroll to the end of the fishing pier at Bradstreet's Landing. (Downtown Cleveland's skyline—nine miles to the east—is obscured by the inlet of the Rocky River, marked by the lighthouse.) Directly visible are steep tree-lined cliffs of Chagrin Shale, which dominate Cuyahoga County's Lake Erie shoreline, especially west of downtown Cleveland and Edgewater Park (see appendix A). Patches of hilly shoreline which front some private residences and Rocky River Park (see note #3) intermingle with the cliffs. Clearly visible to the west are the exhaust stacks of the Avon Power Plant. The small beach here is posted "No swimming."

Bradstreet's Landing is named for a historical event that predates Cleveland's settlement: "Bradstreet's Disaster" of October 1764. British Colonel John Bradstreet was leading 1,500 British and American troops back to Ft. Niagara (near modern-day Buffalo, New York) after helping quell Pontiac's siege of English garrisons in the area around modern-day Detroit (one of the few British-American victories during Pontiac's Rebellion—or "conspiracy"—of 1763–1765). With darkness falling quickly on October 18, 1764, Bradstreet found navigation difficult for his mini-armada of 69 boats (mostly smaller river-navigable boats and canoes) in the normally safe haven of the Rocky River outlet into Lake Erie. He ordered the boats to row 1.7 miles west to a small swale in the cliff-dominated shoreline (the "Landing"). From the end of the fishing pier, one can easily see why Bradstreet chose this spot. It's a wide, flat area of the shoreline, with steep cliffs to both the east and west. Unfortunately, a sudden storm blew in off the lake; high waves destroyed nearly half the boats and severely damaged many others. After a few days of repairs, part of the contingent set off in the remainder of the fleet for the return to Ft. Niagara; bad weather plagued the return of the battered flotilla. Meanwhile—because of the shortage of boats—many others in the party had to return via an overland route. A shortage of provisions made the return journey an arduous struggle, although only one fatality was reported.

Leave Bradstreet's Landing and turn left (east) on Lake Rd. Follow Lake Rd. slightly uphill. Pass by some large lakeside homes on the left and the entrance to the Rocky River Wastewater Treatment Plant on the right (south) side of the road.

**2.** Leave Lake Rd. and bear left (northeast) onto Avalon Dr., a street of fine homes. Continue on Avalon Dr. past Wagar Rd. (0.5 miles).

**3.** Turn left (north) at Beach Cliff Blvd. Residential architecture along this stretch includes fine examples of the Colonial, Georgian, and Tudor styles, as well as some more contemporary designs.

**4.** Continue on Beach Cliff Blvd. to Rocky River Park (left at Parkside Dr.), which boasts a small rocky and driftwood-lined beach protected by a breakwall. It is favored by many local residents because pets are allowed. Parking, restrooms, a picnic area, and benches overlooking the lake are located here. The beach is posted "No swimming."

**5.** (1.0 miles) Leave Rocky River Park, continuing east on Beach Cliff, then turning left (north) on Kensington Oval, which runs along the shoreline and has a few benches along the way from which to enjoy a scenic view of Lake Erie.

Follow Kensington to Frazier Dr. and turn left (east). (1.3 miles) Pass by the numerous cliffside homes, noting especially the Sunset Point estate (opposite Buckingham Rd.), which resembles an Italian villa in design, and River's End at 19486 Frazier Dr., as well as Morningside at 19420 Frazier Dr., with a design reminiscent of a southern plantation home more familiar to Charleston, South Carolina, than to Northeast Ohio. Homes date back at least to the 1920s and command beautiful views of the Rocky River inlet. Many of the residences also have a "seaside fishing village" quality to them, as they are crammed together on the sparse real estate of the cliffs and river inlet bottomland.

NOTE: Please respect the privacy of homeowners by staying on the sidewalks at all times.

Continue on Frazier, which merges back into Beach Cliff Blvd.

CAUTION: You will pass by Yacht Club Drive, which leads down into the Cleveland Yachting Club ("Members Only") and to some private residences. This road has no sidewalk and is heavily traveled by automobile traffic, and therefore it is not recommended for walkers.

**6.** Cross under the Clifton Rd. Bridge on the sidewalk on the west side of the road, and then the railroad bridge. The road becomes Old Lake Rd. and passes by the historic Westlake at 19000 Old Lake Rd., a residential condominium distinguished by its coral pink/peach exterior color and Spanish-style design. Note the decorative exterior lamps. The Westlake is listed on the National Register of Historic Places; visitors are welcome to stop in to see the small inner lobby. (The main lobby is locked.) For a tour of the facility, including its spacious grand foyer and lobby, call ahead at 440-331-1510.

**7.** (2.0 miles) After passing by the Westlake, note the Bridge Building at 18500 Old Lake Rd., constructed over the remnants of the Detroit Avenue Bridge (demolished in 1980). Turn left (east) and cross over the Rocky River Bridge to Lakewood on the other side. On both sides of the bridge are wrought-iron placards describing the history of bridges at that site. If you look across to the Rocky River side, you can see the opposite side of the Bridge Building and its foundation, built from the remnants of the original 1910 bridge. Also note the architectural style of the building itself, which employs arches in its facade to suggest its relation to the basic design of bridges. Cross back over the bridge and proceed west on Detroit Rd.

NOTE: The entrance to Rocky River Reservation of the Cleveland Metroparks is just south of the bridge. (See Chapter 26, Rocky River Reservation-North.)

**8.** Proceed west on Detroit through Rocky River's primary commercial district. To the right (north) is the Old River Shopping Area, which boasts many fine small shops, boutiques, and restaurants. Still proceeding west on Detroit, pass by Beach Cliff Market Square and then the Rocky River United Methodist Church on the right.

**9.** After crossing the entrance to the Clifton Blvd. Bridge (US 6 and SR 2 east), you will reach Linda St., opposite River Square Shopping Center. Turn right (north) on Linda. Pass by the Antique Row shopping area, a unique grouping of crafts and antique shops housed in small, cottage-like former residences. Proceeding north on Linda, pass by some small commercial outlets and businesses and cross the railroad tracks until you come to Lake Rd.

CAUTION: This is an active railroad crossing; use caution when crossing the multiple tracks.

**10.** Turn right (east) on Lake. The grey building at 19621 Lake Rd. is the former site of Cowan Pottery, one of the nation's leading pottery studios in the 1920s and 1930s. It was founded by R. (Reginald) Guy Cowan in the years after World War I, and within a decade the company's expanded staff produced over 175,000 original designs per year. Cowan's pieces sold in department stores throughout the western hemisphere, and were also purchased by prominent art museums. The design styles are considered trailblazing for their use of ceramic "as a medium for sculpture" instead of bronze, marble, or wood. A large collection of Cowan Pottery items is now held at the Rocky River Public Library (1600 Hampton Rd., 440-333-7610); over 400 pieces are on display throughout the library.

Head west again on Lake Road. (3.1 miles)

**11.** Travel on the south side of Lake Rd., noting the decorative stone wall on the right. Pass by two gas stations, a restaurant, and more small shops. At Lake Road Market, cross Lake Rd. to the north side and proceed to the Rocky River Clock Tower.

The Rocky River Clock Tower, originally built in 1912, served as the ornamental entrance marker for the estate of Clifton Bailey Beach (1845–1902), a prominent Cleveland businessman who served in Congress during the 1890s. The 427-acre estate purchased by Beach in 1888 occupied a large portion of Rocky River's current residential and commercial area from Detroit Rd. north to Lake Erie. (Thus the moniker "Beach Cliff," seen in much of Rocky River.) Destroyed by a storm in 1957, the clock tower was rebuilt in 1987. It was rededicated to honor J. Frank Gibson, mayor of Rocky River from 1950 to 1959. (3.5 miles)

**12.** Continue west on Avalon Dr. (which fronts the north side of the clock tower). At Lake Rd., bear right (also west) for the final stretch of the walk back to Bradstreet's Landing.

Rocky River Clock Tower

This chapter prepared by Michael Morgenstern, with assistance from the author.

# 18 Hach-Otis Sanctuary State Nature Preserve

**Distance:** 2 miles

**Hiking time:** 1 ¼ hours

**Description:** The walk is flat, on trails and boardwalks.

**Directions:** I-271 to Exit 36 (Wilson Mills Rd.); east on Wilson Mills; left (north) on Chagrin River Rd. (SR 174); cross Chardon Rd. (US 6), pass Garfield School; right (east) on Skyline Dr. to end.

**Parking:** In a small lot at the end of the drive. No restrooms.

This small 81-acre park offers spectacular views of the Chagrin River Valley 150 feet below. Tall cliffs stand above the river, which is still cutting through glacial drift left in this valley from the last Ice Age, about 12,000 years ago. More than 30 species of trees are found here, including red oak, white oak, sugar maple, beech, tulip poplar, white ash, sassafras, bigtooth aspen, cucumber magnolia, wild cherry, yellow birch, and hemlock. Spring wildflowers such as yellow mandarin, solomon's seal, mayapple, Jack-in-the-pulpit, and large flowered trillium abound in the preserve. Bird-watching is excellent here, as migrants often rest and feed in the tall trees before or after a flight across Lake Erie. Kingfishers and a large colony of bank swallows nest in the steep sides of the cliff. Osprey, turkey vultures, woodpeckers, and a wide variety of songbirds are glimpsed here. Colorful spring wildflowers and brilliant fall leaf colors alike are beautiful in this sanctuary. Because of recent storm damage in the preserve, however, it may be necessary to climb over or hike around trees fallen across the trail.

**1.** The boardwalks near the entrance were built to ease walking over wet spots on this flat plateau. At the entrance sign, take the boardwalk immediately ahead and then turn quickly left (north) at the next boardwalk which soon leads onto a trail (green tree blazes).

**2.** This is a short loop trail which, if you stay to the right at an intersection, ends near the edge of the cliff with a magnificent view of the

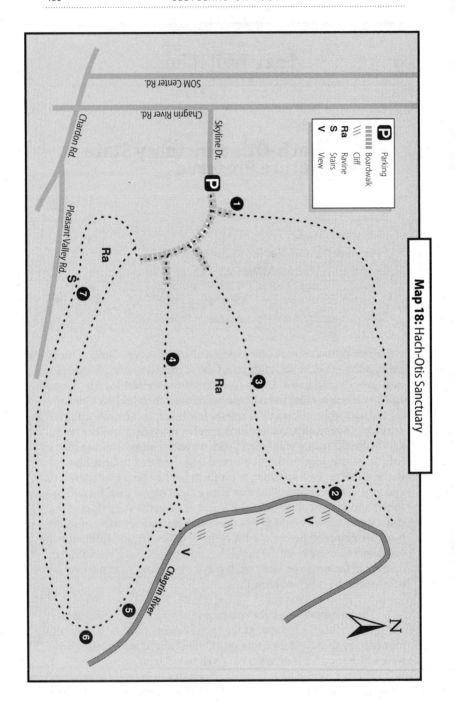

Map 18: Hach-Otis Sanctuary

Chagrin River below. Walk through the brush to avoid taking the badly eroded cliff-edge trail.

> CAUTION: Use much care in viewing the river from this and several other vantage points in the sanctuary because the cliffs are continually eroding and remain highly unstable. Especially in wet, snowy, and icy weather use great caution. STAY WELL BACK FROM THE RIM, and take care to restrain children or pets because of severe cliff-edge erosion.

**3.** Continue on this trail (green tree blazes) going south to the boardwalk again. Rather than returning to the parking lot, turn left, then left again, still on the boardwalk, which soon gives way to a trail.

**4.** Cross a small bridge, reach another sweeping view of the valley and houses below. In the distance is Little Mountain, five miles away.

**5.** Continue east on this trail (red and green blazes) as it loops through a mature forest of beech, maple, and oak trees. As the trail runs parallel to the river below, note the vast commercial nursery located beside the river on Pleasant Valley Rd. The cars you hear are on Chardon Rd. (US 6) to the south.

**6.** The trail loops around to the southwest and passes a connecting trail on the right. Bear left here and walk right to go around the fallen beech tree lying along the cliff edge.

**7.** The path dips down to a ravine, over which a set of stairs takes you north again to the main boardwalk. Follow it back to the parking area.

This chapter reviewed and rewalked by Michael and Lidia Murphy.

# 19 Ohio & Erie Canal Towpath
## Cuyahoga Valley National Recreation Area

**Distance:** 3 miles

**Hiking time:** 2 hours

**Description:** This hike will follow a restored section of the old Ohio & Erie Canal Towpath going south and will return on the same paved towpath. As an option, the flat Towpath Trail can be walked northward to Rockside Rd. (Lock 39 Trailhead) for scenic views of both the canal and the wildlife nearby. That walk is 3 miles round trip from the visitor center and will also take about 2 hours.

**Directions:** I-77 to Exit 155 (Rockside Rd.); east on Rockside to Canal Rd.; right (south) on Canal to Hillside Rd. for 2 miles to Canal Visitor Center.

**Parking & restrooms:** At Canal Visitor Center.

The Cuyahoga Valley National Recreation Area (CVNRA) was created by Congress in 1974 to preserve a valuable 22-mile scenic park corridor between the cities of Akron and Cleveland. The Cuyahoga River runs through this beautiful valley, as do the Cuyahoga Valley Scenic Railroad (CVSR) and the partially preserved Ohio & Erie Canal with its Towpath Trail alongside it. A historic 1853 house at Lock 38 contains the National Park Service's Canal Visitor Center. The Ohio & Erie Canal Towpath Trail extends through the CVNRA for 19.5 miles between Rockside Rd. in the north and Indian Mound trailhead, just south of Bath Rd. Informative signs have been placed along its length describing the canal's history. It is a popular trail for bicyclists. Walkers are cautioned to be aware of fast bicycle traffic and keep to the right to allow bicyclists to pass on the left.

Cleveland Metroparks' newest reservation (Ohio & Erie Canal Reservation) is nearby and extends 6.2 miles north from Rockside Rd. at Lock 39 (Rockside) Trailhead (see chapter 20). Informative signs have been placed all long the towpath.

To reach CVSR, follow signs on Rockside Rd. Turn north on Canal Rd. Just past Lockkeeper's Inn on the corner of Rockside and Canal Rds., turn left (west) on Old Rockside Rd., crossing over the Cuyahoga River. Take a sharp left turn, go under a bridge, and reach the parking lot where rail passengers embark and disembark. For more information and train schedules, call 800-468-4070.

Park rangers and volunteers are in attendance at the visitor center

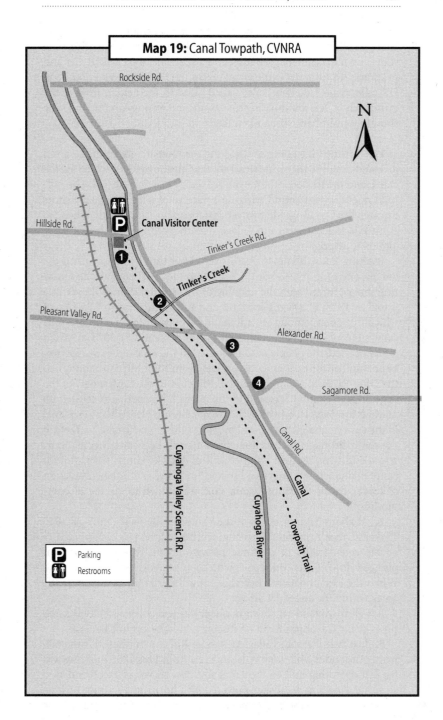

**Map 19:** Canal Towpath, CVNRA

during the day year round. The center contains exhibits on the Ohio & Erie Canal and 12,000 years of human history, an informative slide show and films, and maps, books, and a schedule of park activities and programs. In summer, demonstrations of the restored twelve-mile lock (12 miles from Lake Erie), also called Lock 38, are held in front of the visitor center. It is illuminating to view the interesting exhibits and slide show before embarking on the walk.

**1.** Start the hike going south along the towpath above the restored lock and canal. To the right (west) are the Cuyahoga River, which fed the canal, and the tracks of the Cuyahoga Valley Scenic Railroad. The railroad operates year round, offering a variety of trips that take visitors through the Cuyahoga Valley from Independence, just north of here, to Peninsula, to Hale Farm and Village, near the south end of the CVNRA, and on to Akron.

Walking along this flat towpath, used at one time by mules towing the barges, one cannot help but think back to the canal era and the sensation that occurred with the opening of this section of the Ohio & Erie Canal in 1827. Between Cleveland and Akron there were 42 locks, of which this one is among several that have been restored. The 309-mile canal's 146 locks enabled a complete lift (or descent) of 1,207 feet. When it was opened, the people of Ohio joined in the excitement of vast new opportunities for commerce and travel, from southerly Portsmouth on the Ohio River, to Columbus and Coshocton in the central part of the state, to Akron and Cleveland in the north. The canal also opened up markets for farmers, by way of the Great Lakes, to New York's Erie Canal in the eastern United States, and by way of the Ohio River to markets in the south. Products such as flour, timber, pork, beef, lard, cheese, stone, straw, and whiskey were shipped out of the Cuyahoga Valley. Into it came manufactured merchandise and furniture. With the completion of feeder canals to Pennsylvania, coal was added to the list of commodities.

**2.** At about 0.5 mile south of the Visitor Center is the unusual 1845 Tinker's Creek Aqueduct. This engineering marvel was constructed to enable canal traffic to continue passage above Tinker's Creek as it plunged down to its confluence with the Cuyahoga River to the west. When the canal boats reached this point they simply floated over the creek within the aqueduct bridge.

It is clear why the canal was necessary as you observe the twists and turns of the Cuyahoga River on its course northward to Lake Erie.

**3.** Just past Pleasant Valley/Alexander Rd. and on the left is the tall, white Alexander Mill, now Wilson's Feed Mill. This 1855 building was the last operating mill on the canal and now serves as a feed and seed store. Originally it was water-powered by a horizontal interior turbine engine rather than the traditional waterwheel. Alongside the trail can be seen the 14-mile lock, or Lock 37. Here also is a waste control gate, used to control the canal's water level. By opening the gates the canal could be drained for maintenance and repairs, usually done in the winter when it was not in use.

**4.** Just before Sagamore Rd. on the hill to the left is Frazee House , a red brick Federal-style house that once welcomed canal and stagecoach travelers as overnight guests. Stephen Frazee built this two-story home in 1826, in a prime location for the canal's opening in 1827. The building has been restored by the National Park Service as a museum highlighting the settlement of the Western Reserve. The Frazee House is open only on weekends from 10 a.m. to 5 p.m.

Although this hike ends here, you may continue farther along the towpath if time allows. Return to the visitor center by retracing your steps.

Courtesy Cuyahoga Valley National Recreation Area

Canal Visitor Center

# 20 Ohio & Erie Canal Reservation
## Newest Gem in the Emerald Necklace

**Distance:** 6.2 miles (one way) or 12.4 (round trip)

**Hiking time:** 3–6 hours

**Description:** This path is a flat All-Purpose trail that has been constructed to accommodate hikers, bicyclists, and persons in wheelchairs or strollers. (Horses are not permitted on the trail.) It is best for walkers to stay on the right. Views of both the canal and river are accessible along the trail, which was once the old towpath used by mules that pulled the canal boats between Cleveland, Akron, and points south. The canal opened in 1827 and closed after the Great Flood of 1913. Interesting features of the park include the Mill Creek Aqueduct, Lock 40, and an environmental study area. Picnic areas, playing fields, fishing areas, and interpretive signs have been planned along the route.

**Directions:** I-77 to Exit 155 (Rockside Rd.); east on Rockside, past Brecksville Rd./SR 21, to marked Rockside trailhead on the right (south) side of the road, near the Cuyahoga River. Entry to reservation also available at Cuyahoga Heights Community Park off E. 49th St., south of Harvard Ave., or from Cuyahoga Heights Bocce Park at Old Granger Rd., west of Warner Rd.

**Parking & restrooms:** At the trailheads.

This newest of Cleveland Metroparks' 14 reservations is scheduled to open in fall 1998. For updated information about hiking access to this 400-acre park, please call or write Cleveland Metroparks, 4101 Fulton Pkwy., Cleveland, OH 44144 (216-351-6300).

Ohio & Erie Canal Reservation is part of the Ohio & Erie Canal Corridor, Ohio's first National Heritage Corridor and first National Scenic Byway, designated as such by the federal government in 1996. The 65-mile corridor stretches from Cleveland to Zoar, Ohio, and includes this new reservation north of Rockside Rd. and the current 19.5-mile Canal Towpath Trail that extends south of Rockside through the Cuyahoga Valley National Recreation Area (see ch. 19).

Located along the Cuyahoga River in a valley dominated by industrial plants, the narrow, 6.2-mile Ohio & Erie Canal Reservation follows 5.5 miles of the river and goes through the municipalities of Cuyahoga Heights and Valley View. The land was formerly private property, made available by corporations (including Aluminum Co. of America, American Steel & Wire, BP America, and Cleveland Electrical Illuminat-

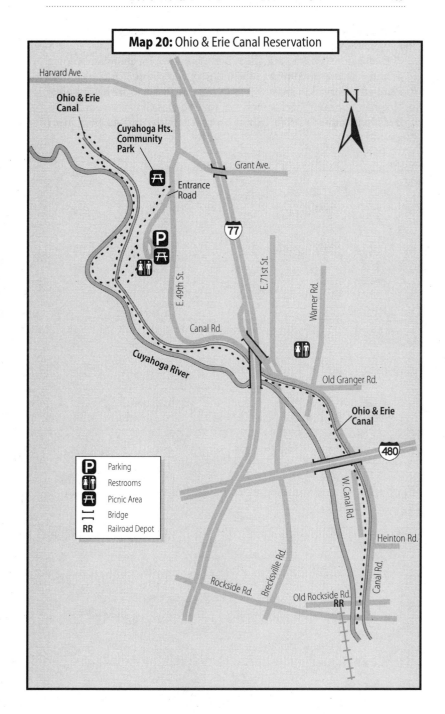

**Map 20:** Ohio & Erie Canal Reservation

ing/Centerior) and government agencies such as the Northeast Ohio Regional Sewer District.

Even before it was a park, the valley was known for abundant wildlife despite its close proximity to the industry and commerce of its locale. Planned observation areas will enable nature lovers to see hawks, great blue heron, beaver, deer, songbirds, waterfowl such as geese and mallards, and other wildlife that prosper, relatively undisturbed, in or around water.

# 21 **Big Creek Reservation**
Lake Isaac

**Distance:** 1 ¼ miles

**Hiking time:** 1 hour

**Description:** This is a short hike on a flat, wide trail that begins at the north end of the parking area and makes a loop through land west of the lake, passing a marsh pond, pine woods, and an old orchard.

**Directions:** I-71 to Bagley Rd. exit in Middleburg Heights; left (east) on Bagley Rd.; right (south) on Big Creek Pkwy. past Fowles Rd. to Lake Isaac, on right.

**Parking & restrooms:** Park in the parking area adjacent to Lake Isaac. Restrooms not available.

Big Creek Reservation, one of 14 Cleveland Metroparks reservations, lies on both sides of Big Creek Parkway and is parallel to Pearl Rd. (US 42) in the towns of Brooklyn, Parma, Parma Heights, Middleburg Heights, and Strongsville. Between Fowles Rd. and Main St. in Middleburg Heights is Lake Isaac, a major waterfowl refuge. This small lake, one of Northeast Ohio's few natural basins, is a glacial pothole created by the melting of a large layer of ice left by the retreat of Ohio's last glacier about 12,000 years ago. This three-acre lake is named for an early Berea settler, Isaac Fowles.

Before Cleveland Metroparks acquired this land in 1975, the lake was lower than it is now because of peat mining along the west and southwest shores. It has been restored to its natural elevation and has become a major attraction for migrating birds, ducks, and other waterfowl. Because Big Creek Reservation is a wildlife sanctuary, the park also attracts deer, fox, opossum, and many other animals, and surprises the visitor with many lovely aquatic plants and wildflowers. A large sign prohibits feeding any of the wildlife in the park to prevent them from becoming dependent upon humans and therefore unable to find their own food, escape predators, or migrate.

It is worthwhile to take along a bird identification guide when visiting Lake Isaac, especially during the spring or fall migrations, when a variety of birds and ducks stop here on their flights north or south. Especially prevalent are wood, mallard, and black ducks, and Canada geese. Less frequently you may see ducks such as the canvasback, hooded merganser, shoveler, pintail, or green- and blue-winged teals;

tall, long-legged great blue herons also find fine fishing here. In mid-May the courtship dance of the male woodcock has often been spotted in the woods behind the lake.

**1.** After stepping down onto the trail and crossing a footbridge over the lake outlet, you will pass a sign for the Meadows Area, home to field mice, rabbits, woodchucks, and other small mammals. Go through a red pine woods and under power lines to reach a trail juncture.

**2.** The trail straight ahead is the beginning of the loop, and the trail to the left is where you will end—either may be taken. Continue straight ahead (west) and you will pass a sign indicating the Ponds Area on the right, home to aquatic mammals such as muskrat, as well as painted and snapping turtles, and frogs. Dragonflies and waterstriders may be seen among the water lilies and cattails.

**3.** The trail passes through an open area, formerly an orchard, and then curves east under power lines and past moisture-loving cottonwood trees.

**4.** At about the halfway point, enter another short red pine woods to reach a bench overlooking Baldwin Creek. You may hear a train whistle breaking the silence of the woods; railroad tracks form the western boundary of the park.

**5.** Follow the path to the next trail intersection, where a sign indicates no trail beyond this point: stay to the left. Pass under the power lines again and return to the trail juncture described in note #2 above. Follow the trail to the right to return to the parking area.

*Optional*

For further trail walking you will find a paved path going both north and south in the center strip of park land adjacent to Big Creek Pkwy. The paved All-Purpose Trail alongside the parkway is also open to hikers as well as bicyclists.

This chapter was reviewed and rewalked by Emily Gregor with the assistance of Jean Znamenek.

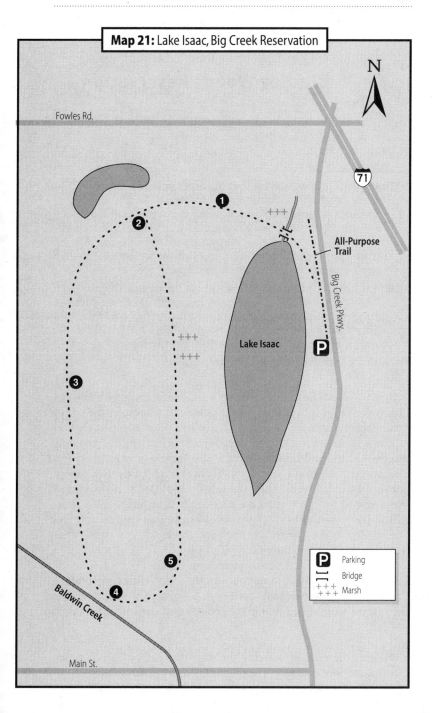

**Map 21:** Lake Isaac, Big Creek Reservation

N

Fowles Rd.

71

❶

❷

All-Purpose
Trail

+++

Big Creek Pkwy.

+++
+++

Lake Isaac

P

❸

❺

❹

Baldwin Creek

Main St.

| P | Parking |
|---|---------|
| Ⅱ | Bridge |
| +++ | Marsh |

# 22 Bradley Woods Reservation

**Distance:** 2 miles

**Hiking time:** 1 hour

**Description:** This short walk leads through woods around Bunns Lake to one of the old shallow quarries where a few large blocks of Berea Sandstone still lie on the ground. The sandstone ledge beneath this park lies only 3 to 5 feet below the soil, causing rainwater to form many small puddles on the surface. Therefore, except for the higher trail around Bunns Lake, the paths in Bradley Woods can be muddy. In summer, mosquitoes breed readily in the stagnant pools.

**Directions:** I-90 to Exit 156 (Crocker/Bassett Rds.); south on Crocker; right (west) on Detroit Rd. (SR 254); left (south) on Bradley past Center Ridge Rd. (US 20); on left; follow White Oak Lane to the end. OR, From I-480, exit at Lorain Rd. (SR 10); east on Lorain; left on Barton Rd.; right (north) on Bradley Rd.; on right; follow White Oak Lane to the end.

**Parking & restrooms:** At Bunns Lake Picnic Area.

Bradley Woods Reservation lies on a massive formation of 360-million-year-old Berea Sandstone (see appendix A) that causes the soil to hold moisture, creating Cleveland Metroparks' only swamp forest. Old sandstone quarries scattered throughout the park produced fine-grade grindstones and millstones until the 1930s. Because of its generally wet environment, beautiful spring wildflowers and lovely fall foliage enhance Bradley Woods. This relatively undeveloped park, located in Westlake and North Olmsted, has a tendency to be buggy in the summer, so it is preferable to visit it in the cooler months of early spring and late fall. Among the trees thriving here are red maples, sour gums, tupelos, yellow birches, and pin oaks.

Hiking on the short, flat trails, picnicking, and fishing in small Bunns Lake, created in 1986, are popular activities for visitors to Bradley Woods. The reservation supports a large population of waterfowl near the lake and white-tailed deer in the undeveloped areas of the park west of Bradley Rd.

**1.** Start the walk by entering the wide dirt pathway south of the Codrington Shelter House. The path is lined with interesting interpretative signs that describe some of the park's history, its wildlife habitat, and the native trees. Because this area was once farm fields and

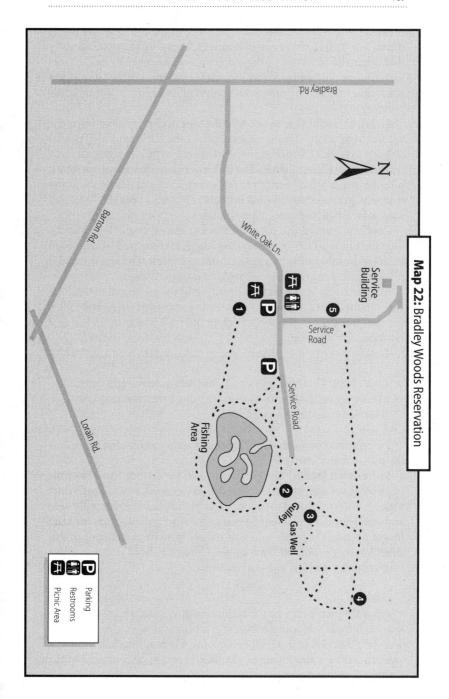

Map 22: Bradley Woods Reservation

orchards, you will see here and there some of the old farm roads still intact. The dam created to form Bunns Lake rises up to impound water that originally filled one of the old quarries. The majority of the trees surrounding the small pond are red maples, gorgeous in the fall, and pin oaks, characterized by downward-pointing lower limbs and upward-pointing higher ones.

**2.** While circling the pond, note the sign declaring "grown over for natural vegetation." This is an example of the Cleveland Metroparks strategy to reclaim natural landscape features. In this instance, this area was once a small, cleared meadow with a narrow path leading north, but now the meadow has been left to regenerate itself with naturally occurring wild grasses. Mowed only infrequently, it also provides food and habitat for small birds and other wildlife.

Continue around the pond on the established trail. Complete the loop near the east parking area. From there, take the park service road (blocked to auto traffic by a posted gate) to the east. The service road is marked with a restricted access sign but is open to hikers.

**3.** Bear right onto a wider dirt path that passes an old natural gas well (on the right). At the next intersection, stay right (east) and follow the trail through deep woods. Stick to the trail, which meanders in a northeasterly direction.

**4.** Where the trail dead-ends into an east–west trail, turn left (west).

CAUTION: This trail intersection has only a left or right turn; beware of small side paths that criss-cross the trail that you traversed from the gas well.

Proceed west on the trail as it opens up onto a small clearing; follow the trail to a service road.

**5.** Turn left (south) and continue down the service road. Note the huge blocks of sandstone that line the service road as you near White Oak Ln. They were used to produce fine-grade sandstone for millstones and grindstones up to about 60 years ago. Nearby shallow quarries (no longer open to the public and now mostly filled in to stimulate marsh development) produced these stones. Continue ahead to reach White Oak Ln. and the picnic and parking areas.

*Optional*
From the picnic area on the north side of White Oak Ln. there are a few small trails that lead northwest to a beautiful, wide clearing to the west (slightly visible from White Oak Ln. where it bends, beyond the western parking area). One of the filled-in quarries is located at the north end of this clearing.

CAUTION: Use extreme care when walking in the vicinity of the filled-in quarry. Hikers should keep a respectful distance: the water and mud can be very deep, and grown-over tilled soil can make footing unstable.

*Courtesy of Cleveland Metroparks Archives*

Bunns Lake

This hike reviewed and rewalked by Michael Morgenstern.

# 23 Garfield Park Reservation

**Distance:** 4 miles

**Walking time:** 2 hours

**Description:** This hike is on short woods trails and abandoned roads, goes up and down several small hills, and past Wolf Creek. It is a pleasant, non-strenuous hike with varied scenery in all seasons.

**Directions:** I-480 to Broadway Ave./SR 14 exit in Garfield Heights; right (north) on Broadway; enter Garfield Park Reservation on left, after railroad overpass; immediate left on Mill Creek Lane to the nature center, on left.

**Parking & restrooms:** At the Garfield Park Nature Center.

Garfield Park Reservation is one of the most recent additions to Cleveland Metroparks. Garfield Park Nature Center (open daily 9:30 a.m.–5 p.m.) was completed in 1987. One of the smaller Metroparks (177 acres), Garfield Park Reservation nevertheless has a long history. This area of Garfield Heights was first settled in 1786 and became known later as Newburg. Because of its higher elevation, it was considered healthier than Cleveland, and for many years it was a haven for people escaping the swampy conditions and diseases of the Cuyahoga River area.

In 1894 the city of Cleveland purchased several properties to form a new country park called Newburg Park, later renamed Garfield Park. It became a pleasant place for city dwellers to enjoy nature in a grand setting of tall trees and hills, to go boating on the upper and lower lakes of dammed Wolf Creek, and to take home water from a mineral spring. The Cleveland Railway Company laid tracks to the park in 1917, opening it up to all. In the 1930s recreational facilities were added, including tennis, football, sledding, swimming, and picnicking.

The southwestern portion of Garfield Park Reservation has been set aside as the Iron Spring Wildlife Preserve for management of upland wildlife species and is especially lovely in spring and fall. Lack of care reduced Garfield Park to a hazardous place in the 1970s until Cleveland Metroparks acquired it in 1986. Now, this lovely small park supports many waterfowl, songbirds, and other wildlife, and numerous varieties of trees, shrubs, and wildflowers. The nature center offers a wide variety of interesting nature programs and events, as well as information and early photographs of the park.

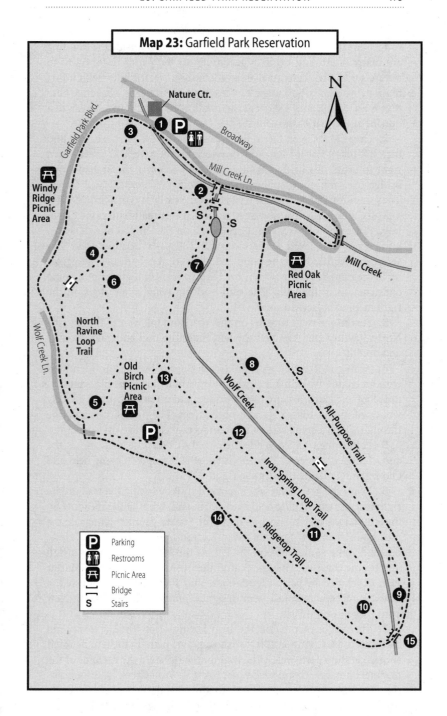

**Map 23:** Garfield Park Reservation

Nature Ctr.

N

Garfield Park Blvd.

Broadway

Mill Creek Ln.

Windy Ridge Picnic Area

Mill Creek

Red Oak Picnic Area

Wolf Creek Ln.

North Ravine Loop Trail

Old Birch Picnic Area

Wolf Creek

All-Purpose Trail

Iron Spring Loop Trail

Ridgetop Trail

P   Parking
👫  Restrooms
🪑  Picnic Area
][  Bridge
S   Stairs

**1.** Start the walk at Garfield Park Nature Center. Inside the building are many interesting exhibits pertaining to the park's history and to nature study. Park personnel are available to assist the hiker with information, brochures, and maps of Cleveland Metroparks. An active beehive is on exhibit, and a short garden walk with interpretive signs is just outside at the rear of the center.

**2.** Cross Mill Creek Ln. to the asphalt-paved All-Purpose Trail and turn left (east) toward the old stonework bridge over Mill Creek. Turn right to cross this bridge, then right again to cross the arched stone bridge over the pond spillway where Wolf Creek enters Mill Creek. These old stone structures are a legacy of the early days of Garfield Park.

Mill Creek is a swiftly flowing stream that eventually enters the Cuyahoga River west of here. Wolf Creek Lake on the left was once a swimming pool and, even earlier—in the 1890s—a boating lake. The sediment that has filled the pond and allowed trees and shrubs to grow up in the mud has come from more than 20 years of highway and home construction in this area. The trail leads up some stone steps on the right to an old blacktop road.

**3.** Stay to the right (north) on this road and follow it to the sign for North Ravine Loop Trail, on the left. Enter the trail going left (south) and uphill.

**4.** At the intersection with the North Ravine Loop Trail (identified with green and white hiker signs), bear right to start this pleasant 0.5-mile loop trail, down steps, over a bridge, and up steps through a lovely woods of maple, tulip, oak, and beech trees. The path circles a ravine through which a small stream runs on its way down to Mill Creek.

**5.** Follow the trail alongside the paved All-Purpose Trail and, at the end of the fence, reenter the woods (north). An open playing field and Old Birch Picnic Area are on the right.

**6.** Leave the green and white marked trail by taking the trail on the right to cross the playing field at its north end, keeping the meadow on the left and the playing field on the right. Stay to your left alongside the meadow. Reach the sign that says "To Iron Spring Loop Trail." Here, descend some stone steps on the left. At the foot of the steps is a sign identifying these as "Historic Stairs" that were part of an 1890 Master Plan developed by early Clevelanders and Frederick Law Olmsted, a noted landscape architect who designed many parks, including New York City's Central Park.

**7.** Turn right (south) on the Iron Spring Loop Trail, a weedy old blacktop road. Continue 200 yards to a gravel path on the left. Bear left (north) at the Y fork. Below the trail on the right are the remains of the original dam that impounded water to create Wolf Creek Lake for boating. Here also are remnants of old stonework walls that edged the boating lake. Future plans for this park include dredging and refilling the once scenic lake to attract more waterfowl.

Continue north on this trail to return to the arched stone bridge over Wolf Creek.

**8.** Head east and then south (away from Mill Creek Ln.) on the Iron Spring Loop Trail. Bearing to the right, continue past the steep flight of steps on the left leading up to Red Oak Picnic Area. The trail here is marked with black and white hiker signs posted on trees.

Interpretive signs are found at frequent intervals along this trail. The first sign points out tall sycamore trees with white trunks and always-peeling bark that thrive in this watery environment. Next on the right is another view of the broken Wolf Creek dam lying across the creek bed. The stairs on the left also lead up to the Red Oak Picnic Area and playing field.

The next sign notes a giant oak that was only a sapling in 1896 when the park opened. On the right are stone steps that lead down to the creek and circle back up again (an optional detour).

Farther along is a sign on the right noting a beautiful stone wall still remaining on the opposite bank of Wolf Creek. This siding was built in the 1930s by the Works Progress Administration (WPA) without mortar by fitting the stone blocks closely together. Amazingly, the wall is still in place after 60 years of spring floods! The erosion-resistant sandstones were quarried near Bedford.

On the left is an interesting sign pointing out ancient layers of sandstone rock with interbedding of more layers of stone. These large blocks of Berea Sandstone were under an inland sea about 360 million years ago and show graphic evidence of periods of drought and water erosion.

Cross a bridge. Farther along on the left is a large witch-hazel bush, the last flower to bloom in late October and early November. Its yellow blossoms resemble frizzy witch's hair.

At a trail intersection, bear left and go uphill where the Iron Spring Loop Trail joins the asphalt All-Purpose Trail.

**9.** Follow the Iron Spring Loop Trail alongside the All-Purpose Trail to the next sign, which describes the early settlements in the area— Moravian communities, beginning in 1786 (ten years before Moses Cleaveland landed in Cleveland), Newburg in 1814, South Newburg in 1919, and, later, Garfield Heights.

The next sign points out the beautiful sandstone ledges over which cascade tiny waterfalls as the creek makes its way down a 70-foot drop to Mill Creek.

**10.** At the 2.0-mile point on this hike, cross Wolf Creek over an old stone bridge. Turn right (north) to follow the west side of the Iron Spring Loop Trail, again on the old blacktop road.

At the next sign is a view of the beautiful arched bridge just crossed. It was built of native sandstone hauled from Bedford in the 1890s. Note the small round indentations that the stoneworkers chiseled to fit hooks and tongs into in order to move the huge blocks to this site.

Next on the right is delightful Green Springs Pool. This beautiful emerald pool was created by large volumes of water falling over erosion-resistant sandstone onto much softer rock, which has eroded away, leaving a pool eight feet deep.

**11.** Opposite the pool and on the left is a small path to the old Garfield Park Quarry. Take this path west past the small natural amphitheater bowl to the small quarry from which stonecutters obtained rock slabs used for the stone steps in Garfield Park. There are still a few stonecutters' marks on rocks and outcrops.

**12.** Return to the Iron Spring Loop Trail. Farther along on the left is Iron Spring, for which this trail was named. Early visitors to the park believed that the dark rust-colored water gushing from this spring was a curative for various ailments. The spring has slowed to only a trickle now because of changes in the groundwater table. The water is not drinkable but still paints the nearby rocks and soil a very dark rust color. Continue north on the Iron Spring Loop Trail.

**13.** Reach the sidewalk on the left leading to Old Birch Picnic Area. Turn left (south) at the sign pointing toward the parking area.

Follow the All-Purpose Trail from the parking area south past the picnic tables; note the magnificent white birch tree on the left.

**14.** Pass the sign for Iron Spring. Along the All-Purpose Trail in this section are Solar Walk signs featuring information about the planets of our solar system. Continue to a bench and the sign on the left indicating the 0.4-mile Ridgetop Trail. This is a most rewarding trail to take in springtime, when many varieties of beautiful wildflowers can be seen. Avoid taking any side trails.

Follow the Ridgetop Trail eastward to a small wooden bridge on the left, and cross it over a tributary of Wolf Creek. Continue on this trail until you reach the paved All-Purpose Trail.

**15.** Turn left (north) on the All-Purpose Trail. Follow it downhill past Red Oak Picnic Area and alongside Mill Creek Ln. to the nature center.

*Optional*

As an option, at point #15 where you emerge from the Ridgetop Trail onto the All-Purpose Trail, you can instead turn right (west) and take the All-Purpose Trail northward past Old Birch and Windy Ridge picnic areas, then alongside Garfield Park Blvd. Turn right at Mill Creek Ln. to reach Garfield Park Nature Center again. You will pass the beginning of the Solar Walk on this section of the All-Purpose Trail.

This chapter reviewed and rewalked by Louis Shainker.

# 24 Huntington Reservation

**Distance:** 4 miles

**Hiking time:** 2 hours

**Description:** This hike contains a variety of terrain and vistas. It winds through lovely woods along Porter Creek, goes along sandy Huntington Beach, and into adjacent Cahoon Park.

**Directions:** I-90 to Exit 159 (Columbia Rd./SR 252); north on Columbia to Wolf Rd.; west on Wolf to sign (on right) for Lake Erie Nature and Science Center/Huntington Reservation. Enter via Porter Creek Dr.

**Parking & restrooms:** Lake Erie Nature and Science Center, 28728 Wolf Rd., Bay Village (440-871-2900). The center is open 1–5 p.m. Sun–Fri, and 10 a.m.–5 p.m. on Saturday. Alternate parking and restrooms at Wolf Picnic Area, east of the center.

Huntington Reservation was named for its owner, John Huntington, a prominent Cleveland industrialist and philanthropist. His vineyard and botanical park were located here long before a reservation was created for public use in 1927. Huntington Beach, with its picnic and fishing areas, is a very popular spot in summer. Lake Erie Nature and Science Center is home to Schuele Planetarium and a wildlife rehabilitation program. Expansion of the center from January to April 1998 will add much-needed space to accommodate visitors and exhibits. Baycrafters and Huntington Playhouse, affiliates of Cleveland Metroparks, are also located in Huntington Reservation, off Porter Creek Dr. Baycrafters presents the popular Renaissance Fayre each year on Labor Day weekend.

**1.** Start this hike by visiting the nature center, if open, to see interesting exhibits and a variety of wildlife. The trail leads from the rear of the center and is bordered by a wooden railing on both sides. It circles around a ravine and, at an opening in the railing, descends downhill on a dirt path above the ravine.

**2.** The trail exits to Porter Creek Dr. at the Wolf Picnic Area sign. Walk on the road downhill under concrete pillars that once supported the Lake Shore Electric Railway. This interurban line carried commuters between Cleveland and the northwestern suburbs in the early 1900s.

**3.** At the foot of the hill cross the bridge over Porter Creek and turn right (east) onto a trail on the north side of the creek.

**4.** The trail winds along the creek. Without crossing the stream, follow this trail through deep cool woods, keeping the creek on your left. Where the trail becomes eroded take the deeply cut path to the left and eventually rejoin the trail. You will come to a short, muddy, rocky section right alongside the water. If necessary, it is best to go off the trail through some bushes to skirt this area.

**5.** Enter Porter Creek Dr. on the left as it crosses beneath Lake Rd. and follow it briefly until you emerge onto sandy Huntington Beach to your right.

**6.** Go north and then west along the beach and enjoy fine views of Lake Erie.

**7.** Ascend the second set of stairs on your left going up the cliff. Walk along the top of the cliff to the far west end of the beach. Return east along the upper walkway to the Huntington Water Tower, an 1890s structure that once pumped water to Mr. Huntington's grape fields. The tower is made of cypress wood, but the outside is covered with siding. The original water pipes, stairway, and water tub enclosure still exist inside the building.

**8.** At the tower, turn right (south) and walk through the marked pedestrian underpass under Lake Rd. Beyond the restrooms and to the west are Huntington Playhouse, Baycrafters Shop, a restored train caboose, and reservation maintenance buildings.

**9.** Descend on the All-Purpose Trail east of the playhouse to the same bridge crossing the creek (see note #3). This is about the 2.0-mile mark on this hike.

**10.** Across the bridge and at the top of the hill, turn left and enter the trail that goes east along the top of the cliff on the south side of Porter Creek. This trail shortly leaves the creek and bears right toward the Wolf Picnic Area. Turn right on wide path. Restroom facilities are in view.

**11.** Turn left (east) on the All-Purpose Trail and follow this paved pathway to Cahoon Memorial Park.

**12.** Continue east through Cahoon Park to Cahoon Rd. and turn left (north) toward Lake Erie. Watching out for traffic, cross Lake Rd. and enter Cahoon Park on a trail on the opposite side of the road.

**13.** Enjoy another view of Lake Erie and the Cleveland skyline to the east.

**14.** Return to Huntington Reservation by crossing Lake Rd. again and following it west to the reservation entrance.

**15.** From the entrance, follow the All-Purpose Trail south back to the nature center parking area.

This chapter reviewed and rewalked by Lynn Schreiber and Warren Davis.

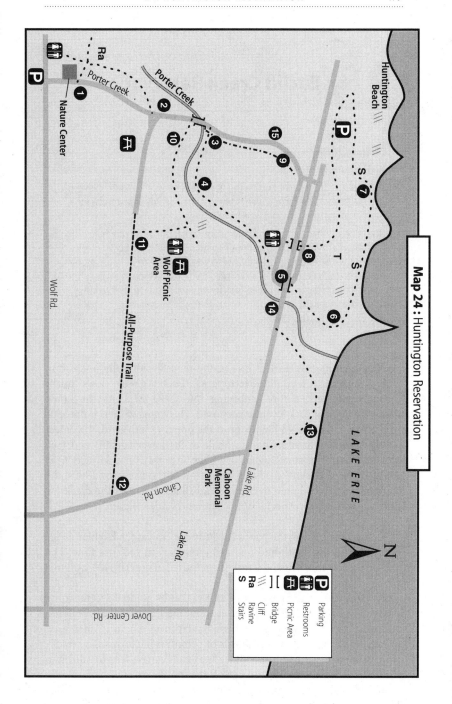

**Map 24 : Huntington Reservation**

# 25 Euclid Creek Reservation

**Distance:** 5 miles

**Hiking time:** 2 hours

**Description:** This hike begins on the paved All-Purpose Trail and follows it uphill alongside Euclid Creek Pkwy. to Anderson Rd., then returns for a part of the distance on a well-traveled woods trail.

**Directions:** I-90 to Exit 182A (Nottingham Rd.); south on Nottingham (becomes Highland Rd.); continue south on Highland to Euclid Creek Reservation entrance, on right (west) side. OR, I-271 to Exit 36; west on Wilson Mills Rd. (becomes Monticello Blvd. past Richmond Rd.); continue west on Monticello; look for entrance signs to reservation before Green Rd.

**Parking & restrooms:** At Highland Picnic Area.

This long, narrow park is one of the most geologically interesting reservations in Cleveland Metroparks. Euclid Creek flows north through the park before emptying into Lake Erie. As the creek descends, ancient rock levels are exposed. The youngest level is the 360-million-year-old Euclid Bluestone at the upper (south) end; the oldest is 400-million-year-old Chagrin Shale at the lower (north) end (see appendix A). The small village of Bluestone was once located near Anderson and Green Rds. From the late 1800s to the early 1900s, the workers who lived here quarried Euclid Bluestone from the creek for use in construction, especially for Cleveland's sidewalks.

**1.** Start the hike on the paved All-Purpose Trail at the Highland Picnic Area heading south and forward (younger) in geologic time. The cliff on the left above Euclid Creek is composed of grayish, 400-million-year-old Chagrin Shale.

**2.** Continue on the paved trail as it makes its gradual ascent, going past the Welsh Woods Picnic Area at about the 1.5-mile mark. Begin to see the darker Cleveland Shale here, its darkness due to its increased organic material content and fossils of primitive life forms. The trackways of some wormlike fish with feathery tails can be seen fossilized in the rocks alongside the stream just off the trail.

**3.** The trail passes under the Monticello Blvd. bridge to the Kelley Picnic Area and a winter sledding hill. The reddish-gray rock of the Bed-

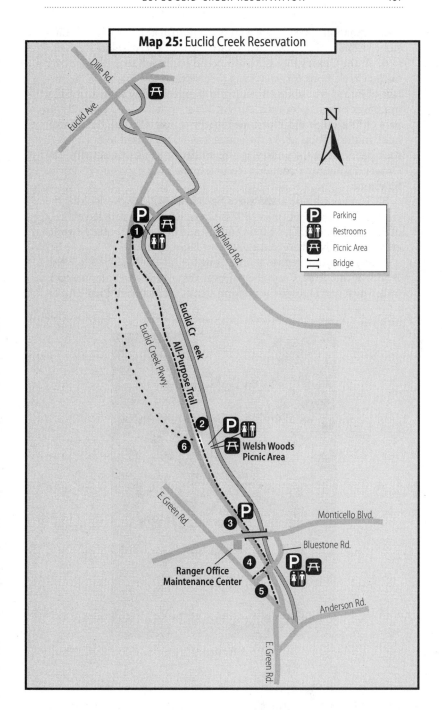

**Map 25:** Euclid Creek Reservation

ford Formation appears here with the grayish, flat slabs of Euclid Blue-stone visible in the creek bed and forming the eastern wall of the trail.

**4.** At the Quarry Picnic Area, descend on the left to the bridge over Euclid Creek. Look for interesting prehistoric ripple marks on the surface of Euclid Bluestone remaining in the creek. They were formed by the waves of an underwater current when an inland sea covered this part of Ohio. The old Bluestone Quarry is now filled in, but an iron hook in the ground above the embankment, once used to hoist heavy rock slabs out of the quarry, is a reminder of its former activity. The Quarry Picnic Area contains the only remaining exposure of Euclid Bluestone.

**5.** The stone house at the top of Euclid Creek Pkwy. overlooking the creek and the house at 1000–1002 E. Green Rd. are constructed entirely of Euclid Bluestone. These were built by, and occupied by, quarry workers who once lived here in the village of Bluestone.

**6.** Retrace your steps to return along the All-Purpose Trail to Welsh Woods Picnic Area. Cross the parkway opposite it and enter a woods trail, which continues to the parking area at the Highland Picnic Area.

*Casey Batiule/Cleveland Metroparks*

Euclid Creek

This chapter reviewed and rewalked by Jerry Berner, president of the Cleveland Hiking Club.

# 26 Rocky River Reservation
## North

---

**Distance:** 6 miles

**Hiking time:** 2 ½ to 3 hours

**Description:** Rocky River Reservation is a long, narrow park through which the Rocky River courses on its relentless flow north to Lake Erie. The valley created by the Rocky River is characterized by steep shale cliffs rising impressively above the river's floodplain and broad valleys. Many beautiful old trees stand in this lush valley, including cottonwoods, willows, and sycamores. This hike begins at the Scenic Park and Marina of Rocky River Reservation and generally follows both Valley Pkwy. and the Rocky River on their winding course northward. The All-Purpose Trail crosses and recrosses the river several times. The hike will retrace the same trail coming back, affording different views of the river and valley on the return.

**Directions:** I-90 westbound to exit for Hilliard Blvd.; left (east) on Hilliard; left (north) on Wooster Rd.; right (east) on Detroit Rd.; cross bridge; right onto Valley Pkwy.; right at the bottom of the hill to enter the Scenic Park & Marina. OR, I-90 eastbound to Exit 161 (Detroit Rd./SR 254); left (east) on Detroit Rd., past Wooster Rd. and across bridge; right on Valley Pkwy.; right at the bottom of hill to enter the Scenic Park & Marina.

**Parking & restrooms:** At Scenic Park & Marina and adjacent picnic area.

---

Rocky River Reservation is one of the largest reservations in Cleveland Metroparks. The reservation's size and shape were determined by the flow of the Rocky River in its twisting, turning course from Strongsville in the south to Rocky River and Lake Erie in the north. (See also chapters 17 and 33.)

Outstanding natural features of this park are its massive Chagrin and Cleveland Shale cliffs that have been exposed by the cutting action of the Rocky River (see appendix A). The oldest Chagrin Shale is near the start of the hike, and the darker, younger Cleveland Shale appears farther along. The shape of the reservation was determined by the flow of the river in its twisting, turning course from Berea in the south to Lake Erie in the north. Nearby streets such as Detroit and Center Ridge Rds. are slightly higher than neighboring terrain. These ridges represent ancient beaches of larger lakes which predate Lake Erie. The geology of Rocky River Reservation is well documented and illustrated in exhibits at the nature center.

The new Scenic Park and Marina, opened in 1996, has boat slips, a restaurant, and a gift shop. Farther down the valley on this hike, off of Hogsback Lane, is the Stinchcomb-Groth Memorial. It pays tribute to city engineer William A. Stinchcomb (1878–1959), whose direction and leadership helped create the Cleveland Metropolitan Park District (now the Cleveland Metroparks) in 1921. Stinchcomb was the district's first director, a post he held until 1957. He was responsible for the building of roads, shelters, bridges, trails, and recreation areas in the 1920s and '30s, as well as the reforestation of park properties by the Civilian Conservation Corps and Works Progress Administration in the 1930s.

**1.** Start at the All-Purpose Trail at the bridge over the river near the parking area entrance. The trail is paved, and mileage is indicated along its full length so distance can be measured. While crossing the bridge, note the massive shale cliff above the river. The river has cut through many layers of earth since the last glacier retreated from Ohio about 12,000 years ago. The soft blue-gray shale on this cliff is Chagrin Shale, the oldest exposed rock in the park. It was formed about 360 million years ago during the Devonian geologic period. The vertical marks penetrating the rock were caused by erosion. Each visible layer probably represents a major storm event when silting occurred in the warm inland sea that once covered Ohio (see appendix A).

**2.** After about a mile, the trail continues under the I-90 bridge and the beautiful Hilliard Blvd. bridge, passing by some physical-fitness trail breaks and picnic tables. Cross Valley Pkwy. with caution. Pass over the bridge, observing the tall trees which abut the river for signs of the many raccoons that inhabit them.

**3.** Soon pass ball fields (on the left) located along a wide bend of the Rocky River. When the last glacier retreated, the river widened in some places and left several broad flat areas in the Rocky River Valley, of which this expanse is an example. In its wake the glacier left huge boulders that can be seen in the river, hence its name.

**4.** At about 2.5 miles, Hogsback Ln. off Valley Pkwy. leads east up to the Stinchcomb-Groth Memorial, a tribute to the founding father and longtime director of the Cleveland Metropolitan Park District. Note how the river has been held in check with a manmade concrete wall. Originally, the river was located farther to the left just below the cliff. At this point note the slight difference in the color of the shale. The darker, black shale now coming into view is the slightly younger Cleveland Shale, also of the Devonian period. Beneath it, of course, lies the older Chagrin Shale seen earlier. Cleveland Shale is black because it contains large amounts of decayed organic matter. Ancient fish and shark fossils have been found in this layer, as well as brachiopods, some examples of which may be seen at the nature center.

Just past the entrance to Hogsback Ln., next to the paved trail, is a

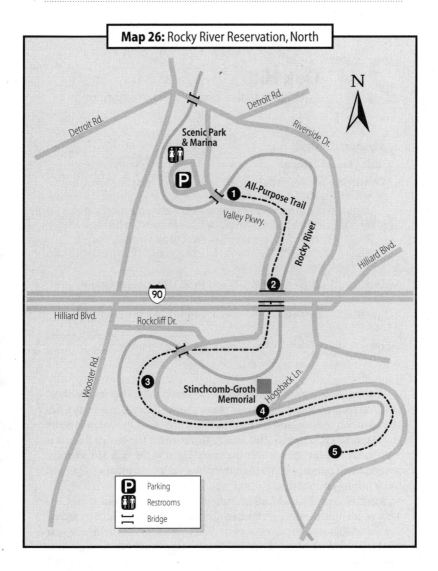

**Map 26:** Rocky River Reservation, North

sign designating Valley Pkwy. as one of America's 10 most outstanding scenic byways.

**5.** At the 3.0-mile mark on the paved trail, turn around if desired and retrace your steps, retreating in time to when this glacial valley was formed about 12,000 years ago. Even today the river continues relentlessly cutting layers of rock.

This chapter reviewed and rewalked by Lynn Schreiber and Warren Davis.

# 27 Oak Hill
## Cuyahoga Valley National Recreation Area

**Distance:** 2.5 miles

**Hiking time:** 1 ½ hours

**Description:** These quiet trails are flat or gently undulating. The walk will take you to Meadowedge and Sylvan ponds and along the top of a high hogback ridge to Hemlock Point. Many oaks grow in the forest as well as maples and hawthorns. Chestnut trees were abundant here until the blight of the early 20th century killed them, but occasionally you will encounter an old chestnut stump. Many beautiful wildflowers dot the fields in the spring, summer, and fall.

**Directions:** I-271 to Exit 12 (SR 303); east on SR 303 (toward Peninsula); immediate right (south) on Major Rd.; just after sharp 15-mph turn, turn right (south) on Oak Hill Rd. to Oak Hill Day Use Area on left, just past Scobie Rd.

**Parking and restroom:** At the entrance near the picnic tables.

Within Cuyahoga Valley National Recreation Area are many short trails on former farm and forest acreage. Oak Hill Day Use Area typifies the adaption of such land for recreational purposes. Opened in 1983 by the National Park Service, this area high above the Cuyahoga River has seen many improvements over the years. Dotting the Oak Hill area are several small ponds, which are enjoyed by a variety of aquatic life as well as by fishing enthusiasts.

South of Oak Hill is Cuyahoga Valley Environmental Education Center, a residential facility for children and adults with a curriculum focusing on ecology and the environment. There are activities held here year round. For information about the center's day, weekend, or week-long programs, call 216-657-2796. CVEEC does not permit hiking on the trails surrounding the center and has posted "No trespassing" signs around the perimeter of its land.

**1.** Begin the hike to the right of the large trail sign at a small brown sign indicating the Oak Hill Trail. Follow the path heading south.

**2.** After about 0.2 mile reach an intersection and bear left so as to remain on the Oak Hill Trail. (The path on the right, the Plateau Trail, returns you to the parking lot.) Cross a bridge.

**3.** At the next trail intersection a sign points southeast toward

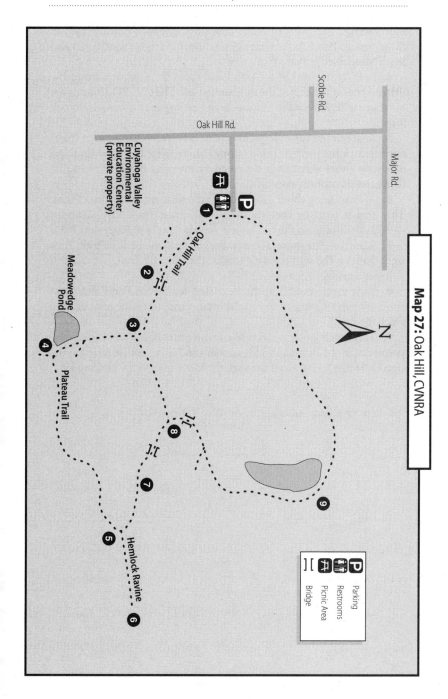

**Map 27:** Oak Hill, CVNRA

Meadowedge and Sylvan ponds. Take this right turn heading toward Meadowedge Pond. At the next intersection, turn right (southwest) and reach Meadowedge Pond (0.5 miles).

**4.** Bear left (south) at the pond and cross the earthen dam to the Plateau Trail at the end of the dam on the left. The CVEEC grounds are on your right. Follow the Plateau Trail heading east toward Hemlock Ravine.

**5.** At about the 1.0-mile point on this hike, reach a right turn (east) for Hemlock Ravine. The trail is along a sharp ridge that drops precipitously on either side and is bordered by towering hemlock trees that thrive in this cool environment.

**6.** After walking about 0.2 mile from the turn, reach Hemlock Point. This area is used by the environmental center for study purposes. (Avoid continuing on the trail as it descends steeply to Riverview Rd.)

**7.** Return on the same trail atop the ravine to the Plateau Trail. Turn right (west) at the sign pointing toward the Oak Hill Trail.

Cross a bridge (1.6 miles).

**8.** Turn right (north) at the next sign for Sylvan Pond and cross another bridge. Continue ahead a short distance to a wide opening and reach the pond.

**9.** This much larger pond is filled with water lilies and bordered by yellow iris in the summer. Cross the dam and at the end, turn left at the sign (2.0 miles). Head west through the forest toward the parking lot.

This hike prepared by the author with the assistance of Elinor Polster.

# 28 Hinckley Reservation
Worden's Ledges

**Distance:** 1 mile round trip

**Hiking time:** 1 hour

**Description:** The trail is not marked, but it can be followed with this description and map or by referring to the map posted on a garage adjacent to the house. The ledges are located directly under the hill below the homestead, and the carvings are not difficult to find. Worden Heritage Homestead is managed by the Hinckley Historical Society, Susen Batke, curator, and is usually open on Sunday afternoons in the summer (330-278-2154). Tours available by appointment.

**Directions:** I-271 to Exit 3 for SR 94 (North Royalton); north on SR 94 (Ridge Rd.); right (east) on Ledge Rd., pass Kellogg Rd. and Ledge Lake Pool to Worden Heritage Homestead, on left (about 1 mile).

**Parking & restrooms:** Very little parking is available at Worden Heritage Homestead, but cars can be parked along the side of the driveway, and in the field east of the homestead, around the loop driveway. A restroom is available inside the museum, when open. Restrooms also available at Ledge Lake.

In 1851 the estate of Samuel Hinckley sold Hiram Worden land in Medina County that would later become part of Hinckley Reservation, one of 14 Cleveland Metroparks reservations, and the only one located outside Cuyahoga County. The Worden Heritage Homestead at 895 Ledge Rd. was built by Hiram Worden in 1862, the year his daughter Nettie was born, and occupied by his farming family and their descendants until the 1980s. Nettie, who lived in the house all her life until her death in 1945, married her third husband, Noble Stuart, 20 years her junior, in 1944. Noble and his son, George Stuart, continued to stay in the house until George's death in 1984, when Cleveland Metroparks acquired the home and the Hinckley Historical Society became its manager.

Noble Stuart, a bricklayer, home builder, wanderer, and, most significantly, folk artist, began carving wood and wet concrete after his marriage to Nettie. He discovered huge sandstone ledges a half mile beyond the Worden home and proceeded to carve figures and faces and other objects in the ledges over a period of six years. The carvings, which are gradually deteriorating, depict people and things that were important to Stuart: a cross over an open Bible; baseball player Ty Cobb, whom he took hunting and fishing in Detroit; a schooner, representing his father's death in a shipwreck on Lake Superior; a bust of Hiram Worden on a corner of a rock with his name inscribed; "Nettie" carved in script; George Washington and the Marquis de Lafayette (reflecting Stuart's historical interests); there is also an eight-foot-long sphinx lying atop a large boulder.

Stuart's concrete carving of Christ on the Cross lies on the ground north of a small shed on the property. Although Stuart was a skillful craftsman, authorities do not consider him a significant artist. He died in 1976 at the age of 94. When asked in 1948 why he did the carvings, he said he simply wanted to keep practicing stone carving and leave something that would last.

West of Worden Heritage Homestead on Ledge Rd. is popular Ledge Lake Pool and Recreation Area (440-234-3026). A small admission charge allows visitors to use the 80-by-100-foot pool, changing facilities, and picnic area. Seniors over 65 and children 5 and under are admitted free. It is open 10 a.m.–8:30 p.m. Memorial Day to Labor Day.

Hinckley Reservation offers hiking trails, picnic areas, and an additional swimming area on Hinckley Lake that can be reached from Bellus Rd. Trail information is available from Cleveland Metroparks. For more information call 216-351-6300.

**1.** From the homestead, reach the trail to the ledges by going west parallel to Ledge Rd. (on your left) and past the sheds (on your right). Turn right (north) just before the barn and follow an old farm lane. Soon the path curves around to the left and gently descends a small hill. This trail may be muddy, as it is also used by horses.

**2.** Near the foot of the slope ignore the minor trail going off to the left and turn right (east) immediately. Follow the trail until you see large sandstone ledges on the path directly ahead.

**3.** At the farthest set of rock outcroppings, you will see on the left a large sphinx carved on top of a rock. This imposing creature seems to guard the entrance to the ledges area. Next is a large rock with "H. M. Worden 1851" carved on its face. On the northwest corner of this rock Stuart carved a bust of his father-in-law, later adding a cement beard when he noticed a photo of him sporting this adornment. "Nettie" is deeply incised in the next rock. A schooner can be seen high up on a ledge to the right, and farther along, also on a ledge to the right, is a cross with a Bible intricately carved into the stone. Ty Cobb's face and name are on a north-facing outcropping nearly obscured by moss.

Worden's Ledges were formed by the same ancient processes that also formed Whipp's Ledges, located in another part of Hinckley Reservation. (These are well worth seeing and can be reached by taking Ledge Rd. east to State Rd. Make a left (north) on State and follow to Whipp's Ledges Picnic Area.) Other ledge formations of Sharon Conglomerate

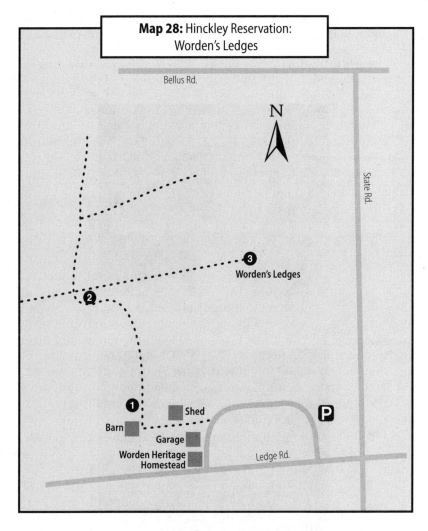

**Map 28:** Hinckley Reservation:
Worden's Ledges

Bellus Rd.

N

State Rd.

**3** Worden's Ledges

**2**

**1**

Shed

Barn

Garage

Worden Heritage
Homestead

Ledge Rd.

P

from the Pennsylvanian Age formed 320 million years ago are found in Nelson-Kennedy Ledges State Park, Chapin Forest Reservation in Lake County, and Virginia Kendall Park in the Cuyahoga Valley National Recreation Area.

Million of years ago this part of Ohio was under a vast inland sea and, over time, mud and sand washed into the ocean as wave action eroded the land. The sand at the ocean bottom solidified into rock, and as the waters receded and the land uplifted, the rocks became exposed. This rock is called Sharon Conglomerate sandstone because it was originally named after Sharon, Pennsylvania. Embedded in it are white quartz "lucky stones" that once were beach pebbles worn smooth by waves at the edge of the sea. Glacial action of 12,000 years ago shaped these sandstone ledges yet further. Erosion and other change still continue today.

Return to Worden Heritage Homestead by retracing your steps in the reverse direction.

*Courtesy of the Hinckley Historical Society*

Naturalist with rock carving by Noble Stuart.

*Courtesy Cleveland Metroparks Archives*

Carving of Ty Cobb

# 29 South Chagrin Reservation
## River Walk

**Distance:** 8 miles

**Hiking time:** 3 ½ hours

**Description:** This hike follows the blue-blazed Buckeye Trail along a scenic section of park land between the Chagrin River and Chagrin River Rd., part of South Chagrin Reservation. An almost flat, wooded trail leads to the main part of the reservation, then follows a paved All-Purpose Trail to Squaw Rock Picnic Area. A set of steep stone steps leads down to the edge of the river, and a short walk along the river leads to Squaw Rock. The walk returns on the same trail.

**Directions:** I-271 to Exit 29 (Chagrin Blvd./SR 87); east on Chagrin; left (north) on S. O. M. Center Rd.; right (east) on S. Woodland Rd. (SR 87); right at entrance to the Cleveland Metroparks Polo Field parking area, just past Chagrin River Rd.

**Parking & restrooms:** At Cleveland Metroparks Polo Field parking area.

The Chagrin River was designated a state scenic river in 1979. This beautiful riverside area is well known for its spring wildflowers and fall foliage. There are many tall hemlock, oak, hickory, beech, and maple trees here. The Cleveland Metroparks Polo Field, where this walk starts, is used by the Cleveland Polo Club for horse and dog shows and periodically for the Cleveland Hunter/Jumper Classic.

**1.** Look for the rectangular two-by-six-inch blue blazes of the Buckeye Trail (BT) painted on trees and poles along the west side of the polo field. Follow these markers going south.

**2.** At 0.7 mile, the BT turns left (east) on a bridle trail toward the Chagrin River and follows roughly parallel to the river along a beautiful stretch of woods. There are a variety of birds and flowers in season.

CAUTION: On this heavily used bridle trail the chances are strong that you will meet horses, especially on weekends. When encountering them, stop well to the side of the trail, remaining quiet and still until they have passed, to avoid startling these large and potentially dangerous animals.

**3.** Continue on BT through open fields and a white pine forest.

**4.** At 1.7 miles, reach the bridge at US 422 (Chagrin Blvd.). Cross the road and continue to follow the trail along the west bank of the river.

**5.** At 2.6 miles cross Willey Creek which, if there is high water, can be crossed by going out to Chagrin River Rd., crossing the bridge, then following the creek back to the BT.

**6.** At about 3 miles the BT crosses another small creek, then goes up a small hill and emerges onto Chagrin River Rd.

**7.** Cross Miles Rd. and bear left (east) across the River Rd. bridge (not Miles Rd. bridge) to enter the park on the right near Sulphur Springs Dr. An asphalt-paved All-Purpose Trail goes south from the small parking area.

CAUTION: Stay to the right on the paved trail. It is heavily used by bicyclists.

**8.** Follow the paved path in a southerly direction, and reach Squaw Rock Picnic Area on the left at about 3.5 miles.

**9.** At the far east end of the parking area is a pathway leading down stone steps to a beautiful view of the Chagrin River and its scenic waterfall below. Descend to the foot of the stairs and follow the riverside trail to Squaw Rock. (NOTE: These steps are closed in the winter.)

*Courtesy Cleveland Metroparks Archives*

Squaw Rock

**10.** This large Berea Sandstone rock (called Squaw Rock) was carved in 1885 by Chagrin Falls blacksmith and artist Henry Church. It depicts a Native American woman surrounded by a quiver of arrows, a sea serpent, panther, skeleton, and eagle, as well as a shield, tomahawk,

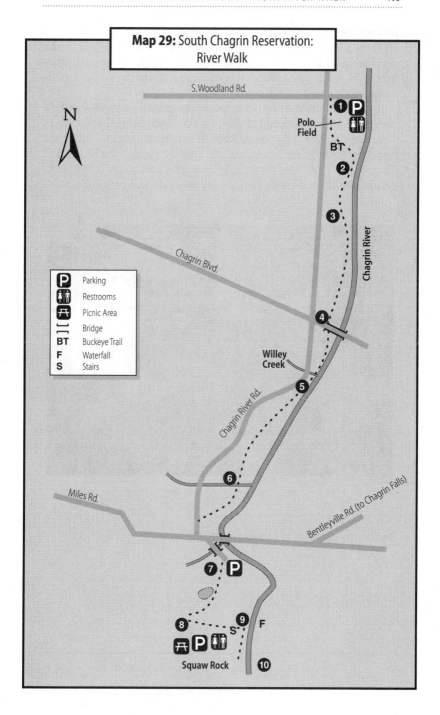

**Map 29:** South Chagrin Reservation:
River Walk

N

S. Woodland Rd.

Polo
Field

BT

Chagrin Blvd.

Chagrin River

P  Parking
🚻 Restrooms
🏕 Picnic Area
⎯ Bridge
BT  Buckeye Trail
F  Waterfall
S  Stairs

Willey
Creek

Chagrin River Rd.

Miles Rd.

Bentleyville Rd. (to Chagrin Falls)

F

S

Squaw Rock

and papoose. On the river side of this huge glacial boulder are more carvings: a log cabin and the Capitol building in Washington, D.C. The significance of these unfinished carvings is obscure. Some think they refer to the white man's plundering of the Indians, or depict the various stages in our country's history.

To return to the starting point, follow the trail in reverse. Ascend the stone steps at the south end of the trail. Turn right (north) at the top of these steps to return to Squaw Rock Picnic Area. Continue along the paved trail behind the restrooms and follow it back to the bridge and Chagrin River Rd. Here continue following the blue blazes of the Buckeye Trail northward until you reach the polo field and parking area.

This chapter was reviewed and rewalked by Art Harvey.

# 30 Mentor Marsh State Nature Preserve Kerven Trail; Wake Robin Trail & Newhous Overlook

Mentor Marsh Nature Preserve is a 750-acre interpretive natural area jointly owned and managed by the Cleveland Museum of Natural History and the Ohio Department of Natural Resources.

The four-mile-long marsh's exceptional features are the diversity of its plants and wildlife, and its interesting history. The Grand River did not always reach Lake Erie at its present outlet at Fairport Harbor. It once flowed through what is now Mentor Marsh and emptied into the lake several miles west of here. Over the 800 to 1,000 years since the Grand River found its present outlet to the lake, the old river channel gradually changed from swamp forest to marsh, and now contains miles of open area enclosing tall plume grass called *Phragmites australis*. Many birds, ducks, reptiles, amphibians, and insects thrive in this rich environment.

The Carol Sweet Mentor Marsh Nature Center, located at 5185 Corduroy Rd. in Mentor, is open on weekends from noon to 5 p.m. from April to October, and, during the rest of the year, on the first Sunday afternoon of each month. Interpretive brochures, reference books, maps, exhibits, a calendar of events, and other materials are available from the naturalist-staffed center during open hours. Classes and guided walks are presented at various times throughout the year. For more information, please call 440-257-0777.

Four marked trails, described below with different access points, are open daily from dawn to dusk. To see all of the nature preserve requires several brief drives. The time needed to complete all the trails will vary depending upon the wildlife and plants that attract the hiker's attention. However, allow a full morning or afternoon to complete them all.

Marsh mosquitoes are part of a wetland ecosystem. It is advisable to take along insect repellent, a hat, a long-sleeved shirt, and long pants when hiking in Mentor Marsh after late May and before the first frost. Open flames and smoking are strictly prohibited, as is the collection of any natural material in the preserve. Pets, motorized vehicles, and bikes are prohibited by state law in the nature preserve.

In 1966 Mentor Marsh became one of the first areas in the United States to be designated a national natural landmark, and in 1973 it was designated a state nature preserve. It is helpful to take along bird and wildflower identification guidebooks to enhance your visit to these natural areas.

# Kerven Trail

**Distance:** ¾ mile

**Hiking time:** Less than an hour

**Description:** The Kerven Trail begins just north of the Carol Sweet Mentor Marsh Nature Center. It is a loop trail on flat forest land with a small enclosed overlook ideal for studying birds of the marsh. Just off the trail is the brief Butterfly Walk, which dead-ends into a field of flowers (in season).

**Directions:** I-90 to SR 2 east to Mentor; north on SR 44; exit left (west) on SR 283 (Lake Shore Blvd.); right on Corduroy Rd. to sign for Marsh House (Carol Sweet Mentor Marsh Nature Center) on right.

**Parking and restrooms:** Park in the nature center parking area. A restroom is located inside the small building attached to the residence of the nature preserve caretaker, who is available during open hours.

**1.** Enter the Kerven Trail just north of the Carol Sweet Mentor Marsh Nature Center. This sometimes wet trail is located on abandoned agricultural land, which has been succeeded by a forest containing a variety of trees and plants. Keep on the lookout for owls and deer, which frequent this forest.

**2.** At the first trail intersection bear right to take the loop in a counterclockwise direction through a grove of white pine. Following closely by private property, you will soon see a white arrow indicating a left turn toward the edge of the marsh.

**3.** Reach the overlook and tarry a while to enjoy the wonderful view of acres of plume grass dotted with occasional dead tree stumps, reminders of the extensive swamp forest that once covered this marshland. The north shore of the marsh originally contained an oak/hickory forest, and the south shore a beech/maple forest. The riverbed contained willow, alder, buttonbush, and cattails. Some of the birds you may observe here are owls, ducks, herons, shore birds, and migrants during May and September.

**4.** The trail continues across a footbridge and past an open field on the left, where the dead-end Butterfly Walk is located. Continue ahead past the trail intersection marking the beginning of the loop and follow the path back to the parking area.

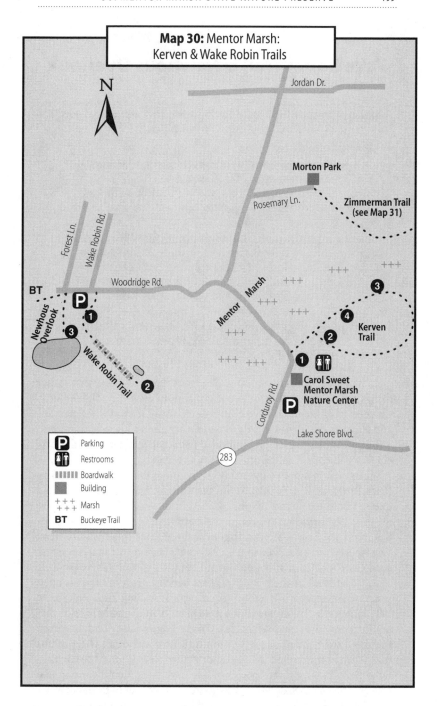

**Map 30:** Mentor Marsh:
Kerven & Wake Robin Trails

N

Jordan Dr.

Morton Park

Zimmerman Trail
(see Map 31)

Rosemary Ln.

Forest Ln.

Wake Robin Rd.

Woodridge Rd.

Mentor Marsh

Kerven
Trail

BT

Newhous Overlook

Wake Robin Trail

Carol Sweet
Mentor Marsh
Nature Center

Corduroy Rd.

Lake Shore Blvd.

283

| P | Parking |
|---|---------|
| 🚹🚺 | Restrooms |
| ‖‖‖‖ | Boardwalk |
| ■ | Building |
| +++ | Marsh |
| BT | Buckeye Trail |

# Wake Robin Trail & Newhous Overlook

**Distance:** The Wake Robin Trail is a 0.7-mile round trip, and the Newhous Overlook is only a 0.1-mile round trip from the road.

**Walking time:** Less than an hour.

**Description:** The Wake Robin Trail is a flat boardwalk leading into the marsh that passes several small ponds containing beaver, muskrat, waterfowl, and wading birds. The Newhous Overlook is a two-level wooden structure overlooking a large pond and acres of tall plume grass growing in the marsh.

**Directions:** For the Newhous Overlook and Wake Robin Trail boardwalk, drive north on Corduroy Rd. across the marsh to Woodridge Rd.; left on Woodridge to mall parking lot on left just before Wake Robin Rd. (Corduroy Rd. originally was originally a bumpy "corduroy" log road. Because of continued sinking, it has recently been widened, raised, and resurfaced.)

**Parking & restrooms:** Park at the small lot identified with a nature preserve sign on the south side of Woodridge Rd. No restrooms.

**1.** The trail from the parking area leads down to a boardwalk that brings the observer directly into the marsh to view the wildlife. Bird-watchers may see the elusive marsh wren, sora rail, and the American and least bittern. Red-winged blackbirds are almost always prominent. The boardwalk is on a slightly elevated path that once served as a short-cut to a golf course on the other side of the marsh.

Freshwater is supplied by springs throughout the marsh as well as by Black Brook and Marsh Creek, but the water remains slightly brackish due to salt-laden runoff that has seeped in from salt mines located on SR 44. Water flows slowly through the marsh from east to west and empties into Lake Erie at Mentor Lagoons, about three miles west of here. The lagoons were dredged in the 1920s for a large resort that was never completed. They remain open, but are not yet a part of the preserve.

**2.** At the end of the boardwalk is a bench to rest on and an open pond where beavers are active. Waterfowl and wading birds nest in the tall plume grass, an invasive salt marsh plant of little nutritive value that tends to crowd out native species. On the edge of the pond, however, there is a small stand of pretty cattails. Beaver and other water mammals, such as mink, muskrat, and short-tailed weasel, might be encountered here. Twenty-three species of fish have been identified in marsh waters. The channel alongside the boardwalk was cut to facilitate water circulation to and from a new pond below the Newhous Overlook. Here you may notice midland painted snapping turtles and green frogs, and you may hear peepers in early spring with an almost deafening sound at dusk.

**3.** Return on the boardwalk to the parking area. Turn left (west) on Woodridge Rd. and continue past five houses to the entrance path for the Newhous Overlook. Here you will enjoy an expansive view of the western end of the marsh and more waterfowl in the beautiful pond below. In summer, hawks and vultures often soar over this part of the marsh, and beaver and muskrats often make an appearance.

*Optional*

To the west of the overlook is Headlands School Forest, owned by the Mentor Board of Education. As an option, you may follow the blue-blazed Buckeye Trail from the overlook, winding through the site of ancient Indian encampments until the trail exits at Headlands School parking lot. Return to the overlook by retracing your steps. In April and May, beautiful wildflowers, especially trillium, dot the landscape. A map of this trail is available at Marsh House.

*Courtesy of Cleveland Museum of Natural History*

The author wishes to recognize the generous consultation and contributions in the original preparation of this chapter by Nancy M. Csider, Cleveland Museum of Natural History naturalist. This chapter reviewed and rewalked by Shirley Pashall.

# 31 Mentor Marsh State Nature Preserve Zimmerman / Buckeye Trail

**Distance:** 4 miles from Morton Park to Headlands Dr. and back

**Hiking time:** 1 ½ to 2 hours

**Description:** The Zimmerman Trail is on a portion of the statewide, blue-blazed Buckeye Trail. It winds along the western edge of Mentor Marsh and undulates gently through a mature upland and swamp forest with lovely wildflowers in season.

**Directions:** I-90 to SR 2 east to Mentor; north on SR 44; exit left (west) on SR 283 (Lake Shore Blvd.); north on Corduroy Rd.; right on Rosemary Ln. to end and large parking lot for Morton Park.

**Parking & restrooms:** Park near the entrance to the Zimmerman Trail. Public restrooms in the pool house building, open only in the summer, or at Headlands Beach State Park.

For an introduction to Mentor Marsh State Nature Preserve, see chapter 30.

**1.** The trailhead for the Zimmerman/Buckeye Trail is at the edge of the woods to the south of the Morton Park parking lot. The trail, named for Willoughby naturalist Harold Zimmerman, is marked with blue two-by-six-inch Buckeye Trail tree blazes. There are turns and side trails, so watch carefully for the tree blazes. Shortly after entering the woods, bear to the left to go east over gently rolling hills, following the edge of the marsh.

**2.** In autumn and winter there are broad views of the marsh on the right. In summer, the trail provides welcome shade from tall beech, oak, and maple trees.

**3.** After about 1.5 miles you will reach a trail intersection. Bear right. (The left spur, Jayne Trail, goes out to Jordan Dr.—where no parking is available.)

**4.** Continue following rolling terrain and cross several small footbridges over wet spots to reach the end of the trail at a parking lot on Headlands Dr. (2.0 miles). A plaque here commemorates Mentor Marsh as a historical landmark. From this point, a short walk east on Headlands Dr. will take you to Shipman Pond, also part of the nature preserve. Ducks, geese, and other waterfowl might be present. Red fox, weasel, raccoon, and opossum may come out to feed at dusk.

**5.** Shipman Pond, a remnant of the old Grand River riverbed, is

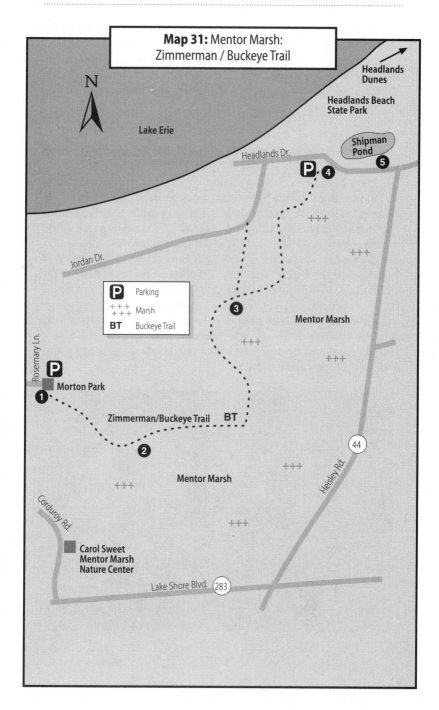

**Map 31:** Mentor Marsh:
Zimmerman / Buckeye Trail

N

Lake Erie

Headlands
Dunes

Headlands Beach
State Park

Shipman
Pond

Headlands Dr.

**P** 4

5

Jordan Dr.

**P** Parking

+ + + Marsh
+ + +

**BT** Buckeye Trail

3

Mentor Marsh

Rosemary Ln.

**P**

Morton Park

1

Zimmerman/Buckeye Trail   **BT**

2

Mentor Marsh

44

Heisley Rd.

Corduroy Rd.

Carol Sweet
Mentor Marsh
Nature Center

Lake Shore Blvd. 283

lined by a buttonbush-willow community. Nearby is the spot where the old Grand River made a sharp turn and gradually eroded through the sand, perhaps in a lake storm or a river flood, to establish its present, more direct course to Lake Erie. The pond commemorates Charles M. Shipman who was a pioneer in the movement to preserve Mentor Marsh in the 1930s.

*Optional*

Nearby and well worth visiting are Headlands Beach State Park and Headlands Dunes State Nature Preserve. The 125-acre Headlands Beach on Lake Erie offers swimming, picnicking, changing facilities, and a concession stand. To the northeast lies Headlands Dunes State Nature Preserve, a vast accumulation of sand along the Lake Erie shoreline that was created by wind and water along the western side of the mouth of the Grand River. Each year the sandy shoreline builds up and extends farther and farther out into Lake Erie. Access to the preserve is from Headlands Beach State Park. This special place is intended for research, nature study, bird-watching, art, and photography. Walking on the dunes is permitted, but visitors are asked not to walk on any growing plants. Monarch butterflies often stop to rest here on their long migration between Canada and Mexico. Plant species found here include dune-making switchgrass and beach grass, and other plants such as sea rocket and beach pea.

*Courtesy of Cleveland Museum of Natural History*

The author wishes to recognize the generous consultation and contributions in the original preparation of this chapter by Nancy M. Csider, Cleveland Museum of Natural History naturalist. Shirley Pashall reviewed and rewalked this hike.

# 32 Bedford Reservation
Tinker's Creek

**Distance:** 3 miles

**Hiking time:** 2 hours

**Description:** This hike follows Tinker's Creek gorge on its northwest side, going steeply uphill with breathtaking views of the gorge at its summit. The trail follows the rim of the gorge to the top and affords beautiful views of the stream as you ascend. This hike returns on the same path to the picnic and parking area. It is an especially impressive hike to take during fall foliage season, and is also a pretty hike when Tinker's Creek is partially frozen and there is snow on the ground.

**Directions:** I-271 or I-77 to Rockside Rd.; Rockside to Dunham Rd. in Maple Hts.; south on Dunham; left on Button Rd. just before bridge over Tinker's Creek (at sign for Hemlock Creek Picnic Area); follow Button to end at Hemlock Creek Picnic Area.

**Parking & restrooms:** At Hemlock Creek Picnic Area.

Bedford Reservation, located in Bedford, Bedford Heights, Valley View, and Walton Hills, is a link in the Cleveland Metroparks "Emerald Necklace." This lovely park on Cleveland's southeast side is also part of Cuyahoga Valley National Recreation Area. Bedford Reservation covers 2,154 acres of public land, through which beautiful Tinker's Creek cuts a gorge that has been designated a national natural landmark. Tinker's Creek drops a dramatic 220 feet during its two-mile course, cutting through many layers of soft grayish Chagrin Shale, and leaving a gorge that ranges from 140 to 190 feet deep.

A wide variety of trees abound here; 29 different species have been identified by the metroparks. Of particular note are tall hemlocks growing in the deep, cooler areas near the streams, reminiscent of more northern climates. Deer are commonly seen in Bedford Reservation.

**1.** Start the hike by heading east from the picnic area and ball field parallel to the wooded hill. The trail parallels Tinker's Creek on the right. Tinker's Creek flows westward to the Cuyahoga River, at which point it goes under the Ohio & Erie Canal beneath an interesting old aqueduct (see ch. 19, Canal Towpath Trail).

**2.** At the first trail intersection, turn right onto the path closer to the creek and view the magnificent cliff across the stream faced with tall hemlock trees clinging to its edge.

These cliffs are composed of very old, grayish Chagrin Shale near the water and darker Cleveland Shale above. These shales were formed of mud and silt laid down by an ancient inland sea about 360 million years ago and have been exposed by the relentless cutting of Tinker's Creek over the millennia (see appendix A). In winter there are beautiful frozen waterfalls here where small streams flow into the creek. This waterside trail continues for about 0.2 mile.

**3.** At the intersection, take the trail on the left that ascends the hill to the main trail. (If you stay on the creekside trail or take the trail that goes off to the right, you will see beautiful wildflowers if it is springtime, and enjoy more views of Tinker's Creek, but both trails eventually dead-end at a steep shale cliff.)

**4.** The upward trail on the left is the old Bridle Trail (now closed) and climbs steeply. In the middle of the trail, about halfway up the hill, is a large boulder covered with ripple marks made by currents at the bottom of the great inland sea that covered Ohio millions of years ago. At the top on the right is a magnificent view of the gorge below.

CAUTION: Do not stray too close to the edge of this cliff. Erosion here has created uneven footing and unstable soil.

**5.** (0.8 mile). As you pass the Bridle Trail sign (hanging by one bolt at this writing!), turn right toward Tinker's Creek gorge and continue on the trail. The road on the left is the north portion of Button Rd., which no longer connects to the southern part. Button Rd. is of interest because it is one of the oldest roads in northern Ohio. It was laid out in 1801 and enabled early settlers living in the highlands to the east of here to reach the Ohio & Erie Canal lying to the west.

**6.** Continue on this flat, winding, woodland path high above Tinker's Creek. Several short side trails veer over closer to the cliff edge, but always return to the main trail. (Use CAUTION if you take these side paths for more views of the gorge below.) At about 1.2 miles the trail begins a gradual descent.

**7.** Reach a trail intersection after another 0.2 mile. Turn right (east) toward the gorge. In another 0.1 mile reach the top of a small hill and another beautiful view of the gorge. Step to the edge for another view amidst the hemlocks.

This is the turnaround point for this hike. Beyond this point, the former trail is closed due to neglect and is barely used. You will return to Hemlock Creek Picnic Area by following the trail in reverse.

This chapter was reviewed and rewalked by Jim Sprague, statewide trail coordinator of the Buckeye Trail Association.

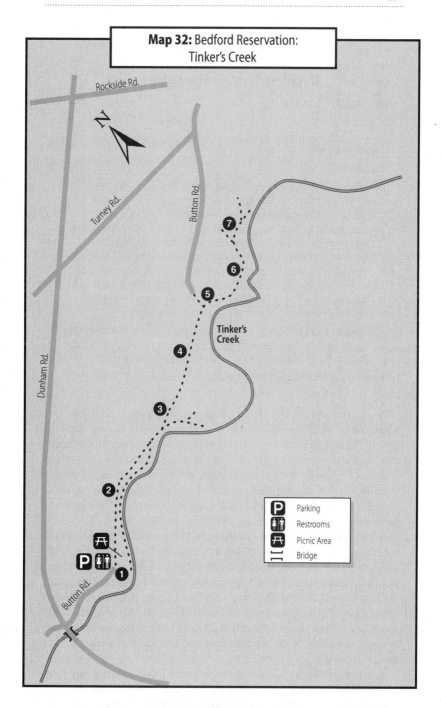

**Map 32:** Bedford Reservation:
Tinker's Creek

# 33 Rocky River Reservation
South

---

**Distance:** 4.2 miles

**Hiking time:** 2 hours

**Description:** This walk includes a variety of well-marked trails in the vicinity of Rocky River Nature Center. Be sure to stop at the center to pick up brochures and see the many interesting exhibits, which describe the forces of nature at work in the creation of the Rocky River valley. Nearby, the East and West Branches of the Rocky River join together at a point close to the bridge over Cedar Point Rd. The former channel of the West Branch once extended to the west and north of where the center now stands. The old channel still exists in pools and marshes below Fort Hill and west of the Wildlife Management Trail. There are steep hills and sets of stairways to climb on this hike.

**Directions:** I-480 to Exit 9 for Grayton Rd.; north on Grayton.; left (west) on Puritas Rd., down hill into Rocky River Reservation; left (south) on Valley Pkwy. to Rocky River Nature Ctr. (on right), just past Shephard Ln.

**Parking & restrooms:** At Rocky River Nature Center.

---

Long, narrow Rocky River Reservation is one of Cleveland Metroparks' 14 "Emerald Necklace" parklands surrounding the city. One of the system's largest parks, it forms the western part of the "necklace" and encompasses eight different municipalities. The reservation encloses the Rocky River and its valley on the river's twisting course from Bagley Rd. in Berea in the south to Detroit Rd. in Rocky River at Lake Erie in the north. (A hike for the northern section of Rocky River Reservation is featured in chapter 26.)

Rocky River Reservation has three golf courses, nine picnic areas, a nature center, a museum, a stables, a marina, and other facilities. A 13-mile paved All-Purpose Trail extends the full length of the park and parallels Rocky River Pkwy. Outstanding natural features of this park are its massive Chagrin Shale and Cleveland Shale cliffs that have been exposed by the cutting action of the Rocky River. At Tyler Field, the lower (and oldest) half of the cliff is Chagrin Shale, while the upper half is Cleveland Shale. In the blacker Cleveland Shale many fish fossils have been discovered (see appendix A).

Rocky River Nature Center, at 24000 Valley Pkwy., offers a variety of exhibits and information about the reservation's natural features. Park naturalists offer programs, guided hikes, and information about the his-

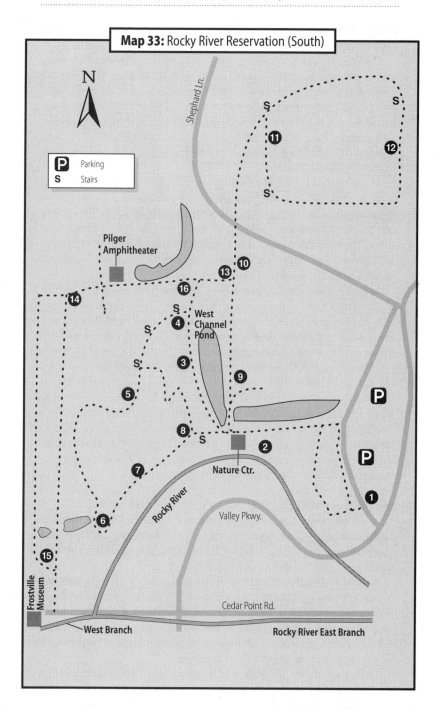

**Map 33:** Rocky River Reservation (South)

tory, geology, and topography of the Rocky River valley. For more information, call the nature center at 440-734-6660.

The valley of the Rocky River was settled early in Cleveland's history and is interpreted at the Frostville Museum, an affiliate of Cleveland Metroparks managed by the Olmsted Historical Society. Housed in several buildings, it provides the visitor with an interesting history of the people who settled the valley in the early 1800s. The museum is just off Cedar Point Rd., west of Valley Pkwy. It is open Sundays 2–5 p.m. Memorial Day through Labor Day, or by appointment. For more information, call 440-777-0059.

**1.** Start the walk on the paved Wildflower Garden Trail, just off the main parking lot. Taking the trail entrance nearest Valley Pkwy., you will follow the path alongside Rocky River, enjoying a nice view of the water. Then continue around to the Ron Hauser Wildflower Garden, a secluded enclave with benches where each flower and fern species is labeled. April and May are prime times to enjoy this garden.

**2.** Enter the nature center. There are descriptions of the various kinds of rocks found in the Rocky River Valley, from the 360-million-year-old Chagrin Shale near Lake Erie to the equally old Berea Sandstone near Bagley Rd. (see appendix A). Of special interest are fish fossils found in the Cleveland Shale layer. On display is a replica of a fierce armored fish found near here, *Dunkleosteus terelli*, the largest sea creature of its time.

The huge boulders scattered throughout the Rocky River gave rise to its name. They were deposited by glaciers that slid across all but the southeastern portion of Ohio. The Nebraskan glacier covered Ohio as far back as 1 million years ago, the Illinoran, 150,000 years ago. Extending the farthest south was the Wisconsin glacier of 70,000 years ago, a mile-thick ice sheet. By 12,000 years ago the last glacier had melted, leaving till and debris covering a vastly widened valley—where the reservation's playing fields and golf courses are now located.

From the center's outside deck there is a beautiful view of the river and Arrowhead Island just across the way. For the next part of this walk you may wish to pick up a Fort Hill map to follow interesting lettered signposts along the way.

**3.** Take the rear exit from the center to the large trail sign. Turn left to begin the walk on the red-blazed Fort Hill Trail (arrowhead symbol). Follow the path past a flight of steep steps on the left. On the right is West Channel Pond, part of the former course of the West Branch of the Rocky River. A variety of waterfowl are usually enjoying this pond. Go down the steps and across a short boardwalk.

The post lettered "B" indicates the obviously rusty water that has leached out of the shale. This mixture of mud and iron eventually hardens into a heavy rock called bog iron. It was once harvested by pioneers, who smelted it down and made tools from it.

The shale cliff at signpost "C" was formed by the West Branch of the Rocky River before it changed its course and joined the East Branch after severing a narrow isthmus between Fort Hill and Cedar Point Hill.

**4.** Bear left up the steps, avoiding the trail that goes off to the right, and remain on the main trail without taking any crossover trails. The path bends left and continues uphill on several sets of steps to make a 90-foot ascent.

**5.** At the top, turn right at the fork. (The trail to the left is a shortcut back to the nature center). Here at the top, evidence has been found that this site may have been occupied by Native Americans about 1,000 years ago.

Oaks and maples grace the woods of this beautiful hilltop. Stay on the main trail, avoiding a trail that goes off to the right and downhill. Continue along the path until you reach the triangular site of Fort Hill.

**6.** Across from Fort Hill is Cedar Point Hill, composed of Cleveland Shale. Between these two hills was the isthmus that over time was eroded away by both the East and West branches of the Rocky River, enabling the latter to join the East Branch's channel and abandon its old riverbed. Below, the Rocky River is formed by the merger of both branches just south of here.

**7.** Continue on the wide main trail along the fence without taking any of the crossover trails. Evidence of erosion is visible in many places—such as the exposed tree roots. Look far below to see the Rocky River, flowing northeast toward Lake Erie, and the nature center, with its deck overhanging the river.

**8.** To the left of the trail are small parallel, finger-like mounds that once were thought to be indicative of Native American earthworks (1000 to 1640 A.D.), but are now considered to be much older and built (perhaps) for native rituals.

Bear right past the juncture with the shortcut trail on the left to a set of 135 steep downward steps. Turn right at the bottom and follow the same trail back to the large trail sign where this walk began.

**9.** Turn left at the sign onto the blue-blazed West Channel Pond Trail, with its flying bird symbol. Follow this path across the manmade dam that impounds water from the old riverbed to form a pretty pond for waterfowl. Stay left past a connecting trail on the right that leads back to the parking area.

**10.** At the next trail intersection, leave the West Channel Pond Trail and stay to the right on the yellow-blazed Mt. Pleasant Trail. This enjoyable path will soon reach busy Shephard Ln.

CAUTION! Cross the road carefully as traffic moves fast on this curving street.

**11.** Follow the wide gravel path to a point where the trail begins to ascend the hill. Bear right at the steps to make a counterclockwise loop.

Another set of steps eases the climb to the summit where a bench invites a rest overlooking Rocky River valley.

**12.** Continue on this pleasant hilltop walk on a dirt pathway. The traffic you hear below on the right is on Valley Pkwy. Next descend the slope on wide steps. The freeway in the distance (on the right) is I-480. At the end of the loop, retrace your steps back across Shephard Lane to the intersection with the blue-blazed West Channel Pond Trail.

**13.** Turn right (west) at this intersection and follow the path past the pond on the right—another remnant of the old riverbed. A variety of waterfowl can often be observed here. Continue now on the brown-blazed Wildlife Management Trail. By remaining on this wide path and without taking any crossover trails, you will pass small Pilger Amphitheater, used for park programs, on the right.

**14.** Cross a service trail and turn left (south) at the next trail intersection, heading toward Frostville Museum and Cedar Point Rd. Keep to the main path (avoid taking any of the crossover trails) and note the marshes that represent more of the former riverbed of the West Branch of the Rocky River.

Admission to the Frostville Museum is free, but donations are accepted. It is open on Sundays only 2–5 p.m., Memorial Day through Labor Day. For more information call 440-777-0059.

Here view the Prechtel House, Briggs House, a one-room pioneer cabin, a barn, and a general store.

**15.** Before reaching Cedar Point Rd. and the museum, the Wildlife Management Trail turns to the right. Rows of apple trees along here attest to the former use of this fertile land for farming. The trail bends to the right again and passes more marshland with cattails growing in the water of the old channel. This trail is also used for cross-country skiing and is marked with a blue-blazed ski sign.

**16.** Reach the same trail juncture passed at point #14, with a bench marked "Generously donated by Fred R. Jones." Continue straight ahead past the service trail and Pilger Amphitheater; turn right at the blue-blazed West Channel Pond Trail. At this right turn there is another bench inscribed like the previous one. Follow the path past the pond on the left to return to the nature center.

This chapter reviewed and rewalked by Lynn Schreiber and Warren Davis.

# 34 North Chagrin Reservation
## Hemlock Trail

**Distance:** 6 miles

**Hiking time:** 2 ½ to 3 hours

**Description:** The first and last parts of this hike are on flat terrain; the middle portion goes over a moderately rolling section of the yellow Hemlock Trail.

**Directions:** I-271 to Exit 36 (Wilson Mills Rd.); east on Wilson Mills; left (north) on S.O.M. Center Rd./SR 91 ; right (east) on Sunset Ln. at park entrance; right on Buttermilk Falls Pkwy; parking lot for North Chagrin Nature Center on right.

**Parking & restrooms:** At North Chagrin Nature Center.

The North Chagrin Reservation of the Cleveland Metroparks is located just east of S.O.M. Center Rd. (SR 91) in both Lake and Cuyahoga counties. It is distinguished by deep ravines, a pretty waterfall, a modern nature center, Sunset Pond, and Sanctuary Marsh. There are many marked trails in North Chagrin, some steep and hilly, some flat, such as the paved All-Purpose Trail, and others moderately hilly over gently rolling terrain. There are five large picnic areas in North Chagrin with picnic tables and shelters, ball-playing fields, and restrooms. North Chagrin Nature Center is a large building staffed by park naturalists who offer information about park facilities, trail maps and brochures, educational programs and activities, and nature exhibits. EarthWords, a bookshop of Cleveland Metroparks, is located in the nature center and offers various nature publications and guidebooks.

**1.** Begin this hike at North Chagrin Nature Center. Circle the building to view Sunset Pond, an excellent habitat for plants and wildlife. Several interpretive signs warn visitors not to feed the ducks and geese. In August 1993, Cleveland Metroparks joined state, federal, and international conservation agencies in adopting a non-feeding policy to better protect the wildlife from overpopulation, disease, and non-migration.

**2.** Leave the nature center and take the wooden marsh deck walk past the nature education building across Sanctuary Marsh. Birds, ducks, and other wildlife can be seen in the marsh, as well as a variety of plants.

At the end of the wooden boardwalk, stay left (west) on the paved trail. On the right, enter the Wildlife Management Loop Trail, identified by an orange footprint sign. Follow this trail along a dirt path to a four-way juncture. Turn left (west).

Cross a wooden bridge over Buttermilk Stream, still following the orange Wildlife Management Loop Trail and now joining the Buttermilk Falls Loop Trail (blue trail markers). Cross the asphalt-paved All-Purpose Trail and continue on the dirt path. (0.4 miles)

**3.** Watch for a left turn at the next trail intersection to continue on the orange Wildlife Management Loop Trail (leaving the blue Buttermilk Falls Loop Trail, which continues straight ahead).

Along this mile-long orange loop, you will find pleasant woods and a soft, flat trail through Sunset Wildlife Preserve. The meadows provide homes for rabbits, songbirds, pheasants, deer, and other wildlife.

**4.** (1.0 mile) At the next intersection (the end of this loop), turn left to the paved All-Purpose Trail, which leads ahead to wooden-platform Buttermilk Falls Overlook. This pretty waterfall flows down over many layers of Cleveland Shale exposed by the stream's cutting action over thousands of years. Looking downstream from the overlook and to the right will reveal the ever-deepening ravine as the water flows eastward to the Chagrin River far below.

**5.** Turn back to the paved All-Purpose Trail and follow it north to Sunset Ln. (Stay to the right on the paved trail).

**6.** Cross Sunset Lane and cross Buttermilk Falls Pkwy. to the second Bridle Trail sign on the right. Enter the marked Bridle Trail and take the right fork to the yellow hiker-marked Hemlock Trail going north (left). This lovely path is parallel to, and high above, a very deep ravine on the right carved by Buttermilk Stream. (The bridle trail is on your left.)

CAUTION: For safety keep well away from the edge of the gorge, because erosion has created loose soil and gravel underfoot. Many large trees have fallen as a result of severe windstorms and some of the yellow hiker signs may be missing. Stay on the hiking trail, rather than the Bridle Trail.

**7.** The Hemlock Trail's gentle ups and downs provide relaxing and enjoyable hiking. At about 2.0 miles the trail begins to bend away from the ravine and crosses three small wooden bridges as it winds north. This is a quiet section of the trail where wildlife may occasionally be observed. Although there are several turns and intersections on this trail, stay with the yellow tree markers on the main trail and you will not get lost.

**8.** At about 2.5 miles cross a fourth wooden bridge over a stream with a shale waterfall and go up a small hill. At the top, bear right, following the yellow marker. (The trail to the left is the Bridle Trail, which leads out to Buttermilk Falls Pkwy. and is a shortcut back to the car if you wish to leave the hike at this point and return via the road). Cross

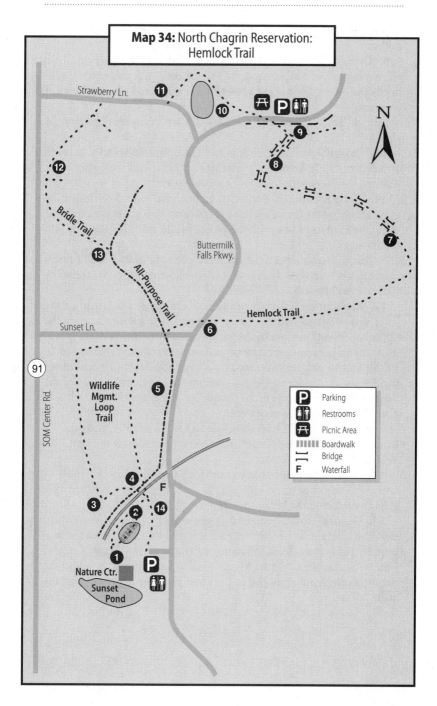

**Map 34:** North Chagrin Reservation:
Hemlock Trail

Strawberry Ln.

N

Bridle Trail

Buttermilk
Falls Pkwy.

All-Purpose Trail

Hemlock Trail

Sunset Ln.

91

SOM Center Rd.

Wildlife
Mgmt.
Loop
Trail

F

Nature Ctr.

Sunset
Pond

P   Parking
🚻   Restrooms
🎪   Picnic Area
▌▌▌▌▌   Boardwalk
⫝   Bridge
F   Waterfall

another small footbridge, noting the rust-colored shale in the stream bottom.

**9.** Cross a sixth footbridge with steps and note the layers of shale worn away by the cutting action of the stream. These shale layers were deposited on the floor of the ancient sea that covered Ohio millions of years ago.

Go uphill on steps cut into the hill, following yellow markers straight ahead.

**10.** Cross the All-Purpose Trail and Buttermilk Falls Pkwy. to reach Strawberry Picnic Area. (3.0 miles). At this picnic area are restrooms, a shelter house, a playing field, and a wildlife pond.

**11.** Circle Strawberry Pond in a counterclockwise direction using the trail behind the picnic shelter. At Strawberry Ln. turn right and walk along the road to just beyond the yellow Bridle Trail sign that you will see ahead.

At this sign turn left off the road and enter the Bridle Trail. Almost immediately turn right at an intersection following the gravel trail. The trail curves close to S.O.M. Center Rd.

**12.** At about the 4.0-mile point on this hike you will reach, on the left, a driveway that leads to a wide, unpaved open parking area. At the right (southwest) portion of the parking area there is a short trail leading to the Daughters of the American Revolution (D.A.R.) Memorial. In 1932 a bronze plaque was placed on a large boulder to commemorate the 200th anniversary of George Washington's birth in 1732. Here the Western Reserve Chapter of the Daughters of the American Revolution planted a large stand of pine trees.

Return to the Bridle Trail alongside S.O.M. Center Rd., and turn left to continue on the Bridle Trail as it enters the woods at the sign, "No Vehicles Beyond This Point."

**13.** Turn right at the intersection with the All-Purpose Trail (4.7 miles) and continue on this paved trail, past Sunset Ln. and Buttermilk Falls Overlook on the left.

**14.** Continue south on the All-Purpose Trail following blue Buttermilk Falls markers to the next intersection and turn right onto the Buttermilk Falls Loop Trail, following the signs to the North Chagrin Nature Center. This loop trail leads back to Sanctuary Marsh and the nature center. A trail just east of the pond goes directly to the parking area.

Buttermilk Falls

This chapter reviewed and rewalked by Jerry Berner, president of the Cleveland Hiking Club.

# 35 Mill Stream Run Reservation

**Distance:** 5 miles

**Hiking time:** 3 hours

**Description:** This trail hike travels over gently rolling terrain, crosses several streams, and reveals a chimney ruin and an abandoned gas well. In the description below, Mill Stream Run refers to the brook flowing from south to north through the reservation.

**Directions:** I-71 to Exit 231 (SR 82); east on Royalton Rd. (SR 82) for one-half mile south on Valley Pkwy. for a short distance; right on Royalview Ln. to picnic area.

**Parking & restrooms:** At Royalview Picnic Area.

Mill Stream Run Reservation is so named because at one time several fast-flowing streams on the property coursed downward about 170 feet to the East Branch of the Rocky River to power the gristmills and sawmills of the early settlers. Today, the streams have dwindled to just a trickle. Because of muddy trail conditions in the spring, it is best to take this hike in the summer or fall. It is also a fine trail for cross-country skiing.

**1.** Begin the hike at the Royalview Picnic Area and find the trail to the right of and behind the shelter. Follow the path northeast into the woods and to a ravine on the right overlooking Mill Stream Run.

**2.** The trail leads north high above Mill Stream Run (on the right) and makes a gradual descent to the creek bottom. (This section of the trail can be very wet and muddy in the spring or after a heavy rainfall.)

**3.** At about 1.0 mile cross Mill Stream Run and climb a short embankment, where the stream now appears on the left.

**4.** Walk another 0.1 mile and turn right (south) onto a wide hiking/skiing trail. Without making any turns, continue along it for about a mile as it gradually ascends to high land. This trail is not blazed but is wide and well traveled. It is also muddy in the spring or after a rainfall. It is necessary at one point to go slightly off the path to circumvent a large fallen beech tree.

**5.** Near the south end of this trail there will be a red hiker blaze affixed to a tree. Directly ahead in the woods is a tall brick chimney ruin. At this point you have hiked about 2.0 miles. The trail bends sharply left. Watch carefully for this southeast (left) turn.

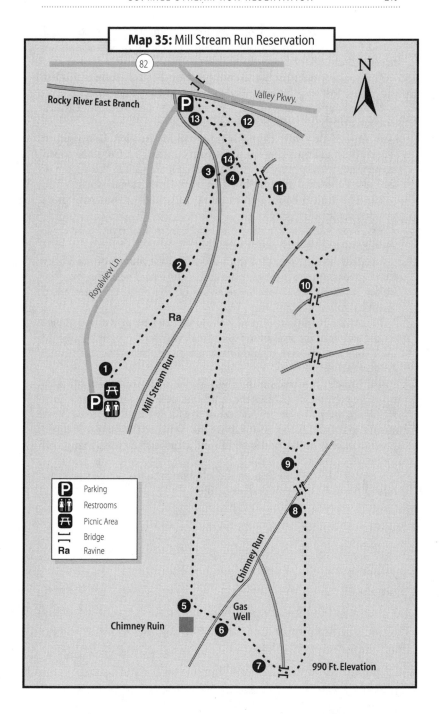

**Map 35:** Mill Stream Run Reservation

**6.** Heading east, cross Chimney Run stream and follow the trail ahead. There will be an active fenced-in gas well on the left. Continue straight ahead on the main trail.

**7.** Cross a small stream and continue east. The trail soon bends left (north). At 990 feet, this is the highest point in the reservation.

**8.** At about 2.8-miles on the left is a huge hollow oak tree. Cross a wooden bridge (constructed primarily for skiers).

**9.** Immediately after the bridge is a trail intersection. Bear right to stay on the main trail, keeping the stream on the right. Continue ahead as the trail bends left (north). Sometimes deer are seen in this stretch of the park. Follow red arrows posted on trees. Cross a small stream.

**10.** The trail follows gently rolling hills and crosses two more wooden bridges.

**11.** Bear left where a trail intersects from the right, and cross another wooden bridge over a stream.

**12.** Stay on the main trail until the wide East Branch of the Rocky River appears on the right near the end of the trail. The bridge over the Rocky River on Royalview Ln. is ahead on the right. You have hiked about 4.0 miles.

**13.** At the road turn left and walk to the parking area ahead. Reenter the woods at the trail sign. Pass a small trail on the right (south). At the Y intersection go right and follow red hiker blazes. The trail is on a gradual incline.

**14.** Watch for a trail on the right off the main trail about 0.3 mile from the parking lot. (This is the same spot described in note #4.) Turn right onto this path. The trail descends to Mill Stream Run, crosses it on stream rocks, and then goes up above the ravine on the same trail hiked previously. Stay on the wider main trail, avoiding side trails that go off to the left or right.

Keeping Mill Stream Run on the left, return to the picnic shelter by hiking north on the same trail as before.

# 36 North Chagrin Reservation
Buckeye Trail Loop

**Distance:** 5 ½ miles

**Hiking time:** 3 hours

**Description:** This hike is primarily on the Buckeye Trail. It includes two nature trail loops, the Overlook and Sylvan trails, and involves a road walk at the end. The hills are steep.

**Directions:** I-271 to Exit 36 (Wilson Mills Rd.); east on Wilson Mills; left (north) on Chagrin River Rd. (SR 174); right (east) on Rogers Rd.

**Parking & restrooms:** Park at Rogers Rd. Field parking lot. Portable restroom available in the parking lot.

There are many kinds of trails in North Chagrin Reservation, which is distinguished by its deep ravines, waterfalls, and large wildlife preserve. Among the facilities here are five large picnic areas, a winter sports area, a nature education building, and North Chagrin Nature Center. Information and maps can be obtained at the nature center. Trail hikes reveal a good portion of the natural beauty of this area. The following hike is mostly in the southern half of this reservation; the northern half is described in chapters 34 and 37. Both this and the hike in chapter 37 have steep hills to challenge hikers.

**1.** Rogers Road Field forms part of the east boundary of North Chagrin Reservation. The Buckeye Trail (BT) enters North Chagrin Reservation on Rogers Rd. You will see the blue blazes on telephone poles along Rogers Rd. going west. Follow them across Chagrin River Rd. and enter Ox Ln. (a paved road).

**2.** BT bends sharply left (south) on the bridle trail at 0.25 mile; at 0.5 mile it crosses the south arm of Ox Ln.

**3.** Bear right as the BT climbs steeply uphill through a mixed beech-maple-hemlock forest.

**4.** Reach the east end of the Overlook Trail on the right at 1.0 mile. This path is marked by an orange bird blaze. This trail offers an interesting nature walk through a mature forest. A portion of the trail is

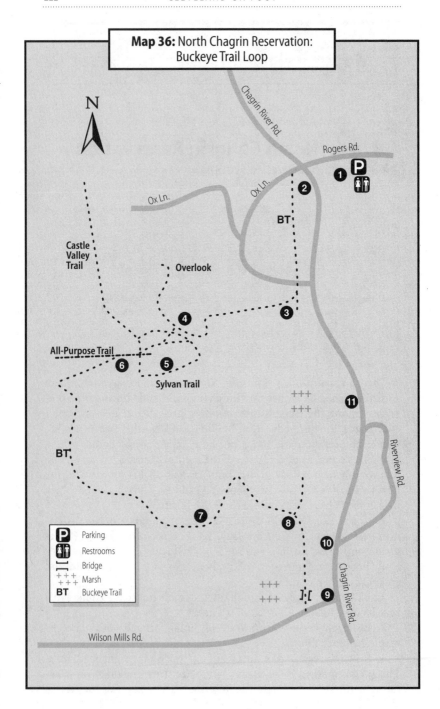

**Map 36:** North Chagrin Reservation:
Buckeye Trail Loop

N

closed for reforestation at a covered shelter overlooking the valley.
Return on the same path.

**5.** On the left side of the Buckeye Trail is the Sylvan Trail (yellow leaf
blaze). Again, if you have time, this 0.5-mile loop is worth exploring
through a beautiful hardwood forest. Continue on the main trail (BT)
going west. This area is dedicated to Arthur B. Williams, the Cleveland
Metroparks' first naturalist. Farther ahead on the right is a commemo-
rative plaque attached to a granite glacial boulder deposited here from
northern Canada about 12,000 years ago or earlier.

**6.** Cross the paved All-Purpose Trail. At 2.5 miles, the BT bends
sharply left (south) away from a parking area and left again. Continue
to follow the blue blazes of the BT.

**7.** The trail winds downhill past an unused paved road and reaches
a trail intersection at 3.4 miles.

**8.** Turn right, still on the BT, and exit the park onto Wilson Mills Rd.
(3.5 miles).

**9.** Turn left onto Wilson Mills Rd. and left again onto Chagrin River
Rd., leaving the BT at this point where it turns right and continues
south.

CAUTION: Chagrin River Rd. is an extremely busy, winding,
hilly road with very fast traffic. Please use considerable care
and walk facing traffic.

**10.** Cross Chagrin River Rd. Turn right onto Riverview Rd., following it as it loops close to the Chagrin River.

**11.** Reaching Chagrin River Rd. again, turn right (north) and continue along the left berm back to the Rogers Rd. parking area.

This chapter reviewed and rewalked by Jerry Berner, president of the Cleveland Hiking Club.

# 37 North Chagrin Reservation
### Buttermilk Falls and Squire's Castle Loop

**Distance:** 5.5 miles

**Hiking time:** 3 hours

**Description:** This loop hike displays the deep ravines for which North Chagrin Reservation is noted, pretty Buttermilk Falls, and Squire's Castle. The terrain is hilly.

**Directions:** I-271 to Exit 36 (Wilson Mills Rd.); east on Wilson Mills; left (north) on S.O.M. Center Rd.; right (east) on Sunset Ln. at park entrance; right on Buttermilk Falls Pkwy., follow the signs to North Chagrin Nature Center.

**Parking & restrooms:** At North Chagrin Nature Center.

This beautiful forest walk is located in popular North Chagrin Reservation, a park with many enjoyable trails. This loop hike goes through the northern part of the reservation and entails some hill climbing. Be sure to visit North Chagrin Nature Center, with its library, EarthWords book and gift shop, and many nature exhibits. Naturalists are on duty daily to assist the hiker with information, maps, and brochures.

**1.** From the North Chagrin Nature Center go north and cross the marsh on the boardwalk. Bear right (northwest) off the paved trail, and right again at the "Once a meadow . . ." interpretive sign. Turn right following the blue waterfall signs for the Buttermilk Falls Loop Trail. Stay on the dirt trail with the stream on your left going toward Buttermilk Falls Overlook.

**2.** Emerge onto Buttermilk Falls Pkwy. Nearby on the left is a wooden platform from which to view Buttermilk Falls (0.5 miles).

Turn left (north) onto Buttermilk Falls Pkwy. and cross the bridge over the deep ravine on right. Continue along the parkway a short distance and bear right onto the Hemlock Trail, identified by a yellow hiker sign.

**3.** The path enters the woods opposite the 15 mph sign and follows the edge of a deep ravine, with Buttermilk Stream far below on the right. Note the big, old hemlock trees here, an indication of the cool climate of this ravine. (A bridle trail is to your left, closer to Buttermilk Falls Pkwy.)

**4.** The yellow-marked Hemlock Trail provides many scenic views of

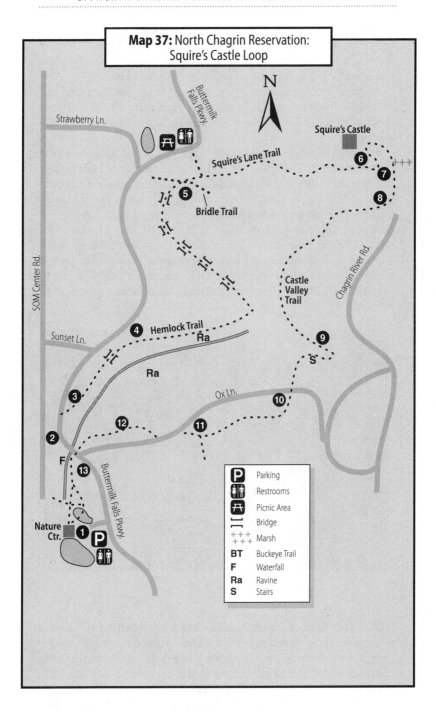

**Map 37:** North Chagrin Reservation:
Squire's Castle Loop

N

Buttermilk Falls Pkwy.

Strawberry Ln.

Squire's Castle

Squire's Lane Trail

6

7

8

5

Bridge Trail

SOM Center Rd.

Castle
Valley
Trail

Chagrin River Rd.

Sunset Ln.

4    Hemlock Trail
Ra

Ra

9

S

3

Ox Ln.

10

12    11

2

F

13

Buttermilk Falls Pkwy.

Nature
Ctr.    1    P

| P | Parking |
| Restrooms |
| Picnic Area |
| Bridge |
| + + + | Marsh |
| BT | Buckeye Trail |
| F | Waterfall |
| Ra | Ravine |
| S | Stairs |

one of the deepest ravines in the park. Cross a footbridge down in a gully. The ravine is on the right and the bridle trail on the left. The trail eventually leaves the ravine behind and crosses five more bridges as it winds north. (The fifth is a stair bridge over a small waterfall.)

**5.** Near Strawberry Picnic Area, cross the Bridle Trail and continue east where the Hemlock Trail soon ends. Turn sharply right and enter the blue-blazed (hiker) Squire's Lane Trail leading to Squire's Castle (2.0 miles).

**6.** Carefully follow the blue hiker signs, continuing on the trail as it curves downhill to Squire's Castle. This three-story stone building was constructed in the 1890s by Englishman F. B. Squire as the gatehouse to a planned country estate (that was never built). Squire and his family used the structure as a summer residence to enjoy the 829 acres of land he owned. The land was acquired in 1925 by Cleveland Metroparks for North Chagrin Reservation. Stripped of all its doors, fixtures, floors, windows, and furnishings, the building now stands as a shell of Squire's dream to build a grand riverfront estate. Restoration in 1997 removed graffiti and added a new roof, flooring, informative signs, and an asphalt path.

*Casey Batule/Cleveland Metroparks*

Squire's Castle

**7.** Just in front of the castle, turn right (east) down a dirt path to a stone water fountain and bear right to reach a trail on the right crossing over a stone bridge/dam. This is the Castle Valley Trail, marked with black-on-white castle signs affixed to the trees. Avoid any side trails going steeply down or uphill (3.0 miles).

**8.** Follow the Castle Valley Trail south as it parallels the Bridle Trail below, on the left. The path goes past Chestnut Shelter in the River Grove Reserved Picnic Area. Cross an open field past the sledding hill, basketball court, and cabins on the right. Reenter the trail and cross a stream on large boulders. The trail soon turns right, following the Castle Valley Trail blazes, with the stream on the right.

**9.** The trail crosses a stream on a wooden bridge, and then goes steeply uphill on railroad-tie steps (4.3 miles).

**10.** Cross Ox Ln. Rd. and continue on the Castle Valley Trail going west.

**11.** After 0.1 mile, bear right and emerge onto Ox Ln. again, leaving the Castle Valley Trail behind, going south.

**12.** Walk west (facing traffic) on Ox Ln. about 0.2 mile to the yellow Bridle Trail sign. Enter the bridle trail on the north (right) side of Ox Ln., going west (left) until it reaches Buttermilk Falls Parkway and the Scenic Overlook.

**13.** Return to North Chagrin Nature Center along the blue-blazed Buttermilk Falls Loop Trail.

*Casey Batule/Cleveland Metroparks*

North Chagrin Nature Center

This chapter reviewed and rewalked by Jerry Berner, president of the Cleveland Hiking Club.

# 38 South Chagrin Reservation
## Buckeye Trail Loop

**Distance:** 5 miles

**Walking time:** 2 ½ to 3 hours

**Description:** This strenuous, hilly hike takes a loop within the park, mostly on the blue-blazed Buckeye Trail. It offers a variety of terrain, from paths in deep woods, to a flat rim trail overlooking the Chagrin River, to the wide Bridle Trail that follows the contours of the hills.

**Directions:** I-271 to Exit 29 (Chagrin Blvd.); east on Chagrin; right (south) on S.O.M. Center Rd. (SR 91); left (east) on Miles Rd. for one mile; right at sign for Look About Lodge.

**Parking & restrooms:** At Look About Lodge parking area.

South Chagrin Reservation is located in Bentleyville, Solon, and Moreland Hills. This lovely, heavily wooded park was enlarged in the 1960s when Cleveland Metroparks purchased property north of Cannon Rd. formerly belonging to a Boy Scout camp. On the east side of South Chagrin Reservation is the Chagrin River, designated a national scenic river in 1979. Prominent in the sheer cliff walls of the river are layers of shale, deposited as silt and hardened into rock by the great inland sea covering this area 350–400 million years ago. At the river's west edge is Squaw Rock, faced with carvings by Chagrin Falls sculptor Henry Church.

The forest in this reservation has many beautiful maples, oaks, hemlocks, hickories, and beech trees, and abundant wildflowers. The park is used most frequently by numerous area horseback riders because of its long, wide trails. Part of the path on this walk is a designated bridle trail. Use caution when encountering horses by remaining quiet and still at the side of the trail until they've passed.

Look About Lodge, where this hike starts, was once operated by the Cleveland Natural Science Club, which still uses it for meetings. The lodge was built in 1938 by the Works Progress Administration to resemble Old Faithful Lodge in Yellowstone National Park. It contains stone fireplaces, chestnut furniture, and cast-iron sconces and chandeliers. It is now a unit of Cleveland Metroparks and has been renovated for use as an outdoor education center.

**1.** Start the hike northwest of the lodge. Soon follow the blue Buckeye Trail tree blazes going into the woods. Pass an old chimney and fire-

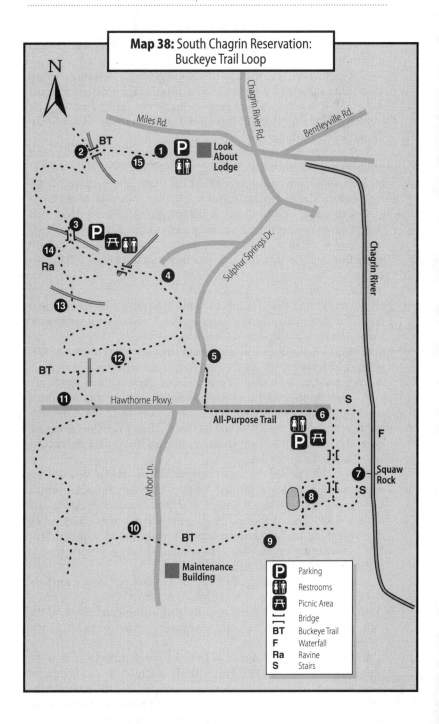

**Map 38:** South Chagrin Reservation: Buckeye Trail Loop

place structure. The trail follows a natural ravine above a quiet tributary of Sulphur Springs stream below on the left. Pass a trail on the right that returns to the lodge.

**2.** The Buckeye Trail soon turns left and gradually descends, crosses a wooden bridge, and joins the gravel Bridle Trail, bordered by an old stone wall (0.4 mile). (Use caution on the Bridle Trail.) This trail was formerly a carriage and vehicular road extending throughout South Chagrin Reservation.

**3.** Turn left (east) onto the Bridle Trail and follow it downhill until it reaches an old stone bridge. At the sign saying "No Horses in This Area," bear left, staying on the Buckeye Trail. (The Bridle Trail continues to the right and will be followed later on during the return portion of this hike.)

**4.** Cross the bridge to the Sulphur Springs Picnic Area, pass restrooms, and enter the picnic shelter. Follow the Buckeye Trail as it continues south of the shelter. Keep to the left at several intersections along this cool, moist trail. At a T-junction, turn left uphill, still following blue blazes.

**5.** Cross Sulphur Springs Rd. to the paved All-Purpose Trail and turn right (south). Pass a triangular traffic intersection on the right and cross Hawthorn Pkwy. Turn left (east) and follow the paved walkway to the Squaw Rock Picnic Area on the right (1.8 miles).

**6.** Squaw Rock Picnic Area has picnic tables, a small shelter, a playground, and restrooms. At the east end of the parking, a path leads down stone stairs to a beautiful waterfall and the scenic Chagrin River.

**7.** You may descend these steps (closed in winter) or continue ahead on the path past two bridges, and go on to note #8. Observe the very pretty waterfall on the left as you go down the steps. Follow along the riverside trail to Squaw Rock, carved in 1885 by Henry Church, a blacksmith and artist from Chagrin Falls.

The significance of the figures carved on the glacial boulder has never been adequately explained. There is a Native American woman surrounded by a quiver of arrows, a serpent, panther, skeleton, and eagle, a shield, and a papoose. On the opposite side are carvings of an incomplete log cabin and of the Capitol building in Washington, D.C. The Berea Sandstone rock has been reinforced with a concrete base to prevent erosion. (See note #10, ch. 29.)

Ascend the stone steps at the south end of this trail. At the top turn right, then left. (Ahead is a bridge, but do not cross it.)

**8.** At the next intersection note the pretty woodland pond on the right, which often attracts playful waterfowl. Turn left here (2.0 miles).

The trail soon bears right.

**9.** Follow an old gravel road westward through mixed woods, passing picnic tables on the left. This is the location of the old Boy Scout camp on land that Cleveland Metroparks added to South Chagrin in the 1960s. Follow the woods road until you reach the service area for the park. There are several maintenance buildings on the left.

**10.** Cross Arbor Lane and again enter the Bridle Trail, still following the blue Buckeye Trail blazes (2.6 miles). At a trail intersection bear right, staying on the Bridle/Buckeye Trail.

**11.** At about 3.1 miles you will reach Hawthorn Pkwy. again. Cross it to continue on the Bridle/Buckeye Trail going north. When you reach a wide trail intersection, turn right (east), still following the Bridle Trail, and leave the Buckeye Trail behind as it continues west.

**12.** Cross a stream on rocks and meet another major trail intersection. Here turn left going uphill (northwest) on the wide gravel trail. This trail winds up and down through beautiful, deep, quiet woods. Soon pass an old stone wall on the left and follow the trail around a U-turn.

**13.** At about 3.7 miles you will cross a stream and go uphill. On the right is another old stone wall, built many years ago when vehicles traveled on this carriage road through the park. Reach another trail intersection and keep to the left. A deep ravine appears on the left.

**14.** Cross the bridge (4.1 miles). You are now at the same point described in note #3, and will follow the blue-blazed Buckeye Trail in reverse. The road goes steeply uphill on yet another ridge. Turn right on the Buckeye Trail when it leaves the road at the foot of a slope and crosses the same stream described in note #2 (4.6 miles).

**15.** Retrace your steps along the Buckeye Trail until it reaches Look About Lodge and the parking area.

Look About Lodge

*Casey Batule/Cleveland Metroparks*

This chapter reviewed and rewalked by Art Harvey.

# 39 Bedford Reservation
## Buckeye Trail from Egbert

**Distance:** 5 ½ miles

**Hiking time:** 2 ½ to 3 hours

**Description:** This hike on the Buckeye Trail will take you to Tinker's Creek Gorge, a national natural landmark. The view from the scenic overlook is particularly impressive during fall foliage season. The terrain undulates up and down small hills.

**Directions:** I-271 to Exit 23 (Broadway Ave./SR 14); north on Broadway; left on Union; right (west) on Egbert Rd. to Cleveland Metroparks entrance on Gorge Pkwy. OR, I-480 to Exit 23 (Broadway Ave. & SR 14/Bedford Frwy.); south on Broadway; right (west) on Union St.; right (west) on Egbert Rd. to Cleveland Metroparks entrance on Gorge Pkwy.

**Parking & restrooms:** At Egbert Picnic Area, on the north side of Gorge Pkwy. just after park entrance.

Bedford Reservation encompasses 2,154 acres of land through which Tinker's Creek flows. The creek has cut a deep and spectacular gorge through the park, which has been designated a national natural landmark. Numerous trees, flowers, ferns—and often deer—provide enjoyment to hikers in Bedford.

NOTE: Watch for sharp turns on the Buckeye Trail. The blue BT blazes may be somewhat far apart but generally follow the Bridle Trail.

**1.** Start the hike from the Egbert Picnic Area. Pick up the Buckeye Trail (BT) behind and to the left of the restrooms. Follow it along the fence and down the ridge overlooking the beautiful Tinker's Creek gorge.

**2.** At 0.2 mile, leave the main trail, going onto the BT (not clearly marked). Turn sharply left, and join the gravel Bridle Trail.

**3.** Turn right at the fence. The BT crosses the paved All-Purpose Trail and Gorge Pkwy. at 0.6 mile and passes Shawnee Hills Golf Course on the left (south).

**4.** At 1.0 mile the BT recrosses Gorge Pkwy. and enters the woods heading west. Stay on the main trail, ignoring the old BT branching off to the right.

**5.** Cross a paved road leading to the Lost Meadows Picnic Area at 1.3

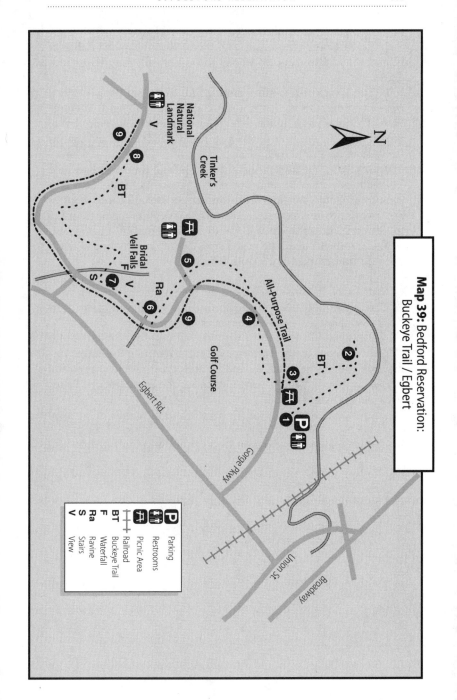

**Map 39:** Bedford Reservation:
Buckeye Trail / Egbert

miles. Soon the trail parallels a deep ravine on the right.

**6.** Reach Gorge Pkwy. again (1.6 miles), and follow the trail as it bears right and reenters the woods above a small stream, Deer Lick Creek.

**7.** The BT crosses another creek at 2.0 miles on a small arched wooden bridge. On the left is a set of stairs descending from Gorge Pkwy. Follow the sign on the right to the overlook for a scenic view of Bridal Veil Falls, a favorite photo spot. The BT leads uphill and continues west on the Bridle Trail.

**8.** Reach Gorge Pkwy. (again at 3.0 miles) and the scenic overlook. This national natural landmark presents a panoramic view of deep Tinker's Creek Gorge, breathtaking in any season. Tinker's Creek drops 90 feet over its two-mile course, and its gorge has depths ranging from 140 to 190 feet as the creek wends its way to the Cuyahoga River to the west.

**9.** Leave the BT at this point and cross Gorge Pkwy. to the paved All-Purpose Trail, marked as the Walk/Bike Trail.

CAUTION: Be careful to walk to the right on the paved trail. This is part of the 20-mile Bedford-to-Akron Bike and Hike Trail, and fast bicyclists may be traveling on it.

Turn left (east) on the All-Purpose Trail to return to the Egbert Picnic Area, passing the Bridal Veil Falls parking area, traversing a graceful steel-arched bridge, and passing the road to the Lost Meadows Picnic Area and the fitness trail.

This chapter reviewed and rewalked by Art Harvey with the assistance of Judy Biscan.

# 40 Bedford Reservation
## Buckeye Trail from Sagamore Grove

**Distance:** 6 miles

**Hiking time:** 3 hours

**Description:** The trail is almost entirely in beautiful, quiet woods on the blue-blazed Buckeye Trail. The terrain is moderately hilly.

**Directions:** I-77 to Exit 155 (Rockside Rd.); east on Rockside; south on Canal Rd.; left (east) on Sagamore to the Sagamore Grove Picnic Area, on left.

**Parking & restrooms:** At Sagamore Grove Picnic Area.

This Buckeye Trail hike offers another route to Bedford Reservation's scenic overlook, and a grand view of Tinker's Creek Gorge, a national natural landmark. It also affords an opportunity to see additional areas of Bedford Reservation and the Cuyahoga Valley National Recreation Area. The trail begins with a steep climb, then follows a flat plateau above scenic Sagamore Creek valley, gradually climbing until it reaches Egbert Rd., Overlook Ln., and Tinker's Creek Gorge.

**1.** From the Sagamore Grove Picnic Area walk east on a footpath just outside the guardrail to the Buckeye Trail (blazed with two-by-six-inch blue tree markers).

CAUTION: Watch carefully for fast traffic on this short stretch of very narrow, winding road.

Very soon pick up the Buckeye Trail (BT) blue tree blazes on the left side of the road. At the point where the trail turns sharply into the woods just before the road goes uphill, the tree blaze may be obscured by foliage.

**2.** Climb steeply to the top of the plateau. At about 0.7 mile on the left is a very pretty waterfall with multiple rock layers exposed. This stream flows down to Sagamore Creek far below. It can be seen only if there is no foliage obscuring the view.

**3.** At 1.4 miles is another, smaller waterfall and a deep ravine on the left. These waterfalls freeze in the winter and are most interesting when they accumulate blue ice. At that time, the intervening ravine also displays a frozen waterfall.

**4.** Reach a set of steep stone steps that lead up to an old railroad bed,

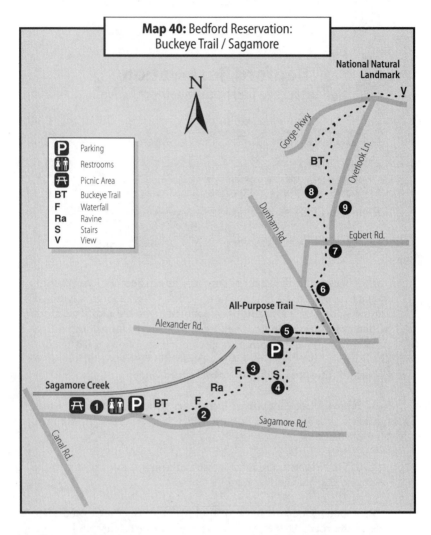

**Map 40:** Bedford Reservation: Buckeye Trail / Sagamore

which is part of the 20-mile Bedford to Akron Bike and Hike Trail. Turn left (north) at the top of the steps and follow this flat trail to Alexander Rd. and a parking area on the left.

**5.** At 1.7 miles, cross Alexander Rd. to the paved All-Purpose Trail and turn right (east). After 300 feet, leave the All-Purpose Trail and turn left into the woods, now following the BT. Cross Dunham Rd. and bear left (northwest) joining the All-Purpose Trail.

**6.** At 2.5 miles, just before Egbert Rd., follow the BT as it makes a sharp right turn (east) on a wide trail leading to Egbert Rd. and Overlook Ln.

**7.** Cross Egbert Rd. Continue north on BT parallel to Overlook Ln.

**8.** Follow the BT blue blazes past an abandoned quarry to Gorge Pkwy. and the national natural landmark, Tinker's Creek Gorge (3 miles). The landmark is about 500 feet east of Overlook Ln. and is not easily visible from here. Take the trail parallel to Gorge Pkwy. to find the gorge overlook platform and parking area. A portable restroom is located here.

**9.** Return south along Overlook Ln. to Egbert Rd. and enter the BT at the same point described in note #7. Follow the BT in reverse past Dunham Rd. and Alexander Rd., then take the Bike and Hike trail south to the stone steps. Descend the stairs and retrace the BT along the top of the ravine above Sagamore Creek to Sagamore Rd. and back to the Sagamore Grove Picnic Area.

This lovely hike provides different views when walking in each direction. Optionally, you may start at the national natural landmark and descend to Sagamore Grove, then retrace your steps upward.

This chapter reviewed and rewalked by Jim Sprague, statewide trail coordinator of the Buckeye Trail Association.

# 41 Hinckley Reservation
## Whipp's Ledges

**Distance:** 5 miles

**Hiking time:** 2 ½ hours

**Description:** This hike, partly on the blue-blazed Buckeye Trail along Hinckley lake, goes to Whipp's Ledges and returns along the east side of the lake to complete a loop. There is one steep hill to climb.

**Directions:** I-271 to Exit 3 (Ridge Rd./SR 94); north on Ridge Rd; right (east) on Hinckley Hills Rd.; right (east) on Bellus Rd.; right (south) on West Dr., entering reservation, for ¾ mile to sign for Johnson's Picnic Area.

**Parking & restrooms:** At Johnson's Picnic Area go to the second (farthest) parking area where the road dead-ends.

Hinckley Reservation surrounds 90-acre Hinckley Lake, into which the East Branch of the Rocky River flows. The river was dammed in 1926 to form this beautiful lake. Hinckley is the only reservation of Cleveland Metroparks completely outside Cuyahoga County. In it are Whipp's Ledges and Worden's Ledges, both formed many millions of years ago.

The Worden Heritage Homestead, managed by the Hinckley Historical Society, is on the north side of Ledge Rd. between State and Kellogg Rds. Here you will find interesting information about the history of Hinckley Reservation. Noble Stuart, the son-in-law of Hiram Worden, after whom the ledges were named, once lived in the homestead. Stone carvings at Worden's Ledges were made by Stuart sometime in the 1940s. They can be seen by taking a trail from the barn located west of the homestead. A map showing how to get to the carvings, a 10-minute walk, is posted on the homestead's garage (see ch. 28).

Hinckley is well known for its celebration of the annual return of the buzzards, or turkey vultures, from the southern U.S. around the middle of March. They find the open fields, rocky ledges and cliffs, and abundant food ideal for nesting and egg-laying. In the spring and summer the buzzards can be seen soaring on the rising thermals created by the open fields.

**1.** Start the hike at Johnson's Picnic Area by finding the blue-blazed Buckeye Trail (BT) heading north on the uphill gravel path just beyond the last parking area. The blue blazes are on the tall trees. The creek will

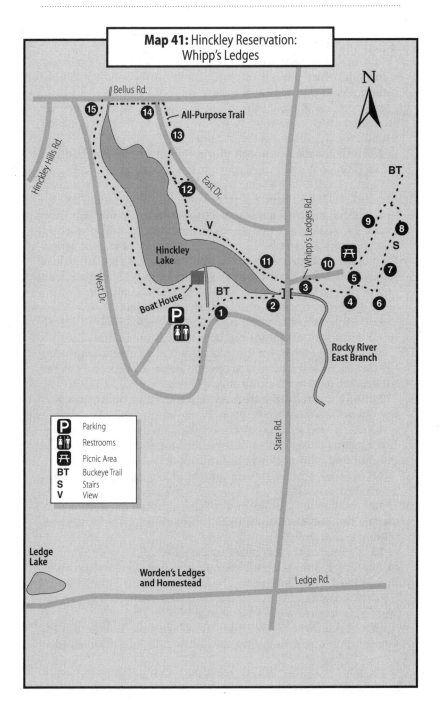

**Map 41:** Hinckley Reservation: Whipp's Ledges

N

Bellus Rd.

All-Purpose Trail

East Dr.

Hinckley Hills Rd.

BT

Whipp's Ledges Rd.

V

Hinckley Lake

West Dr.

Boat House

BT

Rocky River East Branch

State Rd.

S

| | Parking |
|---|---|
| | Restrooms |
| | Picnic Area |
| BT | Buckeye Trail |
| S | Stairs |
| V | View |

Ledge Lake

Worden's Ledges and Homestead

Ledge Rd.

be below on the left. Nice outlooks over Hinckley Lake come into view along this route.

**2.** Turn left on State Rd. at about 0.7 mile and continue on the road across the East Branch of the Rocky River on the sturdy pedestrian/bicycle bridge.

**3.** Cross State Rd. and enter Whipp's Ledges Rd. leading to a picnic area. Immediately to the right the BT turns east from the road alongside a small creek, a tributary of the East Branch.

**4.** The BT continues through a wet area, past the East Branch of the Rocky River on the right, then goes into the woods and uphill.

**5.** At 1.2 miles reach a stone restroom at Whipp's Ledges picnic and parking area. The BT turns right then continues straight ahead uphill.

**6.** Still following BT blue blazes, start a very steep uphill climb to the foot of the moss-covered ledges, which are about 320 million years old (see appendix A). The BT turns left directly under the pockmarked Sharon Conglomerate sandstone. These magnificent rock formations rise about 350 feet above the level of Hinckley Lake. The small shiny quartz pebbles that you see embedded in the sandstone once rolled along the shores of a great inland sea that covered Ohio.

**7.** Hike past small caves and huge boulders, still following BT blazes. At 1.5 miles climb a flight of stone steps between two ledges.

**8.** Hike along the top of the ledges to a trail intersection. Turn left (leaving the BT at this point) and carefully descend a rocky path on the left between the two halves of a large split boulder.

**9.** Reach the trail under the ledges again and turn right onto a path that descends to the Whipp's Ledges Picnic Area (2.0 miles).

**10.** At the picnic area walk down Whipp's Ledges Rd. to State Rd. Cross the road and, without crossing the bridge again, enter the All-Purpose Trail going north alongside Hinckley Lake.

**11.** Fine views of the lake are enjoyed all along this pleasant, well-maintained walkway.

**12.** At 3.5 miles, continue straight ahead past an intersection with another trail joining from the right. Follow the path as it soon curves upward to East Dr.

**13.** Cross East Dr. continuing on the paved All-Purpose Trail, following it left (north) as it leads along the road past Hinckley Lake Bathhouse to Bellus Rd. (3.75 miles).

**14.** Recross East Dr. to continue on the All-Purpose Trail past the swimming area and spillway on the left.

**15.** After a short distance, leave the All-Purpose Trail to turn left (south) at the top of the spillway and follow a dirt trail downhill adjacent to the lake.

Continue along this lakeside trail to the boat launch area and return to Johnson's Picnic Area.

Casey Batule/Cleveland Metroparks

Whipp's Ledges

# 42 Virginia Kendall Park
## Ritchie Ledges and Pine Grove Loop

**Distance:** 4 miles

**Hiking time:** 2 hours

**Description:** Ritchie Ledges and Sharon Conglomerate rock will be seen on this hike, as well as beautiful hemlock and pine trees. The trail slopes down to Ritchie Ledges (the hike is adjacent to them), then farther downhill to Pine Grove. Here the land slopes gently up and down, and you eventually descend a set of steps and steeply ascend another set. You will follow under Ritchie Ledges again, then continue uphill to an overlook before returning to the parking area.

**Directions:** I-271 or I-71 to exit for SR 303; east on SR 303 to Peninsula; south on Akron-Peninsula Rd.; left (east) on Truxell Rd. at sign for Camp Manatoc; continue past Kendall Lake and Octagon Picnic Area to sign for Ledges, on left. Left (north) onto this road, to large picnic area with shelter and playing fields.

**Parking and restrooms:** At Ledges Shelter.

Virginia Kendall Park, one of the first recreational sites to operate within Cuyahoga Valley National Recreation Area (CVNRA), contains the spectacular Ritchie Ledges and Happy Days Visitor Center, operated by the National Park Service. The center was originally built by the Civilian Conservation Corps in the 1930s as a camp for inner-city children. Trail maps and information are available at the center from park rangers, and publications are for sale. It is open daily from 9 a. m. to 5 p. m.; for more information call 330-650-4636.

This section of the park features a set of geologically interesting formations—Ritchie Ledges—that are similar to other ledges in Northeast Ohio. They are composed of ancient Sharon Conglomerate sandstone rock. Millions of years ago this area was covered by a large shallow sea. The conglomerate rock took shape when fast-moving streams from the north and east carried sediment to the inland sea. It was compacted into a cement of sand and small quartz pebbles. You can see these small pebbles, which are round and smooth from the action of the ancient sea, as you walk by the ledges. Some of these pebbles have fallen to the ground, leaving pock-marked rock. These erosion-resistant cliffs, shaped by the action of ancient rivers, were later affected by the scraping action of the glaciers that covered Ohio (see appendix A).

At an elevation of 1,050 feet, the ledges continue to wear away very

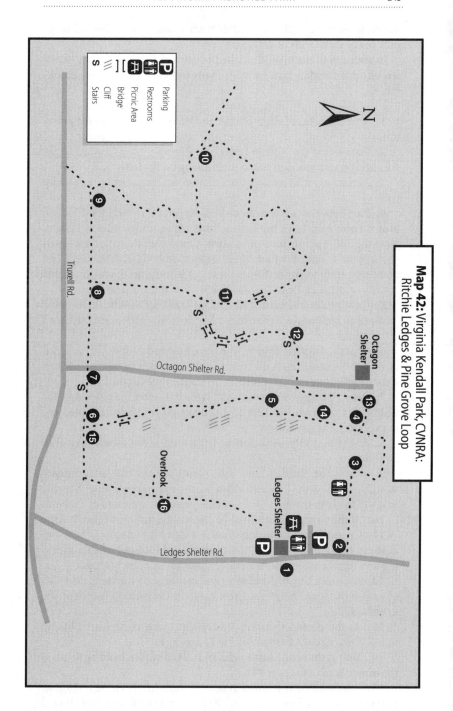

**Map 42:** Virginia Kendall Park, CVNRA: Ritchie Ledges & Pine Grove Loop

slowly. Ice Box Cave (ch. 43) resulted from a fissure that occurred in the rock many thousands of years ago.

In addition to the hikes described below and in the following chapter, Virginia Kendall Park contains many more trails for hiking enjoyment.

**1.** Start the hike at Ledges Shelter and walk north on the wide gravel trail.

**2.** Turn left at the Ritchie Ledges display sign, going toward Octagon. Walk past a wooden restroom building on the left.

**3.** At the next intersection, turn right to descend over a steep rocky trail.

**4.** Pass between two enormous boulders and turn left (south) at the brown trash can. Here the path follows along under Ritchie Ledges. Note the 320-million-year-old Sharon Conglomerate rock mentioned above, with its smooth quartz "lucky stones" embedded in the cliffs. The powdery, sandy soil underfoot is a result of many years of erosion of this conglomerate rock that once was beach sand of the inland sea.

**5.** Continue on the main trail (Ledges Trail), still hiking under spectacular Ritchie Ledges, and disregarding several smaller side trails that go up or down.

**6.** Cross a wooden bridge with a railing and follow the ups and downs of the trail. Reach the top of a set of wooden bar steps and turn right (west). Descend these steps, now on the Pine Grove Trail.

**7.** Reach Octagon Shelter Rd. and cross it to enter the pine grove for which the trail is named. This cool, serene, red pine forest is a pleasure to experience in any season.

**8.** At the first intersection, bear left (west) at the Pine Grove Trail loop sign.

**9.** Where the Kendall Lake sign points toward the left, continue straight ahead on the Pine Grove Trail. The path makes several "S" turns as it winds north through the forest, following the contours of the land.

**10.** At the Camp Butler/Camp Manatoc sign, turn right (northeast).

**11.** Cross a small footbridge. Reach a sign for Octagon Ledges and descend the steps on the left. Continue toward Octagon Shelter, crossing and recrossing Ritchie Run three times on wooden bridges.

**12.** Ascend a long flight of steps and continue on the trail to eventually reach Octagon Shelter Rd. Cross the road and continue north on the gravel trail.

**13.** At the roofed Octagon Shelter sign, turn right (east), hiking uphill. Return to the base of Ritchie Ledges again.

**14.** Bear right on the same main trail hiked earlier, heading south at the brown trash can (note #4).

**15.** Reach the same point as in note #6. Turn left this time and follow the trail east toward the overlook. The path curves left, winding upward to the top of the ledges. Turn left to the Ledges Overlook for a long-distance view of the hills across Cuyahoga Valley.

**16.** A the top of the overlook, follow the trail north, skirting the edge of the woods. On the right is the ball field and Ledges Shelter. Cross the field to the parking area.

Ritchie Ledges

This chapter reviewed and rewalked by Shirley Pashall with the assistance of Saul Isler and the author.

# 43 Virginia Kendall Park
## Ice Box Cave and Boston Run Trail

**Distance:** 5 miles

**Hiking time:** 3 hours

**Description:** This hike on wooded trails entails climbing several hills and passes Happy Days Visitor Center.

**Directions:** I-271 or I-71 to exit for SR 303; east on SR 303 to Peninsula; south on Akron-Peninsula Rd.; left (east) on Truxell Rd. at sign for Camp Manatoc; continue past Kendall Lake and Octagon Picnic Area to sign for Ledges, on left. Left (north) onto this road, to large picnic area with shelter and playing fields.

**Parking & restrooms:** Available at the shelter.

Virginia Kendall Park is a beautiful park with rolling hills, ledges, a lake, cross-country and hiking trails, and the Happy Days Visitor Center. The center, located on SR 303 east of the town of Peninsula and west of SR 8, is open daily from 8 a.m. to 5 p.m., but closed Monday and Tuesday, November through March. Many interesting history and nature programs are held at the visitor center, which offers an abundance of publications, maps, and other helpful information. Park naturalists staff the center. For more information call 330-650-4636 or 800-257-9477.

**1.** From Ledges Picnic Area walk north on the old roadbed past woodland picnic tables on the right. Turn right (east) onto Ledges Trail.

**2.** Turn right at the next trail intersection, now following Ledges Trail toward Ice Box Cave. The trail curves south along the top of the ledges and descends. At an intersection, turn north along the base of the ancient ledges.

**3.** Ice Box Cave is on the left. It is so called because it maintains its cool temperature during the hot summer months within the depths of the overhanging rock. The trail crosses a wooden bridge and climbs a short flight of steps under the Sharon Conglomerate rocks before reaching a Y intersection (see ch. 42).

**4.** After passing a flight of stone steps on the left (built by the Civilian Conservation Corps in the 1930s), bear right at this Y intersection and follow signs to Happy Days Visitor Center.

**5.** The trail descends and goes eastward, crossing a bridge over

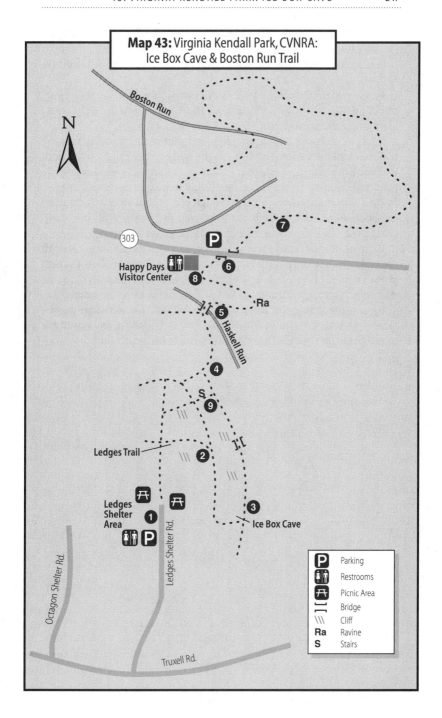

**Map 43:** Virginia Kendall Park, CVNRA: Ice Box Cave & Boston Run Trail

N

Boston Run

303

P

Happy Days
Visitor Center

7

6

8

Ra

5

Haskell Run

4

S

9

Ledges Trail

2

Ledges
Shelter
Area

1

Ledges Shelter Rd.

3    Ice Box Cave

Octagon Shelter Rd.

Truxell Rd.

| | |
|---|---|
| P | Parking |
| | Restrooms |
| | Picnic Area |
| | Bridge |
| \\\ | Cliff |
| Ra | Ravine |
| S | Stairs |

Haskell Run. Ascend the hill and turn left at Haskell Run Trail to Happy Days Visitor Center on a curved and numbered nature trail. Be sure to stop in at the center—its exhibits, trail information, and bookstore are well worth a visit.

**6.** Go east on the visitor center's driveway to a pedestrian underpass under SR 303 to a large parking area. There is a sign to the right (east) identifying the Boston Run Trail, a 3.5-mile loop.

**7.** The entrance to this loop trail is at the far end of the field. Pass the trail exit sign on the left. Continue to the trail entrance sign on the right and enter the wide trail, which traverses low rolling hills and is a favorite for cross-country skiers. It can be muddy in places, because it crosses Boston Run creek several times (though recent trail reconstruction by members of the Sierra Club has improved the path). With one steep climb at the end, this pleasant loop will take about 1¼ hours.

**8.** Back at the Happy Days parking area, retrace your steps through the pedestrian underpass to Happy Days Visitor Center. Follow the sign posted here for Haskell Run Trail and Ledges Shelter. Stay on the same trail, which returns you across Haskell Run and back to the ledges.

**9.** After reaching the ledges, take the flight of stone steps on the right, which were passed earlier (see note #4). Climb these steps to the top of the ledges, turn left, and follow signs to Ledges Shelter.

This chapter reviewed and rewalked by Shirley Pashall.

# 44 Punderson State Park
## Stump Lake

**Distance:** 4.2 miles

**Hiking time:** 2 hours

**Description:** This hike is over rolling terrain, primarily on trails with views of three lakes.

**Directions:** I-271 to Exit 29 (Chagrin Blvd./SR 87); east on SR 87 past town of Newbury to Punderson State Park entrance, on right. Follow park road signs to lodge.

**Parking & restrooms:** Parking lot adjacent to lodge, restrooms inside.

Punderson State Park encompasses 996 acres and includes several glacier-formed lakes and a variety of recreational facilities and accommodations, including a golf course, trails, a small beach, camping area, cabins, tennis courts, a pool, and an 1948 manor house with a dining room. The park is open all year, and in winter it maintains a winter sports chalet for skiing, sledding, tobogganing, skating, and snowmobile riding. This hike will take you on trails to three of the park's lakes. The trails can be enjoyed in any season except in deep winter, when snowmobiles frequently use them. For more information, please call the park office (440-564-2279) or the Manor House (440-564-9144).

**1.** Start the hike by descending the slope to the left (north) behind the lodge. There is a nice view of Punderson Lake ahead. About 12,000 years ago, when the last glacier retreated from Ohio, the melting of the massive ice sheet left depressions called kettles. This spring-fed lake and the others in the park are the result of this kettle-forming process. Punderson Lake, at 90 acres, is the largest glacial lake in Ohio. The trail begins at the Nature Trail sign and leads downhill on a wide path.

**2.** Keeping Punderson Lake on your right (east), continue north along this trail until at 0.3 miles you reach a Nature Trail sign that points to the left (Iroquois Trail). Continue straight past this sign to the sandy beach.

**3.** Walk north across the beach and reenter the trail at the far end, where a sign indicates the concession stand ahead.

**4.** Reach the boat launch/concession stand at 0.8 miles. Walk through the parking area and turn right onto the paved park road leading to the camping area.

**5.** On the left, about 0.2 miles farther, is the entrance to the snow-mobile trail (Erie Trail).

**6.** Turn left to enter the snowmobile trail and very soon reach a fork. Bear left downhill a short distance to see the small, deep, glacier-formed Emerald Lake. (A tree blocks the path at one point.) The cars across the way are on SR 87. Retrace your steps on this short side trail and return to the main trail. Turn left (east) and continue along it.

**7.** At the next trail intersection (1.1 miles) continue straight on the main trail, going past a sign for a snowmobile area and campground to the right. Still on the Erie Trail, the path continues behind the restrooms, although the trail is obscured by this building.

**8.** When the trail reaches a small marsh on the right, bear left onto a wide woods road. At a trail intersection, continue straight ahead. Soon a nice view of Stump Lake appears on the right. The reason for its name is evident from the numerous tree stumps peeking above the water at its south end.

**9.** Keeping Stump Lake on the right, continue close to the shoreline toward SR 87. The trail squeezes between the highway and lake at its north end and continues around to the east shore of Stump Lake.

**10.** At 2.0 miles the trail veers away from the lake. At the next trail intersection, stay right, going toward the lake and hugging the shoreline.

**11.** The trail widens and becomes a more heavily trodden path as it approaches the campground area. Nice views of the lake appear, and waterfowl such as the great blue heron are often seen feeding here.

**12.** The trail ends at a campground road where a sign again identi-fies the path as the Erie Trail (2.8 miles). Cross the road and walk past the check-in station to view Punderson Lake ahead. The lodge and sandy beach can be seen across the water.

**13.** Take the park road north to the boat launch/concession area and return along the trail hiked earlier; continue alongside the lake past the beach, now on your left.

**14.** Just past the beach reach the Nature Trail intersection at 3.8 miles. Instead of returning along Punderson Lake as before, turn right on the gravel Nature Trail. Follow this loop trail uphill past picnic tables and a parking area on the right. Continue on this trail (Nature/Iroquois Trail) as it returns to the lodge parking area.

This chapter reviewed and rewalked by Patricia Spoth.

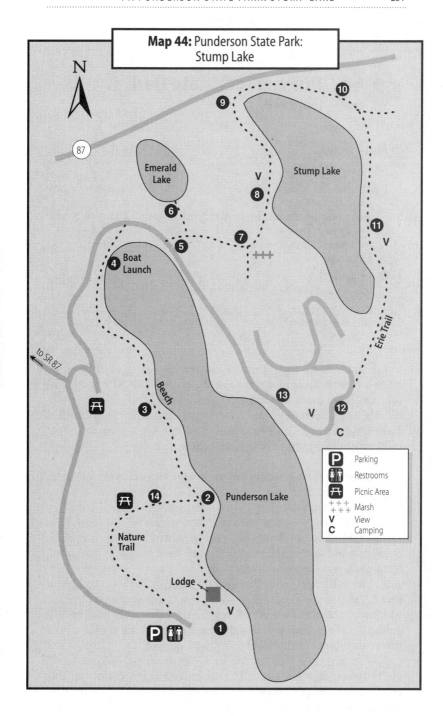

**Map 44:** Punderson State Park: Stump Lake

# 45 Punderson State Park
## Pine Lake

> **Distance:** 5 miles
>
> **Hiking time:** 2 ½ hours
>
> **Description:** This hike crosses rolling terrain on trails used primarily in winter for cross-country skiing, but it is immensely enjoyable in any season. The trail tends to be very muddy in the spring. The route skirts the golf course and affords a view of pretty Pine Lake in the western-most part of the park. This loop hike starts and ends at the lodge parking area.
>
> **Directions:** I-271 to Exit 29 (Chagrin Blvd./SR 87); east on SR 87 past town of Newbury to Punderson State Park entrance, on right; follow park signs to lodge.
>
> **Parking & restrooms:** Parking adjacent to lodge, restrooms inside lodge.

Punderson State Park, described at the beginning of chapter 44, offers a variety of outdoor recreational activities. The park is open all year and offers many opportunities for hiking and cross-country skiing. The trails, up and down gentle hills, are generally well maintained and clearly marked. However, some blazes may be missing and some trails may be overgrown in the summertime.

**1.** Begin the walk at the far west end of the lodge parking lot. There is a sign here indicating the Mohawk Cross-Country Ski Trail. The trail is wide and is marked with round orange tree blazes. After sloping gently down to cross a stream on a platform bridge, the trail then goes uphill to the right. (A left trail turn here, also marked by an orange tree blaze, goes out to the golf course). Shortly there is another trail intersection where you will stay to the right.

**2.** The trail slopes gently up and down before it reaches a paved road leading into the golf course (0.5 mile). Cross this road to a trail marked with a sign showing a variety of cross-country ski trails. Take the trail on the left. Then, continue straight ahead on the main trail, avoiding side trails going off to the right or left.

**3.** Turn left at a sign for the Kaiser Permanente Trail entrance, marked with yellow tree blazes. The Kaiser Trail is a serpentine path that nearly makes a loop, as you will discover on your return. Follow the path westward for pleasant hiking over gently rolling terrain, keeping the golf

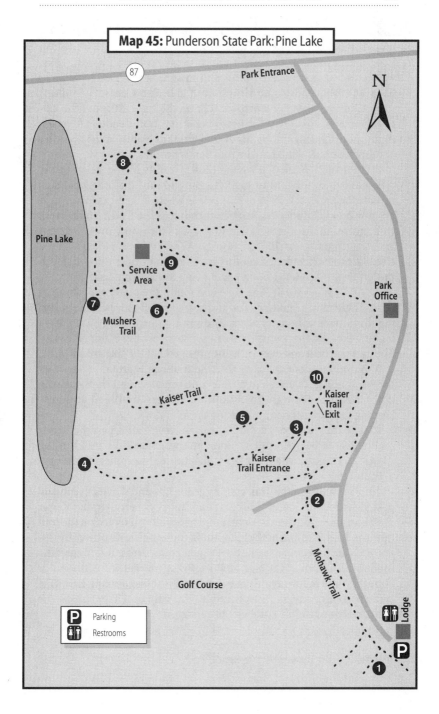

**Map 45:** Punderson State Park: Pine Lake

87

Park Entrance

N

Pine Lake

Service Area

Mushers Trail

Park Office

Kaiser Trail

Kaiser Trail Exit

Kaiser Trail Entrance

Golf Course

Mohawk Trail

P Parking

Restrooms

Lodge

course to the left (south). These beautiful tall trees are beeches, oaks, maples, tulips, and shagbark hickories.

**4.** Just beyond the end of the golf course the trail reaches Pine Lake, which always attracts water birds and in summer is filled with water lilies. The trail bends around in a U-turn to head back east (1.5 miles).

**5.** Continue past the crossover trail on the right. At about the 2.0-mile point on this hike, the now almost flat trail bends west again. Again, note the magnificent hardwood forest of maples and oaks. After another half mile of hiking, the trail bends northeast.

**6.** At a trail junction, leave the Kaiser Trail (which goes off to the right) and take the trail to the left, going toward the fence that surrounds the park service area. This area is where dogsled races are held every winter in Punderson. Just before the fence itself, turn left on a trail (not mowed in the summer) that soon enters the woods on the left and goes toward the west. This trail (Mushers Trail) is now marked with red tree blazes. Shortly there is another trail junction where you will stay to the left on the westward-bound path going toward Pine Lake.

**7.** At 3.0 miles reach Pine Lake and follow the pretty trail along its edge. There may be gulls, ducks, and geese as well as fishermen enjoying this attractive body of water. Midway is a rustic park bench overlooking the lake, from which you can pause to rest and admire the view. The cars you hear and may see at the north end of the lake are on SR 87.

**8.** Continue along the lake until the trail bends around away from the water and goes uphill. At a wide juncture of several trails, take the trail farthest to the right (more of the Mushers Trail) and go south, keeping the park service building on the left (east).

**9.** The trail now goes around the park service area, past the Kaiser Trail taken earlier (3.5 miles). Soon afterward take the trail turning right (east) to enter a path marked with blue tree blazes, near the Adopt-a-Trail sign.

**10.** Continue on this trail with its gentle ups and downs, eventually past signs for the Kaiser Trail Exit and, shortly thereafter, the Kaiser Trail Entrance, both on the right. From here you will return on the trail taken at the beginning of the hike, but in the opposite direction.

Reach the paved road leading to the golf course, cross it, and enter the Mohawk Ski Trail at the sign (the trail is again marked with orange blazes). While following this path back to the lodge parking area, take care not to take any of the side trails to the right or left, but follow the main trail that roughly parallels the park road.

This chapter reviewed and rewalked by Patricia Spoth.

# 46 Three Waterfalls
Cuyahoga Valley National Recreation Area

**Distance:** 9 ½ miles

**Hiking time:** 5 hours

**Description:** The hike from Brandywine Falls is almost entirely on woods trails with several steep hills to climb. The Stanford Trail is well marked and descends into the valley to the paved Canal Towpath Trail. After Riverview Rd. is crossed, the blue-blazed Buckeye Trail is followed to Blue Hen Falls, and a side trail reaches Buttermilk Falls. On this last portion of the hike there are many varieties of wildflowers in the spring; bring a wildflower guide!

**Directions:** I-271 to Exit 18 (SR 8); south on SR 8 ; west on W. Highland; right on Old Route Eight, go under bridge; immediate left, again on W. Highland; left (south) on Brandywine Rd., past Inn at Brandywine Falls on the right, cross bridge; right (west) on Stanford Rd.; parking area for Brandywine Falls on left. OR, I-77 to Exit 149 (SR 82); east on SR 82 to Brandywine Rd.; right on Stanford Rd.

**Parking & restrooms:** Located in the Brandywine Falls parking area.

This chapter and chapters 47–50 describe strenuous hikes in the Cuyahoga Valley National Recreation Area (CVNRA). These hikes explore a variety of scenic trails and are designated as strenuous because of the steep terrain found in this lovely 22-mile green space between Cleveland and Akron. These hikes are also longer than the others in this book and usually require taking a pack with food and water. They are well worth the preparation and effort required to complete them, however. Any of these hikes can be shortened by turning around at any point and retracing your steps back to the beginning.

The three waterfalls that you will see on this strenuous hike are Brandywine Falls, Blue Hen Falls, and Buttermilk Falls. Brandywine Falls is a lovely scenic spot. A wooden walkway and steps lead to a spectacular viewing point close to the foot of the falls. The old foundation of the mill once powered by this waterfall is at the far east end of the walkway. Today hardly anything remains of the village of Brandywine except the 1848 Wallace farmhouse, now used as a bed and breakfast, called The Inn at Brandywine Falls.

The second waterfall, Blue Hen Falls, is far across Cuyahoga Valley and, though not as high as Brandywine, is in a quiet woodland spot and easily accessible by driving your car to the parking area and taking a short hike down to the falls. The third waterfall, Buttermilk Falls, is accessible only by hiking down a streamside trail from Blue Hen Falls when water levels are low.

**1.** After viewing 65-foot-high Brandywine Falls from the walkway, start the hike by walking west along Stanford Rd. to the Stanford Trail entrance, identified by a small brown sign about 0.2 mile on the left, just beyond the Road Closed sign.

**2.** The trail goes downhill and down a set of steps cut into the pathway. Pass a trail on the right. Cross two bridges and two sets of steps.

**3.** At about ³/₄ mile turn left at the intersection where a sign points toward the Stanford House. (Option: take the short trail to the right to view small, pretty Averill Pond and return the same way to this point.)

**4.** Soon the trail bears right, winds up and down ridges, and crosses a bridge (1.2 miles).

**5.** Continue without making any turns, cross one final bridge, then note the large barn in the distance. The path follows a wide swath cut through a meadow to the Stanford House American Youth Hostel, open year round from 5 p.m. to 9 a.m. the following day. This 1843 building has been restored by volunteers and the National Park Service to become Northeast Ohio's first youth hostel. The hostel has 30 beds in two dormitories, common rooms, a large kitchen and dining room, and meeting rooms. For more information, call 440-467-8711.

During much of the 19th century, members of the Stanford family were prosperous farmers, dairymen, lumberers, and influential citizens of the nearby town of Boston.

**6.** Go west across the hostel property to Stanford Rd. Just opposite the hostel's driveway, enter a gravel path heading west across a field.

**7.** At the end of this path turn left (south) onto the Canal Towpath Trail, a wide gravel All-Purpose Trail (heavily used by bicyclists) that closely parallels the old Ohio & Erie Canal. Most of the canal to the left (east) of the towpath is overgrown with trees, but portions of it can be identified. Farther along you can see one of the remaining locks (Lock 32), once needed to elevate boats on their way to Akron, or to lower them on their way to Cleveland. Used until the great flood of 1913, the canal was watered through weir gates entering from the Cuyahoga River to the west. Deer can often be seen along this part of the canal towpath. (See also Ch. 19.)

**8.** At about 2.3 miles reach Boston Mills Rd. and the buildings of what was once the old mill town of Boston. The building next to the unwatered canal on the south side of the road was built in 1836 as the

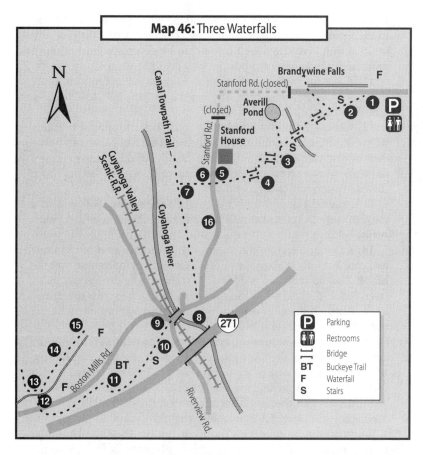

**Map 46:** Three Waterfalls

Boston Land and Manufacturing Company Store. It has been restored by the National Park Service as the "Boston Store" and houses a canal boat exhibit, well worth a visit. Pick up the blue blazes of the Buckeye Trail on Boston Mills Rd. going west.

Cross the bridge over the Cuyahoga River and reach the tracks of the Cuyahoga Valley Scenic Railroad (CVSR). This historic line of the old valley railroad dates from 1870. For information about train rides, call CVSR at 800-468-4070.

CAUTION! A diesel train from the CVSR uses the tracks frequently during the year (especially on weekends).

**9.** Continue west across Riverview Rd. Near the southwest corner of Riverview and Boston Mills Rds., enter the Buckeye Trail at the sign. It ascends a steep hill on small trail switchbacks. The noise of cars you hear is from I-271 to the south.

**10.** At about 3.0 miles descend a flight of 87 wooden steps.

**11.** After crossing a wet area, ascend the hill to property belonging to the National Guard and occupied by a caretaker. Cross the property walking west and follow the hard-to-find blue blazes a short distance until the trail emerges onto Boston Mills Rd. (3.5 miles).

**12.** Cross the road and enter the short drive at the sign identifying the parking for Blue Hen Falls. The paved trail to the falls descends to a serene and cool open area.

**13.** Cross a footbridge over Spring Creek. Do not continue to follow BT (which continues uphill). Follow the wooden fence around for a nice view of Blue Hen Falls. Many layers of dark Bedford Formation (shale) lie below the more erosion-resistant Berea Sandstone cap that lies above this pretty waterfall (see appendix A).

To the northeast is a trail that parallels the stream. Follow it in a northeasterly direction keeping the stream on the right as it carves a ravine below.

**14.** Cross and recross the stream until it reaches a set of old stone and concrete walls that once supported a now-abandoned road over the brook. The old road bed is difficult to see due to landslides and fallen trees. Follow the trail below these walls, and bear left to cross the stream again. As you head up a small embankment, you will begin to hear the waterfall.

**15.** The top of Buttermilk Falls is straight ahead (4.5 miles). Go down to the foot of the falls by means of a trail to the right. This lovely, little-known site is one of the prettiest in our area and contains a 20-foot-high waterfall spilling over Bedford Shale. As is true in many areas of Northeast Ohio, the last glacier finally melted about 12,000 years ago, leaving this high waterfall overlooking the valley below.

Return along the same trail. Watch carefully for the route, because it looks different on the way back. Just above Buttermilk Falls, cross the stream and bear left at the top of the concrete wall. Keep the ravine and stream on the left and follow the trail back to Blue Hen Falls as before.

To return, continue on the Buckeye Trail, going downhill at the National Guard property and across Boston Mills Rd., then continue on the Canal Towpath Trail to Stanford House, and on the Stanford Trail to the Brandywine Falls parking area.

*Optional:*

**16.** For an optional route back from Blue Hen Falls, walk along Boston Mills Rd. east and downhill to Riverview Rd. Cross Riverview and the railroad tracks and bridge. Turn left at Stanford Rd. and follow the road back to Brandywine Falls. Note: Stanford Rd. is permanently closed to vehicles.

This chapter was reviewed and rewalked by Sylvia Banks.

# 47 Jaite to Boston Mills
Cuyahoga Valley National Recreation Area

**Distance:** 8 miles

**Hiking time:** 4 hours

**Description:** This very rewarding hike on the blue-blazed Buckeye Trail includes a steep hill at the beginning, several more moderate hills, and one steep stairway near the end. The last 2 ½ miles are on the flat Canal Towpath Trail.

**Directions:** I-271 to Exit 18 (SR 8); south on SR 8; right (west) on W. Highland; right on Old Route Eight, under bridge; immediately left, again on W. Highland Rd; at the Summit County line (Cuyahoga River), W. Highland Rd. becomes Vaughn Rd. near Jaite. The small yellow buildings on the left, just past the Cuyahoga Valley Scenic Railroad tracks, are the National Park Service headquarters for Cuyahoga Valley National Recreation Area (CVNRA). OR, I-77 to Exit 149 (SR 82); east on SR 82; right (south) on Riverview Rd.; left (east) on Vaughn, cross railroad tracks; Jaite Wayside trailhead is on left.

**Parking:** Parking is at Jaite Wayside on the north side of Vaughn Rd., east of the railroad tracks. There is no restroom here, although on weekdays accommodations are available at the CVNRA office.

This trail offers an exceptional variety of scenery, including a mixed forest of maples and oaks, a fine view of portions of Cuyahoga Valley, open fields, a murmuring brook, and a waterfall. On this hike you may wish to carry lunch and sit down on a mossy spot overlooking a brook for a most enjoyable hiking experience.

**1.** Start at Jaite Wayside Trailhead on Vaughn Rd. just east of the small yellow park buildings. These quaint restored 1906 buildings of the old Jaite Mill Company are offices for CVNRA staff, who welcome visitors and can provide trail maps and information.

**2.** After crossing Vaughn Rd., follow the Buckeye Trail (BT) signs across a field and across railroad tracks to emerge on Riverview Rd.

CAUTION: Be careful crossing these railroad tracks; they are used frequently year round by the Cuyahoga Valley Scenic Railroad on weekends.

Cross Riverview Rd. and stay on the south side of Snowville Rd. Note the sign where the BT comes in from the north and joins the access trail at this point and continues south.

**3.** Turn left (south) and enter the woods on the BT. Climb a set of steep stairs to the top of a ridge through a mixed forest of maples.

**4.** At 1.0 mile reach an open area with an underground pipeline. Bear left and pause for a lovely view of the Cuyahoga Valley to the east. Proceed south under the power line and along the power line access road lined with lovely oaks and dogwood trees. At 1.6 miles descend to a small creek.

**5.** At 2.0 miles the trail descends to a larger creek. Just beyond, the trail ascends another set of wooden steps, and soon emerges onto Columbia Rd. (2.3 miles). Cross the road to a sign that indicates the distance to Boston Mills as 3.3 miles.

**6.** At 3.0 miles there is a beautiful mossy stream overlook, an ideal spot to rest under the tall hemlocks and contemplate the quiet sounds of nature—a true wilderness spot.

**7.** The BT crosses Columbia Run, a broad stream which must be forded; at 3.8 miles it goes under another power line.

**8.** At 4.0 miles the trail reaches Spring Creek and Blue Hen Falls. It is worthwhile to go off the BT on the trail parallel to the fence for a short distance to view the falls, with its cap of Berea Sandstone overhanging softer Bedford Formation shale (see appendix A). There is a bench to rest on at this viewpoint. Another option is to take a half-mile trail eastward along the creek to Buttermilk Falls and return (see ch. 46).

Return by crossing the bridge above Blue Hen Falls and climbing up to the parking area where the trail emerges onto Boston Mills Rd.

**9.** Cross Boston Mills Rd. (4.2 miles) and property owned by the National Guard. Near the caretaker's cabin watch for a sharp turn south. Ahead and on the right is I-271. Pass a creek and ascend the 87-step wooden stairway built to protect the ridge from erosion.

**10.** The BT descends to the junction of Riverview and Boston Mills Rds. (5.4 miles). Bear right and proceed east on Boston Mills Rd., crossing the Cuyahoga Valley Scenic Railroad (CVSR) tracks. Cross the Cuyahoga River and enter the old village of Boston.

CAUTION! Cross the CVSR tracks carefully. This is an active railroad and trains run frequently between Cleveland and Akron, in every season, with the heaviest traffic in the summer and on weekends.

**11.** The first two buildings on the right side of Boston Mills Rd. (5.6 miles) have been restored as historical landmarks by the National Park Service. The Boston Store, formerly a general store, now serves as a canal museum. The M. D. Garage, gas pumps, and sign have been restored to preserve a significant part of the old village. At this point the

## Map 47: Jaite to Boston Mills, CVNRA

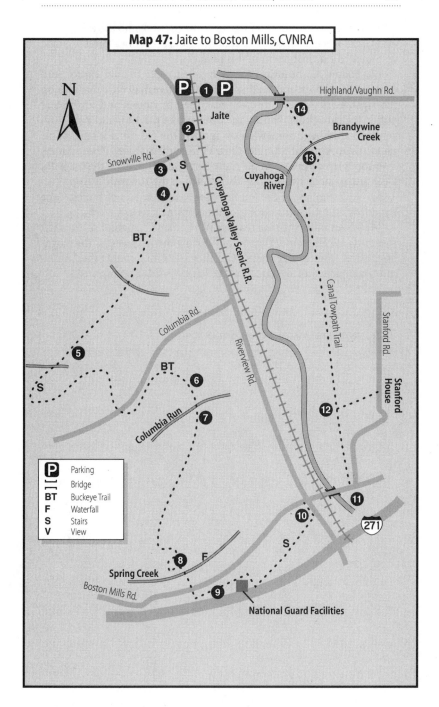

N

P ① P
Jaite
Highland/Vaughn Rd.

②
Snowville Rd.
③ S
④ V
BT

Cuyahoga Valley Scenic R.R.

⑭
Brandywine Creek
⑬
Cuyahoga River

Columbia Rd.

Riverview Rd.

Canal Towpath Trail

Stanford Rd.

Stanford House

BT
⑤
S
⑥
⑦
Columbia Run

⑫

⑪
271

⑧
⑨
⑩
F
S
Spring Creek
Boston Mills Rd.
National Guard Facilities

P  Parking
≡  Bridge
BT  Buckeye Trail
F  Waterfall
S  Stairs
V  View

BT continues south, but this hike turns north (left) onto the wide, grav-eled Canal Towpath Trail. (The Stanford House is about a tenth of a mile up Stanford Rd., just north of this point.)

**12.** Follow the beautiful towpath north. Note the old church and cemetery on the left and, farther along, the interesting old canal lock on the right, Lock 32. The towpath was used by horses and mules that pulled the canal boats during the canal era of the 19th and early 20th centuries. Although somewhat overgrown, the old canal is still visible on the right. At about 6.1 miles the trail from the Stanford House American Youth Hostel enters on the right. Continue straight on the towpath. Deer are frequently seen along this stretch of the Towpath Trail.

**13.** At 7.0 miles on the left the trail passes the site of the old Jaite Paper Mill (1906) and passes over Brandywine Creek.

**14.** At 7.4 miles the trail reaches W. Highland/Vaughn Rd. Turn left (west) on W. Highland/Vaughn and follow the road across the Cuya-hoga River. This bridge marks Cuyahoga-Summit county line. At 8.0 miles complete the hike circuit at the Jaite Wayside parking area.

This chapter reviewed and rewalked by Sylvia Banks.

# 48 Brecksville Reservation
## Buckeye Trail to Pinery Narrows

**Distance:** 11 ½ miles

**Hiking time:** 5+ hours

**Description:** This hike, entirely on the Buckeye Trail, begins at Oak Grove Picnic Area and descends the hill to a beautiful section of the Cuyahoga Valley National Recreation Area (CVNRA). The trail is marked by single blue blazes—except for turns, indicated by double blazes (see p. 19)—and follows the flat Ohio and Erie Canal Towpath Trail through one of the most beautiful and scenic areas of Northeast Ohio, Pinery Narrows. (However, the pines are long since gone.) Wildlife abounds here in the valley of the Cuyahoga River. This portion of the trail has recently been improved to accommodate bicycles, strollers, and wheelchairs on the paved pathway. It is best to stay to the right on the Canal Towpath, facing oncoming bicyclists.

**Directions:** I-77 to Exit 149 (SR 82); east on SR 82 to just past Brecksville Rd. (SR 21) in Brecksville.; right on Chippewa Creek Dr. at park entrance; right on Valley Pkwy. to the entrance for Oak Grove Picnic Area on left.

**Parking & restrooms:** At Oak Grove Picnic Area.

Brecksville Reservation, largest of the Cleveland Metroparks, is deeply carved into seven separate valleys and has many different trails throughout its beautiful forested land. Chippewa Creek, in the northern section of the park, cuts through a magnificent gorge formed by the final retreat of Ohio's last glacier about 12,000 years ago. Within another scenic gorge is Deer Lick Cave, an unusual outcropping of rock formed many years ago. The Brecksville Nature Center on Chippewa Creek Dr. is a good place to stop in for a visit to learn more about the reservation and to obtain a hiking trail map.

**1.** From the Oak Grove Picnic Area driveway, take the east exit to Valley Pkwy. Turn right onto the paved All-Purpose Trail on the south side of the road. Continue to follow the blue blazes.

**2.** At the double-blue blaze, turn right(east) into a beautiful woods of tall beeches, maples, and oaks. The Buckeye Trail (BT) is also blazed along here with orange hiker signs.

**3.** At 0.7 mile turn left (north), continuing to follow the BT and orange hiker signs to Chippewa Creek Dr.

**4.** Cross the drive and follow the BT right (east) on All-Purpose Trail.

**5.** Continue on the All-Purpose Trail east to the Station Rd. Bridge parking area.

**6.** Ahead are the railroad tracks of the Cuyahoga Valley Scenic Railroad (CVSR).

CAUTION! Cross the tracks carefully—this is an active railroad line.

The recently rebuilt Station Rd. bridge spanning the Cuyahoga River is ahead. Many years ago there was a railroad depot here, and this was an important stop on the line between Cleveland and Akron. The tracks are now used for scenic train rides from Independence to Hale Farm and Village and Quaker Square in Akron.

**7.** Cross the bridge (closed to vehicles) and note the old wooden bricks used to pave the bridge surface (1.5 miles).

**8.** Continue east along the All-Purpose Trail and turn left (north) onto the Canal Towpath Trail. Bear left (toward the river) at the next intersection. Near the river are the remains of an old canal gate once used to regulate water levels from the river on the left to the canal feeder on the right. Overhead is the strikingly beautiful SR 82 bridge. Pinery Dam, a pretty spillway on the Cuyahoga River, often brings fishermen to try their luck at this spot.

**9.** The Canal Towpath/Buckeye Trail closely parallels the straight, shallow canal on the right and keeps the wider Cuyahoga River on the left, all through the valley. The river continues gently twisting for several miles through the attractive Pinery Narrows. There may be deer, waterfowl, and evidence of beaver activity all along this enjoyable stretch of the Narrows.

Stay to the right on this path, watching for bicycle traffic, which is fast-moving along here.

**10.** At about 4.3 miles cars can be seen or heard on Canal Rd. to the east. Continue past another of the original weir gates and an overflow dam just beyond it.

**11.** Reach a wooden pedestrian bridge and turn right to cross it to busy Canal Rd. Turn right (south) on Canal Rd. and follow the BT blazes to Sagamore Rd.

**12.** Turn left (east) at Sagamore Rd. and follow the road to Sagamore Grove Picnic Area on the left, where there are restrooms and picnic tables (5.3 miles).

**13.** Return along the same trail, retracing your steps through the Narrows, and enjoy new views on the right. Cross the old Station Rd. bridge to the paved All-Purpose Trail on Chippewa Creek Dr.

Watch carefully for the double-blue blazes of the BT on the left (south) side of the road. Ascend the hill to Oak Grove Picnic Area.

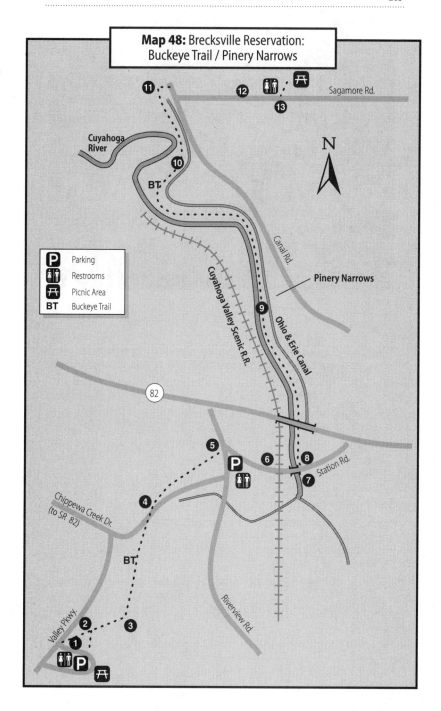

**Map 48:** Brecksville Reservation:
Buckeye Trail / Pinery Narrows

Marsh in fog

This chapter reviewed and rewalked by Shirley Pashall with the assistance of Richard Kana.

# 49 Brecksville Reservation
## Buckeye Trail to Jaite

**Distance:** 10.8 miles (with a 1.7-mile optional extension)

**Hiking time:** 5 ½ to 6 hours (7 hrs. with option)

**Description:** This long hike descends from Brecksville Reservation to the Cuyahoga Valley on the Buckeye Trail over rolling hills. There are many stream crossings and a few areas that can be very wet in the spring or after a heavy rain. This pleasant, challenging hike is strenuous because of its length and the hilly terrain it traverses. It is marked in its entirety with blue rectangular six-by-two-inch Buckeye Trail blazes painted on trees and posts.

**Directions:** I-77 to Exit 149 (SR 82); east on SR 82 to Brecksville; south on Brecksville Rd.; left (east) on Valley Pkwy.; right on Meadows Dr.; right at the Cleveland Metroparks Brecksville Stables.

**Parking & restrooms:** At the stables parking area.

Brecksville Reservation, one of 14 Cleveland Metroparks reservations, lies within Cuyahoga Valley National Recreation Area. Steep ridges and deep valleys cut by glacier-fed streams characterize Brecksville Reservation, a 3,090-acre park with rugged hiking trails. The Brecksville Trailside Museum (1939) on Chippewa Creek Dr. is open daily and contains interesting nature exhibits. Helpful park naturalists are on duty daily to supply information to visitors.

**1.** Begin the hike at the stables and cross Meadows Dr. to find the blue blazes of the Buckeye Trail (BT) a short distance down the road on the left. Enter the trail going east and follow it until it emerges onto the drive to Ottawa Point Reserved Picnic Area.

**2.** Reach the picnic area via the entrance drive and follow the blue blazes as they continue northeast from the parking lot on a hogback ridge overlooking a deep ravine on the right, and later, on the left as well.

**3.** The trail descends and makes a sharp right turn off the wider trail. Watch for this turn as it is easy to miss. The double-blue turning blaze is on a post at this point.

**4.** At about 1.0 mile cross a brook on a wooden bridge. Follow the trail upward along the edge of the hill on the right until it leads out to an old, overgrown former blacktop road. This is the old portion of Parkview Rd. that once went through the reservation.

**5.** Follow this old pavement trail about 0.1 mile, watching for a double blaze indicating a sharp right turn (south) where the BT enters the woods. (This is another easy-to-miss turn.) The trail continues for about a half mile on mostly flat terrain. This area can be very wet in the springtime. (Be sure to wear waterproof boots during this season.)

**6.** Cross a stream and soon ascend another hogback ridge.

**7.** (2.0 miles) The trail begins to descend, crosses a stream, and goes up and down another hogback ridge.

**8.** The BT goes up and down another hill and crosses two small streams twice, then goes up and down the side of a ridge (3.0 miles). One point of interest is a rusty old automobile (1930s vintage) left by the farmers who formerly owned the property.

(3.0 miles) Still following the BT blazes, cross a larger stream twice and climb another hill.

CAUTION!: It is easy to lose the trail here. Be careful to watch for blue blazes.

**9.** Reach an open area, a former farm with an abandoned woods road (4.0 miles). The trail then enters a wooded section on the right and goes south on the old woods road past an open field. (Blue birdhouses are here.) The BT then enters the woods, crosses a gas line right-of-way, and finally reenters the woods (4.5 miles).

**10.** The trail continues down a steep ridge, crosses a stream twice, then another stream. (Watch carefully here for BT turn blazes.) Soon emerge onto Snowville Rd. at 5.4 miles.

**11.** Although the BT continues south across the road, this is the turn-around point on this hike.

Return to Brecksville Stables by taking the trail in reverse and watching carefully for the BT blue blazes at each turn and stream crossing. When hiking in the reverse direction, entirely new vistas open up for continued pleasurable hiking.

*Optional:*

Walk east on Snowville to Riverview Rd., and north on Riverview to the yellow buildings in Jaite at the corner of Riverview and Vaughn Rds. for a stop at CVNRA headquarters. The buildings are usually open only on weekdays.

Another option while in Jaite is to follow Vaughn Rd. east to the Canal Towpath Trail at Red Lock Trailhead. Then follow the Towpath Trail north to its reconnection with the Buckeye Trail at the Station Rd. Bridge parking area (see ch. 48, note #6). Cross Riverview Rd. (still on

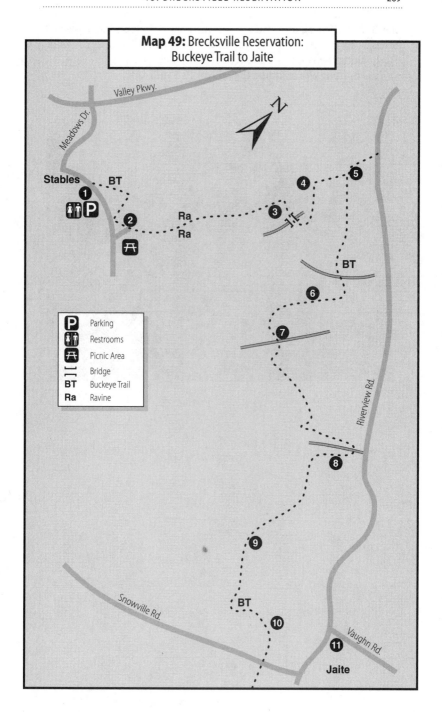

**Map 49:** Brecksville Reservation:
Buckeye Trail to Jaite

the Buckeye Trail), and you'll reach the area described in chapter 48, notes 5–13. Follow the BT to Deer Lick cave, then follow it across Valley Pkwy. along the Bridle Trail to return to the stables.

This options will lengthen the hike to 12.5 miles.

Casey Batule/Cleveland Metroparks

This chapter reviewed and rewalked by Elizabeth McQuaid.

# 50 Brecksville Reservation
## Deer Lick Cave Loop

**Distance:** 5 miles

**Hiking time:** 3 hours

**Description:** This hike starts at the nature center on the yellow and white trails, continues along Chippewa Creek Gorge on the green trail, and then takes the red Deer Lick Cave Trail in a clockwise direction back to the nature center. Traversing all seven of Brecksville's ridges, it is quite a strenuous hike, although not long in mileage, because of its many hills.

**Directions:** I-77 to Exit 149 (SR 82); east on SR 82, past Brecksville Rd. (SR 21) in Brecksville; right on Chippewa Creek Dr. at park entrance; continue past Meadows Dr. to parking area for Brecksville Nature Center, on right.

**Parking & restrooms:** Near Brecksville Nature Center.

Brecksville Reservation's most outstanding feature is its topography. Seven separate valleys and ridges have been cut through the hills by rivers and streams over many thousands of years. Chippewa Creek has cut a magnificent gorge through the northern section of the park. This gorge was left behind by a retreating glacier about 12,000 years ago as water flowed east to the Cuyahoga River. Large granite rocks from northern Canada also remain behind in the gorge and park. The fall foliage is beautiful in all of Brecksville, but especially from the Chippewa Creek Gorge Scenic Overlook.

Brecksville Nature Center, listed on the National Register of Historic Places, is an interesting building to visit to learn more about this Metropark and to obtain a map of the trails in the reservation. Opened in 1939, Brecksville Nature Center is the oldest nature center still standing in Cleveland Metroparks. Built by workers of the WPA (Works Progress Administration), it is constructed of chestnut, walnut, and cherry wood, and reflects the fine craftsmanship of its era.

**1.** Follow the sign from the parking area on the paved All-Purpose Trail to the nature center. Primitive restrooms are in the woods to the right of the walkway. Before starting the hike, take a moment to view the exhibits in the nature center.

Just before the building is the yellow-blazed Valley Stream Trail on the right. Begin the hike on this trail with its useful tree identification signs. This is the Harriet L. Keeler Memorial Trail, named in honor of a well-known naturalist, botanist, teacher, and author who died in 1921.

Follow the yellow blazes. The trail soon turns to the right to a wooden observation deck for the Prairie Restoration Project. This project was created to encourage the growth of plants that once were common here but no longer are readily found. These plants include big and little blue stem, Indian grass, tall coreopsis, prairie dock, and coneflower.

The yellow trail continues to the west, left of the prairie, and reaches a large glacial boulder with a plaque in memory of Harriet L. Keeler.

**2.** Here, leave the yellow trail (which goes left) and continue straight ahead beyond the boulder to the white trail. Cross Chippewa Creek Dr. to the All-Purpose Trail, identified with both green and white markers. You may begin to hear the rushing waters of Chippewa Creek far below on the right.

**3.** Almost immediately the trail turns right (east) downhill to a small enclosed shelter. This scenic overlook affords a fine view of the gorge looking north toward the stone bridge at SR 82. Berea Sandstone blocks that have fallen into the gorge are resistant to erosion even though the creek continues its persistent cutting as it flows eastward to the Cuyahoga River.

**4.** Follow the green and white trails to the right along the wooden fence; there are broad views of spectacular Chippewa Creek Gorge far below on the left. Proceed straight ahead on the Chippewa Gorge Trail (blazed with green tree markers).

**5.** Stay on the Chippewa Gorge Trail along the fence, noting that the gorge becomes deeper as you progress, a result of the continued cutting action of the creek. (A side trail leads off to the right to the Harriet L. Keeler Picnic Area and the car parking area.)

**6.** The trail gradually winds downhill to a marsh and at its foot meets the Bridle Trail coming in on the left. Very soon the green trail turns right. Staying on the green trail, bear left at the Y intersection. Cross a wooden footbridge over a side stream.

Cross another side stream on a wooden suspension bridge constructed by the Ohio National Guard in 1981. Soon after the bridge follow the green trail as it turns right and goes out to Chippewa Creek Dr. (1.8 miles.)

**7.** Cross the road and you will be on a driveway that leads into Maple Grove Picnic Area (may not be identified). Here, go south on the red Deer Lick Cave Trail, which will lead all the way back to the nature center in a counterclockwise direction. The red trail begins to the left of the driveway.

**8.** Follow the red trail on a long, steep uphill trek. Valley Pkwy. is below on the left. This ridge is one of the seven finger-like ridges that lie across Brecksville Reservation. Far below on the right is the stream that long ago cut this ravine and today slowly continues to deepen it.

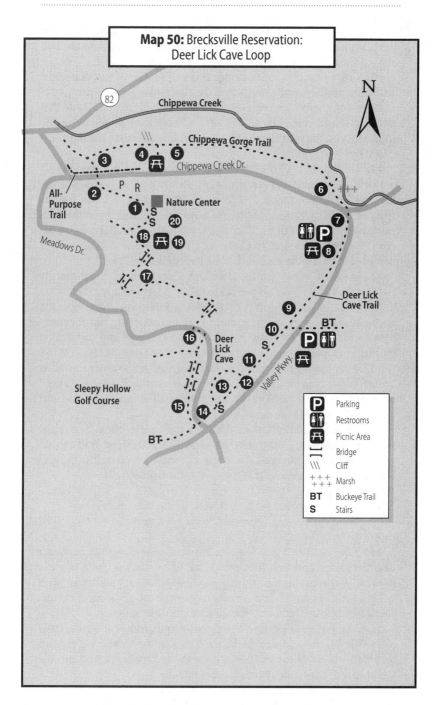

**Map 50:** Brecksville Reservation:
Deer Lick Cave Loop

N

Chippewa Creek

82

Chippewa Gorge Trail

Chippewa Creek Dr.

3

4

5

Nature Center

All-
Purpose
Trail

2

1

P    R

S
S

20

6

7

P

8

18

19

Meadows Dr.

17

Deer Lick
Cave Trail

9

16

Deer
Lick
Cave

10

S

BT

P

11

Valley Pkwy.

12

13

Sleepy Hollow
Golf Course

15

14

S

BT

| | |
|---|---|
| P | Parking |
| | Restrooms |
| | Picnic Area |
| | Bridge |
| \\\ | Cliff |
| +++ | Marsh |
| BT | Buckeye Trail |
| S | Stairs |

**9.** At 2.3 miles the red trail is joined by the blue-blazed Buckeye Trail (BT). Signs for the blue ski trail and the orange trail point to the left. Stay on the red trail as it goes downhill in tandem with the BT.

**10.** Cross a small wooden bridge and ascend a set of wooden steps. To the left and across the parkway is the Oak Grove Picnic Area.

**11.** Continue on the red Deer Lick and blue-blazed BT. (Note that the Bridle Trail comes in on the left and continues downhill on the right.) Stay on the red trail; the BT loops off the red trail to the right (2.6 miles) but later rejoins it.

**12.** On the red trail is a bench near a few picnic tables overlooking the peaceful woods and stream below. Reach a kiosk placed for the Buckeye Trail Association by Cleveland Metroparks. It identifies this spot as the "Crossroads of the Buckeye Trail." From here the trail extends in three directions: 522 miles south to Cincinnati through eastern Ohio, 441 miles west to Cincinnati through western Ohio, and 65 miles north to Headlands Beach State Park and Lake Erie.

The overlook viewpoint for Deer Lick Cave is ahead. Turn sharply right on the red trail to go downhill to the cave. It is actually a rock overhang composed of erosion-resistant Berea Sandstone. Note how the enormous rock lying on the ground to the left once fit into the overhang. Birds make their nests in and among the foliage and crevices on this beautiful rock.

**13.** After leaving the Deer Lick Cave area, turn left to cross a wooden bridge, continuing on the red trail, then over another bridge. Go uphill on a set of stone steps. Note the pretty waterfall on the right. The trail bends to the right at the top of the steps.

**14.** Cross Meadows Dr. At the next trail intersection bear right (north) to continue on the red trail—leaving the Buckeye Trail behind where it goes straight ahead. Continue following the red trail all the way back to the nature center. This trail is also the Bridle Trail.

CAUTION: If you meet horses, step to the side and remain quiet and still until the horse and rider have passed.

**15.** At about the 3.2-mile point, the trail goes downhill, crosses a wooden bridge, and then goes uphill. The Sleepy Hollow Golf Course is now on the left. The trail soon goes downhill again, across another bridge, and rises uphill. You are now crossing some of the most beautiful valleys, streams, and ridges in Brecksville Reservation.

**16.** The ski trail, identified by blue skier signs, comes in on the left to join the red trail. Continue on the red trail. Recross Meadows Dr. again and turn left along the road. Watch for the red trail's reentry into the woods a short distance ahead on the right.

**17.** At 4.1 miles the trail descends another ridge, crosses a bridge, and goes uphill. Bear left at the top of the hill. Soon there is a view of an open meadows area on the left. The red trail goes downhill again, bends to the right, crosses a small stream on another bridge, curves around another ridge, then crosses another side stream on yet another bridge. Here you are still crossing more of Brecksville's ridges.

**18.** At about 4.5 miles the red trail again goes up a steep hill along the edge of still another of Brecksville's ridges. At the top of this hill, turn right to continue on the red trail.

**19.** Next the red trail turns left away from the Bridle Trail just before the playing field, which is on the right. Reach the Meadows Picnic Area and cross through it, going past restrooms and picnic tables to continue into the woods.

**20.** The red trail is joined by the green trail at the top of a set of steps. Descend the steps, following the sign to the nature center. The red trail meets the yellow trail at the foot of the steps. Cross the small bridge on the right and ascend another set of steps to arrive back at the nature center. The paved walkway to the parking area is just in front of the building.

Casey Batiule/Cleveland Metroparks

This chapter reviewed and rewalked by Sylvia Banks.

# Appendix A

## Generalized Geological Column for Northeast Ohio

Source: Joseph Hannibal, Cleveland Museum of Natural History, 1996

# Bibliography

Abercrombie, Jay. *Walks and Rambles in Ohio's Western Reserve.*
Woodstock, Vt.: Backcountry Publications, 1996.

Armstrong, Foster, Richard Klein, and Cara Armstrong. *A Guide to
Cleveland's Sacred Landmarks.* Kent, Ohio: Kent State University
Press, 1992.

Blakeslee, C. T. *History of Chagrin Falls and Vicinity.* Chagrin Falls, Ohio:
Exponent Publishing Co., 1903. (Written by Blakeslee in 1874).

Brockman, C. Frank. *Trees of North America.* N.Y.: Golden Press, 1968.

Chagrin Falls Historical Society. *Village Victorian.* Chagrin Falls, Ohio:
Chagrin Falls Historical Society, 1983.

Committee for Public Art. *A Walking Tour and Guide to Public Art in
Downtown Cleveland.* Cleveland: Committee for Public Art, 1995.

Cuyahoga Valley Trails Council, Inc. *Trail Guide Handbook, Cuyahoga
Valley National Recreation Area.* Akron, Ohio: Cuyahoga Valley
Trails Council, Inc., 1991.

*The Cuyahoga Valley: An Official Map and Guide.* Washington, D.C.:
National Park Service, 1995.

Ellis, William Donohue. *The Cuyahoga.* Dayton, Ohio: Landfall Press,
Inc., 1966.

*Field Guide to the Birds of North America.* Washington, D.C.: National
Geographic Society, 1983.

Fletcher, Colin. *The Complete Walker.* N.Y.: Alfred A. Knopf, 1972.

Folzenlogen, Robert. *Hiking Ohio: Scenic Trails of the Buckeye State.*
Glendale, Ohio: Willow Press, 1990.

*From Town to Tower.* Cleveland: Western Reserve Hist. Society, 1983.

Gaede, Robert C., and Robert Kalin, eds. *Guide to Cleveland Architecture,* 2d ed. Cleveland: Cleveland Chapter of the American Institute
of Architects, 1997.

Gieck, Jack. *A Photo Album of Ohio's Canal Era, 1825–1913.* Kent, Ohio:
Kent State University Press, 1988.

Hannibal, Joseph T., and Mark T. Schmidt. *Guide to the Building Stones
of Downtown Cleveland: A Walking Tour.* Guidebook No. 5. Columbus, Ohio: Department of Natural Resources, Division of Geological
Survey, 1992.

*Heritage on the Heights.* Cleveland Heights, Ohio: Heights Community
Congress, 1977.

Johannesen, Eric. *Cleveland Architecture, 1876–1976.* Cleveland: Western Reserve Historical Society, 1979.

Lewis, Joanne, and Richard Karberg. *In Our Day.* Cleveland Heights, Ohio: Heights Community Congress, 1978.

McCray, R. Y., ed. *Representative Clevelanders.* Cleveland: Cleveland Topics Co., 1927.

Miller, Carol Poh. *Cleveland Metroparks, Past and Present: Celebrating 75 Years of Conservation, Education, and Recreation 1917–1992.* Cleveland:Cleveland Metroparks, 1992.

Newcomb, Lawrence. *Wildflower Guide.* Boston: Little, Brown and Co., 1977.

Ohio Department of Natural Resources, Division of Natural Areas and Preserves. *Directory of Ohio's State Nature Preserves.* Columbus, Ohio: Ohio Department of Natural Resources, 1996.

Ohio Department of Natural Resources, Division of Natural Areas and Preserves. *Ohio's Natural Areas and Preserves: A Directory.* Columbus, Ohio: Ohio Department of Natural Resources, 1987.

*Pathfinder: A Guide to the Cleveland Metroparks.* Cleveland: Cleveland Metroparks, 1996.

Ramey, Ralph. *Fifty Hikes in Ohio.* Woodstock, Vt.: Countryman Press, 1990.

Rose, William Ganson. *Cleveland: The Making of a City.* 1950. Reprint, Kent, Ohio: Kent State University Press, 1990.

Sego, Mickey. *Then There Was None: A History of the Berea Sandstone Quarries.* Berea, Ohio: King's Court Communications, Inc., 1996.

Van Tassel, David D., and John J. Grabowski, eds. *The Encyclopedia of Cleveland History,* 2d ed. Bloomington: Indiana University Press, 1996.

———. *The Dictionary of Cleveland Biography.* Bloomington: Indiana University Press, 1996.

Weber, Art. *Ohio State Parks, A Guide to Ohio's State Parks.* Clarkston, Mich.: Glovebox Guidebook Publishing Co., 1994.

Williams, A. B. *Geology of the Cleveland Region.* Pocket Natural History No. 9, Geological Series; No. 1. Cleveland: Cleveland Museum of Natural History, 1940.

# Index

**A**

Adam Poe House, 79
Adelbert Hall, 95
Administration Building (Riverside Cem.), 82, 84, 87, 89-90
Alexander Mill, 160
Alfred Fritzsche House, 118
Allen Memorial Library, 94
Alta House, 95
Amasa Stone Chapel, 95. See also Stone, Amasa
American Automobile Association, 13
American Hiking Society, 28
American Institute of Architects, 38, 87
Antique Row Shopping Area, 152
Appalachian Mountain Club, 28
Appalachian Plateau, 96, 112
Appalachian Trail Conference, 28
Arcade, 35, 48, 86, 107
Archives, 58, 72, 87, 92
Archwood United Church of Christ, 76, 80-81
Audubon Society of Greater Cleveland, 23

**B**

Bach Memorial Library, 134
Badgley, Sidney R., 70, 85
Baldwin, John, 130, 134-135
Baldwin Creek, 132, 166
Baldwin Lake, 133
Baldwin-Wallace College, 130, 132, 134-135
Bandstand (Chagrin Falls), 128
Bank One Center, 36
Barber, Josiah, Sr., 88
Battle of Lake Erie, 53
Bay Village, OH, 148, 177
Baycrafters, 177-178
Beach, Clifton Bailey, 153
Beaver, 164, 200-201, 264
Bedford, OH, 21, 24, 175, 205, 207, 232-233, 235-237
Bedford Formation, 258, 260
Bedford Heights, OH, 205
Bedford Reservation, 205, 207, 232-233, 235, 237
Bedford-to-Akron Bike and Hike Trail, 234
Bellamy, John Stark, 64, 111
Ben-Brae, 108
Berea, OH, 32, 42-43, 113, 130-137, 165, 168, 175, 183, 194, 208
Berea Area Historical Society, 137
Berea Quarry, 132
Berea Sandstone, 32, 42-43, 113, 130, 132, 168, 175, 194, 210, 230, 258, 260, 272, 274, 278
Big Creek, 76, 165-166
Big Creek Reservation, 21, 165–166
Big Quarry (Berea), 132, 136
Birds & Birdwatching, 12, 16-17, 62, 116, 155, 165, 170, 193, 197-198, 200, 204, 213, 254, 274
Black Brook, 200
Blue Hen Falls, 255-256, 258, 260
Blue heron, 164, 250

Bluestone Quarry, 182
Board of Education Building, 37
Bomante House, 78
Boston Mills, OH, 256-261
Boston Run, 248
Boston Run Trail, 246, 248
Boston Store, 257, 260
BP America Building, 34, 37, 92
Bradley Woods Reservation, 167-169, 171
Bradstreet's Landing, 148, 150-151, 153
Brainard family, 76, 78, 80, 82, 85-86
Brandywine Creek, 262
Brandywine Falls, 255-256, 258
Bratenahl, OH, 138-145, 147
Bratenahl Place, 143-144
Brecksville, OH, 25, 263, 265, 267, 271
Brecksville Nature Center, 263, 271
Brecksville Reservation, 263, 265, 267, 269, 271-275
Brecksville Stables, 267-268
Brecksville Trailside Museum, 267
Breezy Bluff, 141
Bridal Veil Falls, 234
Bridge Building, 152
Bridle Trail, 14, 193, 206, 214, 216, 221, 224, 226-228, 230-232, 234, 270, 272, 274-275
Brightwood, 140-141
Brooklyn, OH, 165
Brooklyn Centre, 76-81, 84
Brooklyn Centre Burying Ground, 76, 80
Brooklyn Memorial United Methodist Church, 76, 81
Brooklyn Savings & Loan Co., 81
Brookside Reservation, 21
Brush, Charles F., 34, 99
Buckeye Carriage Shop, 128
Buckeye Trail, 19, 23-24, 27-28, 193, 196, 201-202, 206, 221, 223, 228-232, 235, 237-238, 255, 257-259, 263-264, 267-268, 270, 274
Buckeye Trail Association, 27-28, 206, 274
Buckeye Trail Loop, 221, 223, 228
Buckeye Trail Tree Blazes, 19, 202, 235
Bullard House, 123
Bunns Lake, 168, 170-171
Butterfly Walk, 198
Buttermilk Falls, 213-214, 216-217, 224-225, 227, 255-256, 258, 260
Buttermilk Falls Loop Trail, 214, 216, 224, 227
Buttermilk Falls Overlook, 214, 216, 224
Buttermilk Stream, 214, 224
Buzzards, 238

**C**

Cahoon Memorial Park, 178
Cain Park, 107-108
Cambrian Period, 45, 47
Canal Visitor Center, 158, 161
Cancer Survivors Plaza, 92
Carabelli, Joseph, 98, 101

Carnegie West Branch Library (CPL), 56
Carol Sweet Mentor Marsh Nature Center, 197-198
Carrying In and Carrying Out, 18
Carter, Lorenzo, 52
Carvings, 37, 43, 85, 87–89, 94, 98, 113, 189-190, 192, 196, 228, 230, 238
Case Western Reserve University, 88, 90, 94–95, 112
Castle Valley Trail, 226-227
Cathedral of St. John the Evangelist, 36, 47, 72
Cedar Point Hill, 211
Central Market, 50
Chagrin Falls, OH, 79, 120-129, 136, 194, 228, 230
Chagrin Falls Historical Society, 122, 124, 129
Chagrin River, 23, 121, 125-126, 155, 157, 193-194, 196, 214, 221, 223, 228, 230
Chagrin Shale, 150, 180, 183-184, 205-206, 208, 210
Charles Selzer House, 79
Chestnut Shelter, 227
Chimney Run stream, 220
Chinese Cultural Garden, 92
Chinese inscriptions, 86
Chippewa Creek, 263-264, 267, 271-272
Chippewa Gorge Trail, 272
Church, Henry, 128, 194, 228, 230
Church of the Covenant, 94
Civil War, 32, 42, 58, 66, 87–88, 136
Civilian Conservation Corps, 21, 184, 242, 246
Clayton Townes House, 80
Cleaveland, Moses, 32, 100, 102, 175
Cleveland Botanical Garden, 91, 94, 147
Cleveland Browns, 31, 38, 48, 132, 135
Cleveland City Hall, 34, 38, 104
Cleveland Convention Center, 37
Cleveland Heights, OH, 96, 98, 104, 106-110, 112-114, 142-143
Cleveland Heights Historical Society, 107
Cleveland Hiking Club, 28, 182, 217, 223, 227
Cleveland Indians, 50
Cleveland Institute of Music, 94
Cleveland Lakefront State Park, 63, 138, 140
Cleveland Metroparks, 10–11, 13, 22–23, 86, 130, 133, 152, 158, 162, 165, 169–170, 173–174, 177, 181, 183, 189–190, 193, 205, 208–210, 214, 221–223, 226, 228–230, 232, 238, 263, 267, 271, 274
Cleveland Metroparks Zoo, 21-22
Cleveland Museum of Art, 91, 95, 141
Cleveland Museum of Natural History, 23, 28, 40, 48, 91-92, 197
Cleveland Police Historical Society, 54
Cleveland Public Library, 30, 34, 36, 45, 56, 68, 78, 85, 88, 101
Cleveland Public Library, Louis Stokes Wing, 36, 45-47
Cleveland Shale, 113, 180, 183-184, 206, 208, 210-211, 214
Cleveland Trust Co. Building, 35, 142
Cleveland University, 65-66, 71
Clothing and Footwear, 14
Cloud Series IV, 1981, 52
Cobb, Ty, 189, 192

Codrington Shelter House, 168
Coe Lake, 130, 132, 137
Coe Lake Park, 130, 132
Coffinberry, James M., 85, 88
Coit House, 144
College Club, 110, 115
Collinwood, 102, 138
Colonial Arcade, 35
Columbia Run, 260
Commerce, 34
Commercial Survey Company, 13
Concerts, 63, 74, 91, 94, 128
Convention & Visitors Bureau of Greater Cleveland, 21
Coventry Library, 109, 115
Cowan Pottery, 152-153
Crane's Canary Cottage, 127
Crawford Auto-Aviation Museum, 92
Crile, Dr. George S., 58, 100, 114
Cumberland Park, 106
Cuyahoga County, 21-22, 42, 120, 127, 133, 136, 140, 150, 189, 238
Cuyahoga County Archives, 58, 87
Cuyahoga County Courthouse, 34, 38
Cuyahoga County Fairgrounds, 126, 132, 136
Cuyahoga Heights, OH, 162
Cuyahoga Valley, 158, 160, 245, 259-260, 267
Cuyahoga Valley Environmental Education Center, 186
Cuyahoga Valley National Recreation Area, 11, 13, 24-25, 158, 161-162, 186, 191, 205, 235, 242, 255, 259, 263, 267
Cuyahoga Valley Scenic Railroad, 24, 158, 160, 257, 259-260, 264
Cuyahoga Valley Trails Council, 28

**D**

Daffodil Hill, 100
Daughters of the American Revolution, 216
Davis House, 79
Deer Lick Cave, 263, 270-275
Deer Lick Cave Loop, 271
Deer Lick Cave Trail, 271-272
Deer Lick Creek, 234
Denison Cemetery, 80
Detroit Avenue Bridge, 152
Detroit-Superior Bridge, 59
Devonian Period, 45, 47, 124, 184
Disclaimer, 10
Dittrick Museum of Medical History, 94
Doan Brook, 113
Downtown Cleveland, 31, 33, 35, 37, 39-41, 43, 45, 47-49, 51, 53-54, 65-66, 85, 88, 91, 114, 116, 138, 147-148, 150
Duck Pond, 118
Dugway Brook, 99, 103, 107
Dunkleosteus terrelli, 210
Dyer, J. Milton, 38, 81, 141

**E**

Eagle Creek State Nature Preserve, 27
Early Settlers Association, 102
EarthWords, 213, 224

East Cleveland, OH, 96, 98, 100
Eastman, Linda, 46, 85
Eastman Reading Garden, 36, 46, 85
Easy and Moderate Trail Hikes, 11
Easy Urban and Suburban Walks, 11, 31
*Edge, 1977,* 53
Edgewater, 146
Edgewater Park, 43, 63-64, 140, 150
Egbert Picnic Area, 232, 234
Emerald Lake, 250
Emerald Necklace, 21-22, 86, 162, 205, 208
Engine Company No. 24, 78
Environmental education, 27, 186
Erie Trail, 250
Erieview, 48
Erosion, 18, 40, 45, 113, 157, 175, 176, 178, 184,
    191–192, 204, 206, 211, 214, 230, 244, 260, 272
*Étoille VIII,* 34
Euclid Arcade, 35
Euclid Bluestone, 99, 103, 180, 182
Euclid Creek, 21, 180-182
Euclid Creek Reservation, 179-181

**F**

F. A. Shepherd House, 80
Fairmount Presbyterian Church, 113
Fairview Park, OH, 148
Falls Loop Trail, 214, 216, 224, 227
Federal Reserve Bank of Cleveland, 36
Feller, Bob, 50
Findley State Park, 26
Fine Arts Garden, 91
First Church of Christ, Scientist, 78, 111, 122
First Presbyterian Church, 43. *See also* Old Stone
    Church
Fish & Fishing, 24, 50, 63, 133, 140, 148, 150-151,
    162, 166, 168, 177, 180, 184, 186, 190, 200, 208,
    210
Flats, 40, 55, 59, 65, 74
Food and Liquid, 12, 15
Fort Hill, 208, 210-211
Fort Hill Trail, 210
Fort Huntington Park, 53
Fossils, 31, 40-42, 44-47, 48, 98, 180, 184, 208, 210
Foster, Claud H., 88
*Fountain of Eternal Life,* 35, 37
*Four Benches,* 53
Franklin Circle, 55, 58, 87
Franklin Circle Christian Church, 58
Franklin Circle Masonic Temple, 87
Frazee House, 161
*Free Stamp,* 37-38
Frostville Museum, 210, 212

**G**

Gardens, 26, 36, 46, 60, 89, 91–92, 94, 107-108,
    112–113, 115, 124, 140, 145-147, 210
Garfield, Abram, 110, 112, 115, 141, 143-144, 146
Garfield, James A., 84, 96, 98, 110, 124, 141, 143
Garfield Heights, OH, 172, 175
Garfield Monument, 84, 87, 96, 98, 110. *See also*
    Garfield, James A.
Garfield Park Nature Center, 172, 174, 176

Garfield Park Reservation, 13, 21-22, 172-173, 175
Gateway Plaza, 49-50
Geauga County, 24, 26, 121
Geauga Park District, 26
Geese, 164-165, 202, 213, 254
Generalized Geologic Column for Northeast Ohio,
    276
Geology, 31, 40-42, 43, 45, 47, 180, 183–184, 210
Ginkgoes, 98
Glaciers, 155, 165, 184–185, 192, 196, 210, 223,
    230, 249, 258, 263, 271–272
Goff, Frederick H., 142
Gold Coast, 60, 62
Gordon, William J., 138, 140
Gordon Park, 53, 113, 138, 140, 147
Grand River, 197, 202, 204
Granger, Alfred Hoyt, 110, 114, 147
Granite, 33-34, 36-37, 42-45, 47, 49-50, 85, 87-88,
    99-100, 223, 271
Great Lakes Brewing Co., 56, 87
Great Lakes Science Center, 31, 38, 48
Greater Cleveland Peace Officers Memorial, 53
Greek Orthodox Church of the Annunciation, 71
Green Lake, 118
Group Hiking, 14, 28
Group Plan, 34-35, 37-38, 46
Guidebooks, 198, 213
Gund Arena, 31, 49-50
Gwinn, 145-146
*Gyratory III,* 35

**H**

Hach-Otis Sanctuary State Nature Preserve, 23, 27,
    155
Hale Farm, 160, 264
Halle Family, 112, 118
Hamilton, James M., 112–114, 142-143, 146
Hanna Family, 60, 62-63, 87, 92, 103, 114, 143-144
Hanna Mansion, 92, 144
Happy Days Visitor Center, 26, 242, 246, 248
Harriet L. Keeler Memorial Trail, 272
Harrison, General William Henry, 53
Haskell Run, 248
Haskell Run Trail, 248
Haysmar, 142
Headlands Beach State Park, 23, 202, 204, 274
Headlands Dunes State Nature Preserve, 23, 204
Headlands School Forest, 201
Heisman, John, 58
Hemlock Creek Picnic Area, 205-206
Hemlock Point, 186, 188
Hemlock Ravine, 188
Hemlock Trail, 213-215, 217, 224, 226
Henn House, 114
Heritage Park, 52
Highland Picnic Area, 180, 182
Hiking Preparation, 13, 15, 17, 19
Hiking Resources, 13, 21, 23, 25, 27
Hiking Resources, Local and national, 28
Hinckley, OH, 21-22, 189-192, 238-241
Hinckley Historical Society, 189, 192, 238
Hinckley Lake, 190, 238, 240
Hinckley Reservation, 189-191, 238-239, 241

Historic Warehouse District, 52
Hogback Ridge, 186, 267-268
Holden, Liberty Emery, 100, 138, 141
Holden Arboretum, 26, 141
Holy Ghost Byzantine Catholic Church, 71
Hopkinson, Charles W., 84, 87
Horses, 78, 162, 190, 193, 228, 230, 262, 274
Horseshoe Lake, 118
Hunt Farm Visitor Center, 13, 26
Huntington Reservation, 177-179

**I**

Ice Box Cave, 244, 246-247
Iconography, 66
Independence, OH, 39, 160, 264
Indian Mound trailhead, 158
Indians, 196. *See also* Native Americans
*Integrity,* 36, 47
Iron Spring Loop Trail, 174-176
Iron Spring Wildlife Preserve, 172
Iroquois Trail, 249-250
Irving House Hotel, 125
Ivex Paper Mill, 120, 126

**J**

Jacobs Field, 31, 50
Jaite Paper Mill, 25, 262
Jaite Wayside Trailhead, 259
James A. Garfield Monument. *See* Garfield
    Monument.
Japanese garden, 94
Japanese pagoda trees, 96
Japanese threadleaf maples, 100, 102
Jayne Trail, 202
Jefferson Branch (CPL), 68
Jeptha Wade Memorial Chapel, 96, 101
John Hartness Brown House, 110
Johnson, Tom L., 32
Johnson's Picnic Area, 238, 240
Jones, Carlos, 85
Judson Manor, 92
Judson Retirement Community, 92, 112
Jurassic Period, 42, 44
*Jurisprudence,* 34
Justice Center, 53-54

**K**

Kaiser Permanente Trail, 252, 254
Kelley Picnic Area, 180
Kendall Lake, 242, 244, 246
Kerven Trail, 197-198
Key Center, 31
Key Tower, 33, 43
KeyBank, 33, 43
Keystone Trails Association, 28
Kirwan Lake, 24
Kroehle House, 80

**L**

Lake County, 23, 191
Lake Erie Nature and Science Center, 177
Lake Erie Shoreline, 138, 148, 150, 204
Lake Isaac, 165

Lake Metroparks, 22-23
Lake View Cemetery, 82, 84, 87, 95-97, 99, 101, 103,
    110, 140, 143
Lakewood, OH, 60-64, 148, 152
Lakewood Historical Society, 60
Lakewood Park, 60, 62, 64
Lamson-Sessions monument, 86-87
*Last,* 52
Ledge Lake, 189-190
Ledges Overlook, 245
Ledges Picnic Area, 190, 240, 246
Ledges Shelter, 242, 244-245, 248
Ledges Trail, 244, 246
Leisy Brewing Company, 85
Lemko Hall, 66
*Liberty,* 42
Limestone, 41-42, 44-48, 68
Lincoln, Abraham, 37, 66, 99
Lincoln Park, 65-66, 69, 72
Little Italy, 95, 98-99, 101, 106
Longwood, 99, 108
Look About Lodge, 13, 22, 228, 231
Lorain County, 26, 43
Lorain County Metro Parks, 26
Lost Meadows Picnic Area, 232, 234

**M**

Mall A & Mall B, 35, 37
Mallo House, 78
Map Symbols, 29
Maple Grove Picnic Area, 272
Maps, 13-14, 22, 25-26, 28-29, 160, 174, 197, 213,
    221, 224, 242, 246, 259
Marble, 34-39, 41-42, 44-47, 68, 71-73, 91, 101, 114,
    153
Marina of Rocky River Reservation, 183
*Market Place/Meeting Place: An Urban Memorial,* 50
Market Square District, 55
Market Square Park, 55
Marsh Creek, 200
Marshall Lake, 118
Mather, Samuel, 101, 145-146
Mather, William Gwinn, 145
Matzen, Herman N., 32, 99, 100, 102-103
May Company, 34
McClentic Building, 128
Meade, Frank B., 110, 112, 114, 118, 142-143
Meadowedge Pond, 188
Meadows Area, 166, 275
Meadows Picnic Area, 232, 234, 275
Medina County, 21, 189
*Meet Me Here,* 49
Memorial Plaza, 37
Mentor Lagoons, 200
Mentor Marsh State Nature Preserve, 23, 197, 199,
    201-203
Metro Parks Serving Summit County, 26
Middleburg Heights, OH, 165
Mill Creek, 162, 172, 174-176
Mill Creek Aqueduct, 162
Mill Pond, 132
Mill Stream Run, 130, 132, 218-220
Mill Stream Run Reservation, 13, 130, 132, 218-219

Mississippian Period, 42
MK-Ferguson Building, 50
Moderate Trail Hikes, 11, 197
Moderately Strenuous Trail Hikes, 11, 221
Mohawk Cross-Country Ski Trail, 252, 254
Monarch butterflies, 204
*Mondrian Linear/DIA, 1977,* 53
Moreland Hills, OH, 228
Morton Park, 202
Motch House, 116
Moyenage, 146
Mt. Pleasant Trail, 211
Murals, 32, 34-39, 44, 50, 53, 73
Murray Hill School, 95, 114
Mushers Trail, 254
Music Hall, 34, 37
Music Mound, 132

**N**

National City Center, 35
National Heritage Corridor, 162
National Historic Landmark, 55
National Park Service, 24-25, 161, 186, 242, 256-257, 259-260, 277
National Register Historic District, 76, 113, 124
National Register of Historic Buildings, 82, 106
National Register of Historic Places, 62, 73, 76, 82, 96, 101, 152, 271
National Scenic Byway, 162
Native American earthworks, 211
Native Americans, 194, 211, 230. *See also* Indians
Nature Center at Shaker Lakes, 118
Nature Center at Shaker Lakes, 118–119
Nature Centers, 118-119, 172, 174, 176-178, 183-184, 197-198, 208, 210-213, 216, 221, 224, 227, 263, 271-272, 274-275
Nature Conservancy Ohio Chapter, 28
Nature Trail, 221, 248-250
Nebraskan Period, 210
Nelson-Kennedy Ledges State Park, 24, 191
Ness, Eliot, 100-101
Newbury, OH, 24, 249, 252
Newhous Overlook, 197, 200-201
Nickel Plate Railroad, 150
*Night Sky,* 37
Nike missile site, 140-141
Nine Mile Creek, 144
North Chagrin Nature Center, 213, 216, 221, 224, 227
North Chagrin Reservation, 213, 215, 217, 221, 223-227
North Country Trail Association, 28
North Olmsted, OH, 168
North Ravine Loop Trail, 174
North Royalton, OH, 189

**O**

Oak Grove Picnic Area, 263-264, 274
Oak Hill Day Use Area, 186
Oak Hill Trail, 186, 188
Octagon Ledges, 244
Octagon Picnic Area, 242, 246
Octagon Shelter, 244

Ohio & Erie Canal, 21, 24, 158-163, 205-206, 256, 263
Ohio & Erie Canal Corridor, 162
Ohio & Erie Canal Reservation, 162-163
Ohio & Erie Canal Towpath Trail, 24, 158-159, 161, 263
Ohio & Erie Canal Towpath Trail, 24, 158–159, 161–162, 205, 255-256, 258-259, 262-264, 268
Ohio Canal Corridor, 75, 162
Ohio Department of Natural Resources, 23, 27, 197
Ohio Division of Geological Survey, 40
Old Arcade, 86
Old Birch Picnic Area, 174, 176
Old Federal Building, 34-35
Old Stone Church (First Presbyterian), 32-33, 43, 144
Oldest Stone House, 60, 62
One Cleveland Center, 47
Opera House, 127-128
Ordovician Period, 41
Osprey, 155
Ottawa National Wildlife Refuge, 28
Ottawa Point Reserved Picnic Area, 267
Our Lady of Mercy Roman Catholic Church, 72
Overlook House, 111
Overlook Trail, 221
Owens, Jesse, 53

**P**

Pace, 11, 14, 17-18
Painesville, OH, 23
Park Synagogue, 104
Parker's Restaurant and Catering, 58
Parma, OH, 165
Parma Heights, OH, 165
*Passing Years,* 52
Patrick Calhoun House, 110
Peninsula, OH, 26, 160, 186, 242, 246
Pennsylvanian Age, 47, 191
Perkins Beach, 63
Perry, Commodore Oliver Hazard, 53
*Phragmites australis,* 197
Pilger Amphitheater, 212
Pilgrim Congregational Church, 70, 87
Pine Grove Loop, 242, 244
Pine Grove Trail, 244
Pine Lake, 252-254
Pinery Dam, 264
Pinery Narrows, 263-264
Plants, 52, 165, 197-198, 204, 213, 272
Plateau Trail, 186, 188
Playhouse Square, 31, 39
Ponds Area, 166
Popcorn Shop, 120-122, 128
Portage County, 24, 27
Portage Escarpment, 112
Portage Lakes State Park, 27
*Portal,* 53
Prairie Restoration Project, 272
Preyer House, 106
*Primal Energy,* 34
Public Art walks, 31–40, 49–54
Public Auditorium, 34, 37

Public Square, 31-32, 34, 37, 39-43, 45, 49, 53-54, 102, 114
Punderson Lake, 24, 249-250
Punderson State Park, 24, 249, 251-253

**Q**
Quarry Picnic Area, 182

**R**
Rails-to-Trails Conservancy Ohio Chapter, 28
Red Lock Trailhead, 268
Red Oak Picnic Area, 175-176
Rhodes, James Ford, 87
Ridgetop Trail, 176
Riemenschneider Bach Institute, 134
Ritchie Run, 244
Ritz-Carlton Hotel, 32
River Grove Reserved Picnic Area, 227
Riverside Cemetery Association, 84, 86, 90
Riverside Park, 126-127
Riverside Walk, 126
Robert Russell Rhodes House, 58
Rock and Roll Hall of Fame and Museum, 31, 38, 48
Rockefeller, John D., 52, 95, 98, 103, 106-107
Rockefeller Building, 52, 106
Rockport Township, 148, 150
Rocky River, OH, 148-154
Rocky River, East Branch, 211, 218, 220, 238, 240
Rocky River, West Branch, 208, 210-212
Rocky River Bridge, 152
Rocky River Clock Tower, 153
Rocky River Nature Center, 208
Rocky River Park, 148, 150-151
Rocky River Reservation (North), 183–185
Rocky River Reservation (South), 208–212
Rocky River Valley, 184, 208, 210, 212
Rogers Rd. Field, 221
Roseneath, 62
Royalview Picnic Area, 218
Ruetenik Family, 89

**S**
Safety, 17, 100, 214
Sagamore Creek, 235, 237
Sagamore Grove Picnic Area, 235, 237, 264
St. Alban's Episcopal Church, 110
St. Ann Church, 114
St. Augustine's Roman Catholic Parish, 70
St. George Orthodox Church, 69
St. Ignatius High School, 56
St. John Kantu (Cantius) Roman Catholic Church, 68
St. John's Episcopal Church, 58
St. Patrick's Church, 56
St. Paul's Episcopal Church, 8, 113
St. Philip the Apostle Episcopal Church, 80
St. Theodosius Russian Orthodox Cathedral, 73-74
Sts. Constantine and Helen Greek Orthodox Cathedral, 104
Sts. Peter and Paul Ukrainian Catholic Church, 74
Sanctuary Marsh, 213, 216
Sandstone, 32-33, 42-43, 47, 63, 70, 99, 110, 113, 121, 123-124, 128, 130, 132-135, 137, 168, 170, 175-176, 189-192, 194, 210, 230, 240, 242, 258, 260, 272, 274
Scenic Overlook, 227, 232, 234-235, 271-272
Scenic Park & Marina, 183-184
Schuele Planetarium, 177
Schweinfurth, Charles, 33, 39, 43, 63, 144, 146
Security, 36, 47
*Sentimental Scale,* 53
Settler's Landing, 52
Severance, John L., 99, 107
Severance Circle, 104, 107-108
Severance Hall, 94, 99
Severance Town Center, 99, 104, 107
Shaker Heights, OH, 100, 116–119, 142, 144, 147
Shaker Historical Society and Museum, 118
Shaker Lakes, 113, 116-119
Sharon Conglomerate, 190-191, 240, 242, 244, 246
Shipman Pond, 202
Shoreby, 144-145
Sierra Club, 27, 248
Sokolowski's University Inn, 75
Solar Walk, 176
Soldiers and Sailors Monument, 32, 37, 42
Solon, OH, 228
*Sommer's Sun,* 37
Songbirds, 155, 164, 172, 214
South Chagrin Reservation, 13, 21-22, 128, 193, 195, 228-231
*Sports Stacks: Gateway Plaza Columns,* 50
Spring Creek, 258, 260
Squaw Rock, 128, 193-194, 196, 228, 230
Squaw Rock Picnic Area, 193-194, 196, 230
Squire's Castle, 224, 226
Squire's Castle Loop, 224
Squire's Lane Trail, 226
Standard Building, 39, 54
Stanford House American Youth Hostel, 256, 262
Stanford Trail, 255-256, 258
State Office Building, 52
Station Rd. Bridge, 264, 268
Statues, 32, 36-39, 42, 47, 50, 53, 72–73
Steamship William G. Mather, 38
Stinchcomb, William A., 184. *See also* Cleveland Metroparks
Stinchcomb-Groth Memorial, 184
Stone, Amasa, 43, 95, 99, 144. *See also* Amasa Stone Chapel
Strawberry Picnic Area, 216, 226
Strawberry Pond, 216
Strenuous Trail Hikes, 11, 221, 255
Striebinger, Frederick, 78-79
Strongsville, OH, 165, 183
Stuart, Noble, 189, 192, 238
Stump Lake, 249-251
Suburban Walks, 11, 31
Sulphur Springs Picnic Area, 230
Summit County, 26, 259
Sunset Pond, 213
Sunset Wildlife Preserve, 214
Superior Schoolhouse, 104, 107
Sylvan Pond, 188
Sylvan Trail, 223
*Symphonic Suite,* 37

## T

Temple Etz Chayyim, 110
Temple Museum of Religious Art, 92
Temple-Tifereth Israel, 92
Terminal Tower, 21, 32, 100
*The Plain Dealer,* 100, 140-142
*The Spirit of '76,* 38
*The Trailblazer,* 28
*Three Figures,* 53
Three Waterfalls, 6, 255, 257
Thwing Hall, 94
Tinker's Creek Aqueduct, 160
Tinker's Creek Gorge, 205-206, 232, 234-235, 237
Tinker's Creek State Nature Preserve, 27
Tinker's Creek State Park, 27
Tower City Center, 21, 31-32, 39-41, 48-50, 54
Trail Sense, 19
Tremont, 65-75
Tremont West Development Corporation, 68, 75
Triangle Park, 123, 128
*Triple L Excentric Gyratory,* 35
Turkey vultures, 155, 238

## U

Ukrainian Museum and Archives, 72
Underground Railroad, 58
United States Geological Survey, 43
University Circle, 21, 91, 93-96, 99, 101, 113, 141, 146
University Hospitals of Cleveland, 94
Upson Memorial, 96

## V

Valley Stream Trail, 271
Valley View, OH, 26, 162, 205
Van Sweringen, Mantis J. & Oris P., 99, 116, 118, 144
Veterans Memorial Bridge, 52
Viaduct Gateway, 52
Virginia Kendall Park, 26, 191, 242-247
Visitor Centers, 26, 158, 160-161, 242, 246, 248
Voinovich Park, 38

## W

Wade, Jeptha H., 82, 96, 101, 103
Wade Memorial Chapel, 100, 102
Wade Oval, 28
Wade Park, 53, 91-92, 101
Wade Park Lagoon, 91, 85
Wake Robin Trail, 197, 200
Waldmere, 64
Wallace Lake, 133
*War Memorial Fountain,* 35, 37
War of 1812, 53
Washington, George, 37, 190
Waterfowl, 100, 164-165, 168, 172, 174, 200-202, 210-212, 230, 250, 264
Weldon Davis House, 79
Welsh Woods Picnic Area, 180, 182
West Branch State Park, 24
West Channel Pond Trail, 211-212
West Side Market, 55, 59, 88
Western Reserve Historical Society, 91-92, 101
Westlake, OH, 168

Westlake Hotel, 152
*Where Men and Minerals Meet,* 38
Whipp's Ledges, 190, 238-241
*Who's On First,* 50
Wildflower Garden Trail, 210
Wildflowers, 12, 16, 155, 165, 168, 172, 176, 186, 193, 201-202, 206, 228, 255
Wildlife, 26, 28, 158, 164-165, 168, 170, 172, 177, 197, 200, 208, 212-214, 216, 221, 263
Wildlife Management Loop Trail, 213-214
Wildlife Management Trail, 208, 212-214
Wildlife Preserve, 26, 172, 214, 221
Willard Park, 37
Willey Creek, 194
William H. Warner House, 115
William R. Coates House, 79
Williams, Arthur B., 223
Willoughby, OH, 23, 202
Willoughby Hills, OH, 23
Winton, Alexander, 60, 62
Wolf Creek, 172, 174-176
Wolf Creek Lake, 174
Wolf Picnic Area, 177-178
Worden, Hiram M., 189-190, 238
Worden Heritage Homestead, 189-190, 192, 238
Worden's Ledges, 189-190, 238
Works Progress Administration, 21, 107, 133, 175, 184, 228, 271
World War I, 70, 118, 129, 136, 152
World War II, 37, 50, 72, 106, 127
Wright, Frank Lloyd, 112

## XYZ

Zimmerman Trail, 23, 202
Zion United Church of Christ, 72-73
Zoar, OH, 162